CW01333212

**Lieut.-General Baden-Powell C.B.
1908 Chief Scout of the World**

In Scouting

Colin Walker

Gilwell 2009

Acknowledgements

My wife Fran, without whose patience support and active involvement with research and proof reading, this book could never have been contemplated.

My friends John Ineson and Ian Leonard for their many hours in proof reading

UK Scout Association, Paul Moynihan, Pat Styles
Girlguiding Scotland Archives

The Hon. Michael Baden-Powell
Rob Bolton, Boys' Brigade and Church Lads' Brigade Historian
Angela Booth, Sydney Australia, John Banjo Booth's great niece
Frank Britain, Archivist Hertfordshire Scout Association
Nick Dale Royal Canadian Mounted Police
John Day, Worcester - Humshaugh Diary
Bob Dring, Baden –Powell Scout Association.
Martin Eggmont, Guisborough
Girl Guiding Scotland Archives
Jean-Marc Bonello, Figura, Malta
Kelvin Holford: Kent.
Justin Dawson, Scouting Radio, The Station That Loves To Talk Scouting
Bruce Hardy, Jonathon Oakley (Humshaugh) grandson
Mrs Hatfield, Archivist Eton College
Paul Jones, Birkenhead District Scout Council
Michael Loomes, Be Prepared The Story Scouting Museum, Waddecar, Lancs
Mercers' Company Archives
Scott Park, GSL 1t Stirlingshire Scout Troop
Stoatbringer. High Force Photograph p.46
Geoff Pocock and the Legion of Frontiersmen
Robert Preece 1st Nairn. Scotland
Joppi Ranta, Wild Rover Finland
Louis Robdrup, Look Wide Campsite, Northumberland
Dave Scott, US Scout Historian, Texas, USA
Dr Stephan Schrölkamp, Berlin.
Ian Webb of 1st Claremont Scout Group, South Africa
Brian Woolgar, Brownsea Scout Fellowship.
YMCA Birkenhead.

Foreword: The Hon. Michael Baden-Powell

It is a great pleasure to write the foreword for this book. Colin Walker, is an eminent researcher of the Founder, Lord Baden-Powell and of historical events relevant to the Scout Movement.

Recently, World Scouting celebrated the first 100 years since B-P undertook his now famous experimental camp on Brownsea Island, 1st August 1907. Its significance cannot be overstated. It was though the events of 1908 that established, worldwide, the pattern for our future success. The impact on people was enormous and far-reaching, enabling Scouting to become, without question, the world's largest youth organization and perhaps the greatest Peace Movement in history.

The winds of change have brought many new challenges which, fundamentally, have had an enormous impact on our way of life, expectations and family values. Many of our traditional pillars of social support have changed and therefore the need for Scouting and Guiding is probably greater now than at any time during the past 100 years. Thus we need to become even more mindful of our social responsibilities towards the young people who are the greatest asset we have. Young people are our prime responsibility, irrespective of what changing values and expectations may prevail, our objective must always be focused on the ongoing "development of character, regardless of colour, class or creed".

In a nutshell, we are an educational Movement but we use recreational means to achieve our purpose. This is why the key points of our Law should always continue to be the very core of our existence. Over the past 100 years, the Movement has thrived and whilst we have a wonderful history of achievement, we must continue to look wide by presenting the benefits offered to the citizens of tomorrow through our Scout and Guide training.

Congratulations Colin, continue to research and catalogue our precious heritage. By recording important events mentioned in your books, you are not only playing a pivotal role with the education of today's young people but you are also preserving Scout and Guide heritage, which can only benefit citizens of tomorrow.

In summary, history has shown that *B-P was a man of his time and indeed before his time*.

Michael Baden-Powell
22nd February 2008

1908: The Dawn of the World Scout Movement

	Introduction: Brownsea, The Aftermath	5
1	**Baden-Powell's Diary 1907/08**	7
2	**1908 Influences**	15
	The Brigades/Brother Organisations	16
	The Seton Influence	22
	The Legion of Frontiersmen	29
3	**1908 Publications**	
	The Writing of a Best Seller: Scouting for Boys	41
	The Boy Scouts Scheme	48
	The Scout Magazine	57
4	**The First Troops**	61
	Primmer and the Washhouse Patrol	63
	Everett and the 1st Elstree	65
	1st Glasgow	67
	1st Newport	70
	'Wilkie' and the 1st Blackpool	71
	1st Birkenhead	72
	Harold Price and the 1st Chiswick	73
	1st Sunderland and 1st Hampstead	74
	What Two Girls Did: The Henfield Group	78
	Scouting for Girls	78
	Alison Cargill and the Cuckoo Patrol, Glasgow	82
	Social Scouting in the Missions	84
	School Groups/Work Groups	85
	Cycle Patrols	85
5	**Lt.-Gen. Baden-Powell, Chief Scout of the World**	
	Gibraltar	87
	Malta	88
	Canada	89
	Australia	90
	South Africa	92
	New Zealand	93
	Asia Minor	94
	United States of America	95
	Germany	95
6	**Organisation and Structure**	
	The Origins of the Uniform	96
	Badges	108
7	**Humshaugh: B-P's Holiday Camp**	110
8	**The Rest is History?**	149
	Appendix: First UK Troops Database	150

Introduction

Brownsea: The Aftermath.

In 1907 Lieutenant-General Baden-Powell was a fifty-year-old bachelor. He had gathered ideas from every conceivable source to promote his contention that training in scouting/woodcraft could be used to turn Britain's mainly urban youth into better citizens which, in the General's view, was unfortunately all too necessary.

He used his fame as the Hero of Mafeking to promote his ideas and had received favourable comment from influential citizens, as well as support from Arthur Pearson, a noted publisher. He lacked however one very necessary credential. He had no experience whatsoever of working with children! Since leaving school, Baden-Powell had served as an Imperial Officer in the very hierarchical world of the British Army. It is true that he had observed the Mafeking Cadets[1] carry out useful work during the famous Siege, with which he will forever be associated, but contrary to popular belief he had had no role in their formation or training.

The Experimental Camp on Brownsea Island in August 1907 was then a very necessary exercise to test not only his training scheme, but also to demonstrate his ability to work with and inspire young people. For his scheme to be accepted across the nation, it had to appeal to, and succeed with, boys from every social class. Again, in truth, B-P had little informal contact with the working classes.

The ex-public schoolboy and now famous officer found it easy to gather together twelve of his friends' children including his young nephew Donald. Naturally they, as he had been, were being educated through the (fee-paying) public school system. To provide the necessary contrast, the would–be youth leader had to borrow 'Town Boys' from the Boys' Brigade, with two of their leaders, to join him in a camp that would prove, he hoped, that both he and his ideas were up to the task. Could young Britons, from different social classes, work together as equals? A revolutionary concept in 1907.

That you are reading this book is testimony to the fact that the future Chief Scout of the World passed his self-imposed tests with flying colours.

B-P wrote[2],

Since this experimental camp I am more than ever convinced of the possibilities which underlie the scouts' training as an educator for boys of all classes. Prepared as I was for enthusiastic endeavour on the part of the lads, I was surprised at the effect on their character, which became visible even in the few days that we were at work. I have not trusted merely to my own observation, but have had reports from all the parents bearing out this conclusion, and giving incidentally some very useful hints from the parents' point of view. That the boys enjoyed the training is evident from the letters that I have had from them....

---

[1] *The Mafeking Cadets* on the author's Scouting Milestones Website. See web-based resources.
[2] In the *Boy Scouts Scheme* published December 1907 and also *Scouting for Boys* 1908.

One of the 'working boys' from the Boys' Brigade wrote,

> *The most important thing that a great many boys need to learn is to look on the bright side of things and to take everything by the smooth handle. I myself found that a great lesson, and I should never find words enough to thank you for teaching me it. I have already found it a great help even in everyday life.*

Another letter[3] was from a boy, who wistfully thought that adults too might benefit from B-P's wisdom,

> *It would be a very good thing if you could have a course for **parents**, to teach them how to train their sons.*

It was not just the boys who were impressed. Pearson's Literary Agent, Percy Everett, attended the camp for the last day, including the final campfire. He was to write,

> *...to see the chief dancing round the Camp Fire leading the Eengonyama Chorus[4], to hear his inimitable yarns, to watch with wonder the ready way he tackled any question that was fired at him, to listen to his imitation of the songs of the birds and the calls of wild animals. All this is a memory, which will remain with me.*

Everett's day visit to Brownsea was the start of a lifetime's involvement in Scouting, culminating in his appointment as Deputy Chief Scout. (See Page 65)

There was no doubt, the experiment was successful. It was time to take the message that inspired 22 boys on the small island of Brownsea, to the boys and girls of Britain and then across the British Empire, soon to be followed by every other country in the world[5]. Twenty-nine million Scouts and eleven million Guides are the proof of this success.

But now, the year is 1908, the dawn of The World Scout Movement.

Colin Walker

15 January 2008
(The 100th Anniversary of Scouting for Boys)

---

[3] Sir Percy Everett, The First Ten Years, p.17
[4] See Image on Page 149.
[5] There are currently only five countries where Scouting is not permitted, but all of these at some stage in their history have had Scouts. Though Scouting is not permitted in Mainland China, there are Scouts in both Hong Kong and Macau.

Baden-Powell's Diaries 1907/1908

The period following the Brownsea Camp from August 10th 1907, to the opening of the Humshaugh Camp on August 24th 1908, was just over a year, 375 days to be precise. This was the most decisive time in the history of Scouting. So much was achieved and decisions were made, for better or for worse, that endure to this day. The man at the centre of it all was of course Lieut.-General Baden-Powell. He was a consistant diarist, but his wife, Lady Baden-Powell, gave these records, after her husband's death, to the Boy Scouts of America. The BSA however provided the UK Scout Association with microfiche copies of the diaries. These provide a unique insight into B-P's daily life and the prevailing social conditions of the time. Factual evidence from the diaries underpins nearly every page of this work. Until this time however they have seldom been quoted.

Baden-Powell, it must be said, never intended his diaries to be read by anybody other than himself. His handwriting is often illegible even to those who have become accustomed to it. Apart from his visits abroad they can perhaps best be described as 'appointment diaries', seldom offering thoughts or description. The Founder was very careful to note down the people he met, especially if of interest or status, places visited, the number of people who attended his talks, and what he caught and shot!

Each page is only four by six inches (10 x 15cms), and is in the modern jargon 'two weeks to view'. Each day has a space, ¾ inch (2cms) by 4 inches (10cms) including the printed date, in which to write. The microfiche rolls are now somewhat ancient and this, with the poor handwriting, makes an unfortunate combination that does not help in their transcription.

Baden-Powell has often been called 'a man of his time and ahead of his time'[6] and this is absolutely true, but his time was fixed within a period of history, which by happy chance yielded a social structure and a physical infrastructure that was vital for the success of the 'Scouting Scheme'. The period between say 1905, with the advent of the motorcar, and 1914 when great country house parties came to an end with the advent of the First World War, was a 'window of opportunity' that was never to be seen again.

Lecture Tours

The Founder gave 60 talks to youth organisations between September 1907 and the Humshaugh Camp in August 1908, mainly as part of a lecture tour across Britain in January and February 1908.

The total number of people attending the meetings has not been recorded, however 12,000 people attended just 14 of these talks, so statistically around 51,000 people could have heard the founder promote his scheme during this time. In the absence of radio and television this face-to-face contact with significant numbers of 'the right people' was essential to the scheme's success. His schedule was so punishing that on one occasion his voice failed him completely and the meeting's Chairman had to read out his notes.

---

[6] See the Foreword to this book by the Founder's grandson the Hon. Michael Baden-Powell.

On May 7th 1907 B-P retired as Inspector General of Cavalry. He then accepted a post, on March 31st 1908, of Commanding Officer of the Northumbrian Territorial Army (volunteers who lived at home). The promotion of his Boy Scout scheme, via lecture tours and the writing of *Scouting for Boys,* was, in the main, undertaken during this period of 'leave'.

1908　　Baden-Powell's Diary - Three weeks in January

09.Jan	London to Plymouth stay with Gnl Leach - Mrs Johnson- lecture 700 mostly boys BB and YMCA
10.Jan	Plymouth to Bristol. Stay B Beverly Wills, Clifton. YMCA reception Col Savil Chair. Sir Matthew Dodsworth, keen, called on YMCA to go Scouting, Fry, CLB
11.Jan	Bristol to Wolverhampton, visit Bristol Cathedral, Drill Hall Wolverhampton, Lord Dartmouth, Col. Crombie, Stay Slaverly Hill, MP Oxley Manor. 700 mainly boys
12.Jan	Wolverhampton to Cheltenham, Mrs Stavely Hill interested in my Kashmeri sketches
13.Jan	Cheltenham. Tea with Estella. Lectured at Cheltenham, 900-mixed YMCA
14.Jan	Cheltenham, Sturgess Northumberland - refuses to join scheme no loss. Esking vg but self assertive
15.Jan	Hanley North Staff Hotel, R Heath Pres. YMCA Victoria Hall 2000 enthusiastic
16.Jan	Burton on Trent. Col E Soer Good Meeting CLB
17.Jan	Worcester, went over Brewery Co-op works, A C Cherry, Mrs Levy, Good Meeting
18.Jan	Dale End YMCA Birmingham …outlined scheme
19.Jan	Birmingham stay with AM Chance, Edgbaston, - saw orchid
20.Jan	Shrewsbury, stay with Gnl Hill, Shelton Oak Priory, Lecture at Masonic Hall
21.Jan	Wrexham. Lectured in Drill Hall, Col Edwards, Oswald Flower, 1200, satisfactory. Capt T O Bury
22.Jan	Chester to Carnarvon, Stayed with J Greaves Glangwna - lectured at the Pavilion 1200, mixed- satisfactory, Mr J de Grichjuy Gaudin MA
23.Jan	Carnavon to Crew. Lectured Crew Mayor in chair, 550 good audience, Mayor to hold meeting next Monday. Buckley Johnson sec.
24.Jan	Liverpool, stay with Pilkington, Hyton. Addressed boys Liverpool anti-cig league. Lecture Birkenhead YMCA Hall, 500 mean well. Sir John Gray Hill in Chair
25.Jan	Liverpool, lectured Liverpool Gymnasium, 600 good audience - presided at Gymnastic comp between Liverpool and Birmingham
26.Jan	St Helens, Rain all day, lectured 600 boys from the works on the duty of boys to the country, Capt Wilcocks agreed to get up next meeting. Crouch ex RSM 13th Hussars. See P's works has a corps of Boy Scouts of his own
27.Jan	Wigan. Lectured at Wigan Technical School, 700 very enthusiastic YMCA organising sec with Mayor to do next meeting
28.Jan	Salford Manchester visited St Helens with Pilkington, went over glassworks - went to Beecham's Pills factory. To Manchester put up at JG Groves at Midland Hotel. Lecture on Mafeking and Boy Scouts to 600 to the Salford Lads Club
29.Jan	Manchester, lunched Haywoods, Light Oaks. Lectured YMCA, 1000 v g audience L T Broadhurst in chair, E Haywood proposed vote of thanks
30.Jan	Manchester, went with Groves to hippodrome in aid of Crimea vets. Saw Bernard Shaw's play Widowers, fair
31.Jan	Manchester to York, attend meeting of combined county assocs of TA

The above entries show the hectic pace that B-P maintained. This was typical of the man *until he finally retired to Africa aged eighty.

He would, with the same intensity, set himself schedules focussing on his charitable work, his Scouting, his social life and particularly his fishing. Sometimes they would be intermixed at such a pace as would be beyond most ordinary individuals. In modern terms Baden-Powell was a 'driven' man.

The distances travelled would not have been possible without the advent of the overnight sleeper train, as it was by this means that B-P was able to visit distant places on consecutive days. It needs to be remembered that during this time B-P was without a secretary (being on his travels) and yet was initiating correspondence and sending off drafts by post for the later editions of the part series *Scouting for Boys*.

Big Houses and Country sports and 'networking'

Though B-P devoted a considerable amount of time to his Scouting lectures, writing *Scouting for Boys* and articles for *The Scout* magazine, it was not the first call on his free time. Between the 1907 and 1908 camps, Baden-Powell spent at least 81 days indulging his passion for fishing and shooting. Fifty-five days were spent fishing, 19 days shooting and one otter hunting. These activities were carried out on the estates of his wealthy and often titled friends. Over thirty such houses were visited during this period including some of the most famous in the land, such as Harewood House near Leeds and Alnwick Castle in Northumberland.

B-P recorded the names of those he met, many of whom were the 'glitterati' of their day, such as the Prince and Princess of Wales, the Duke of Gloucester, the Earl of Harewood and the Duke of Connaught whom he had known over several years. During the year he dined with no less than 25 Lords and Ladies, politicians such as Haldane, the then Secretary for War, industrialists like Lord Armstrong, owner of the biggest armament factories in the country and the most influential and important members of society. These contacts were not wasted but carefully recorded in his diary, 'names' ready to be pressed into service as and when the opportunity arose.

It should be remembered that B-P met the Van Raaltes, who kindly loaned Brownsea Island, at a fishing lodge in Ireland and Pearson, his sponsor and publisher, at another weekend house party at the newspaper magnates' home in Surrey. The Duke of Connaught became the first President of the Scout Association and many of the other titled hosts took on influential non-uniformed positions in Scouting e.g. Presidents of Scout Counties. (Every member of the Royal Family had a Scouting position by 1936.)

This 'social networking' was the basis on which Baden-Powell built and extended his influence. Through the support of the 'gentry', District Organising Committees were set up and Local Association campsites found. More often than not they could be relied upon to provide financial support for the local administration of Scouting, enabling it to be 'rolled out' so speedily to find ready acceptance across the nation.

Ernest Thompson Seton's contribution to Scouting is documented later in this work. (See Page 22) There are those who believe he that deserves the accolade of 'Founder of the Scout Movement'. Whatever the level of his contribution, he did not enjoy, as B-P did, this easy access to, and patronage of, the 'great and the good' without which no idea, at that time, was likely to spread much beyond the backyard of its originator.

The thirty or so country estates that BP visited during this period required immense wealth to fund the army of servants, gardeners and cooks that were necessary to maintain them. Only six years after the Humshaugh camp, these same young men who had responded to Baden-Powell's call to play the great game of Scouting went, on the call of a whistle, 'over the top' of the Flanders' trenches to walk obediently into near-certain death from machine-gun fire. Those that returned wanted more out of life than to be another man's servant. The era of the house parties was at an end. Many of the large houses were too big and too expensive to maintain. They were sold off or given to the nation in lieu of death duties. In 1908 however they were an invaluable part of B-P's 'social network'. If you want to tread in the footsteps of Baden-Powell, you could do worse than join the National Trust, or check the history of Country Hotels, especially those by a trout stream.

1907	Baden-Powell's Diary – One week in September
7 Sept	Left Dinmara Grouse Shoot Scotland for Chillingham Northumberland
8 Sept	Chillingham-walked to see their white cattle- with the children
9 Sept	Netted the river am fished pm
10 Sept	Grouse drive. Guns: George, Saxton, Humphrey, Col Vaux, Sir Alex 29 brace….fished evening
11 Sept	5 children slept out in the park with me. Partridge shooting got 26. Lady Trevelyan from near Elsdon
12 Sept	Chillingham, sultry day, Saxton George etc went rough shooting I got 2 grouse 2 rabbits. **To London.**
13 Sept	Spent the day in **London returned by night mail to Newcastle**
14 Sept	Reached Chillingham 8.30 shooting with Saxton, Mr Humphrey Ward (art critic Times) Miss Ward interested in children's education

The above extract is of interest for several reasons. It shows that Baden-Powell, in pursuit of his pleasures, went directly from one great country house to the next. Chillingham Castle was then the home of the Noble family, who provided two boys for the Brownsea Camp, one being Humphrey who also attended the 1908 Humshaugh Camp (See Page 110). His father, Saxton Noble[7], funded the deficit
B-P incurred on the Brownsea Camp just a month previously. The September 12th and 13th entries show that B-P amazingly undertook a return journey of 675 miles from a remote Northumberland Castle to keep an appointment in London and be back shooting in Northumberland the following day.

One hundred years ago trains were naturally not as fast as those of today, but they could average a mile a minute. The journey time from London to Edinburgh, for example, was around eight and a quarter hours, which could be accomplished in some style leaving Kings Cross on the overnight sleeper at midnight, arriving Waverley, Edinburgh just after breakfast.

The railway network in 1908 was far more extensive than it is today. (Progress is not always a straight-line graph.) It was to a great extent dictated by

---

[7] Brownsea: B-P's Acorn, p.153

geography. Railway engines cannot anything but the gentlest of gradients and so there were still many places that could be reached directly by train. The country houses B-P wanted to visit in Scotland and Northumbria were far more likely to be closer to a river or grouse moor than a railway station.

In 1907 motoring was the province of the wealthy and it was still more of an art than a science. Baden-Powell was a 'motor' enthusiast and his diary shows he attended the Paris Motor show in 1903 at a time when most people would never have seen a car, (The first British Motor show was held at Crystal Palace also in 1903.) He also attended the London Motor shows of 1907 and 1908.

Baden-Powell could not possibly have navigated himself around the north of England and Scotland without a car or a 'motor', as they were called. In the period between the 1907-1908 camps, B-P was still sufficiently impressed by the novelty and sense of adventure that car journeys entailed to mention 45 separate occasions in his diary when he was '*motored to...* or he himself *motored out.* There are many references that detail just how the 'motor' behaved,

> *May 21st 1908 ... two big hills but she took them both beautifully, (near Sunderland).*
>
> *May 29th 1908, Spurn Point, visited church a miniature cathedral, Patrington, motored back to York. Saw Col. Altham – motored on to Richmond arriving 10.30. Motor running beautifully.*

Reading his notes it is possible to feel the sense of euphoria that was engendered when 'the motor' was running well, but also the annoyance of the all too common puncture (near Chollerford August 23rd 1908) and even the black despair when the machine was malfunctioning.

> *April 13th 1908, Broken spark plug near Darlington.*
> *April 20th 1908, Car going very badly, valve loose.*
> *April 21st 1908, Car needs decarb.*
> And worst of all.... *June 2nd Car broken down (near Richmond)*

All of these entries relate to B-P's Thornycroft 18 horsepower car that was supplied to him direct from the manufacturers. The original sales ledger[8] is still in existence and shows the following information.

4. Lt Gen R Baden-Powell, H4 Car, 7-3-08

'H4' was the manufacture's reference, in this case an 18 horsepower four-seater open tourer, delivered to the customer on March 7th 1908. Another purchaser of this model was Lord Beaulieu, a man whose name is synonymous with early motoring. There are references to this particular vehicle as an 'alternative Rolls Royce', a marque to which B-P aspired, eventually owning a total of three, including the famous 'Jam Roll', presented to him with the Eccles caravan by the Boy Scouts of the world at the 1929 World Jamboree.

B-P describes his Thornycroft car, in his draft advert below, as being of 'Staff Officer's Pattern'. The listed modifications such as the *lying down accommodation* and the lamp and sliding table were probably fitted by Thorneycroft's, as other

---

[8] http://www3.hants.gov.uk/thornycroft-car-sales-register.pdf

customers listed in their sales ledger include the War Office and the Indian Civil Service.

Unfortunately the draft advert is undated, but B-P gives as his reason for the car's sale that he had no further use for it, as he was moving back to London. His official appointment as Officer Commanding the Northumbrian TA Division ended on 31st March 1910.

Motor caravans were rare beasts in 1908 though there were examples of custom-built models prior to this. One of the earliest, a 'maison automobile', was exhibited in Paris in 1904 by architect Tony Selmershem. There is little evidence of car conversions at this time, though it is such an obvious idea that B-P surely would not have been the first to have thought of it. He maintained his interest in 'car camping' and was President of the Camping Club of Great Britain from 1919 until his death in 1941. Besides conventional camping, the club has always shown an interest in cycle, caravan and 'motorised' camping.

There is no doubt that B-P used his Thornycroft 'camper' for the purpose it was intended. His diary records that in 1908 he slept in the car on July 28th near Maske - North Yorkshire, on July 11th near Whitby, on July 25th near Dalton- North Yorks and again, on August 9th, near Guisborough also in North Yorks.

John Ineson collection

Loyalty

Baden-Powell's diary also provides excellent evidence of his commitment and loyalty to any organisation lucky enough to have him as a member. The diaries for the period between the first Scout camps show no less than eight occasions when B-P attended the Royal United Services Institution, an organisation devoted to the study of Military History. The meetings took the form of lectures and B-P, a member of the Committee, was a speaker on several occasions. He talked, on 23rd March 1911 for example, on why Scout Training was better than that received by Officer Cadets (in public schools).

© Mercers' Company Archives 2008

B-P was a member of the Mercers' Company, an ancient City of London trade guild. An ancestor of his, Thomas Powell, was admitted to the Company in 1508 and his descendants are still members. During the period between the two Scouts Camps, B-P was only in London for a total of 95 days, including 12 at Wimbledon where he decided to isolate himself, in order to deliver the manuscript of *Scouting for Boys* on time. He was not then in a position to attend committees and events throughout the year, but did manage to attend the annual Mercers' Dinner and one or two other events.

Once freed of his army responsibilities in 1910, B-P became a regular attendee at the Mercers' Court and other committees. He was a Governor of two of the Mercers' charitable institutions, the St Paul's Boys' and Girls' schools. This often involved travelling from his home 'up' to London two or three times a week. He was elected Master of the Company in 1913.

Another annual event in B-P's calendar that was clearly of central importance to him, was 'Mafeking Day', as May 17th became known to the world after the 217-day siege. The Garrison was finally relieved by Col. Mahon's flying column together with Col. Plumer's men who were part of B-P's own Frontier Forces. Celebrations took place in London and every other major city of the Empire on such an unprecedented scale that a new verb, *to Maffick*, was coined. (Check your dictionary).

John Ineson Collection

13

From 1900 onwards a celebration took place each year, involving men from both the besieged town and its relieving forces. On Mafeking Day 1908, the previously mentioned Mahoon and Plumer, along with Colonel Panzera, Mafeking's Senior Gunnery Officer, Lord Charles Bentinck of the Garrison's Protectorate Regiment and Colonel Vyvyan, the 'Base Commandant', lunched with B-P. In later years Relief of Mafeking reunions would be commemorated with lavish dinners, many more guests and printed commemorative menus etc.

Another annual ritual was 'Founders Day', commemorating the death of Thomas Sutton, the Founder of B-P's old school Charterhouse, on December 12th 1611. Baden-Powell took this event very seriously indeed and, wherever he was in the world, he would make every effort to contact other Old Carthusians, as old boys of the school are called, for the purpose of holding a commemorative dinner. As bizarre as this might seem, whilst besieged in Mafeking, its 'Colonel Commanding' (B-P) advertised in the Mafeking Mail, for any of the garrison who had been at Charterhouse to make themselves known, in order to hold a Founder's Day Dinner. Unfortunately the only other person who would have qualified was Captain, The Hon. Douglas Marsham [9] who had been killed in a Boer attack on the 31st October 1899.

The Charterhouse School Crest

In 1907, B-P attended the Founder's Day dinner at Charterhouse which required the use of the overnight sleeper to enable him to arrive in York the following morning.

Baden-Powell's first Charterhouse headmaster was Dr W Haig-Brown. B-P corresponded with him and, when able, visited him until the headmaster's death in 1907. The author has in his possession correspondence and also a Christmas card sent by B-P to Haig-Brown's daughter, Hilda, shortly before his death in 1941, representing a continuous association with the family for over 70 years. Similarly Baden-Powell kept in touch with his Charterhouse housemaster, Frederick Girdlestone. During the 1st World War, in his retirement, Girdlestone manned one of the Scout run 'Rest and Recuperation' Huts at Hythe in Kent. It was there that he first caught pneumonia, brought on by overwork, which eventually caused his death in 1922.

---

[9] Mafeking Siege Register, Write Books, C.R. Walker 2007

Chapter 2

1908 Influences

Describing the numerous influences on the life and work of Baden-Powell would require an entire book. He was a man who deliberately sought out interesting people and kept abreast of modern ideas. He was much influenced by his mother and also his brothers whom he accompanied on holiday expeditions. Of course, B-P's schooldays at Charterhouse were also important. The purpose of this chapter however is to document those influences which can be demonstrated to have had an effect on Baden-Powell's 1907/8 writings and the formation of the Scout Movement.

Brother Organisations

Initially B-P believed that his Scouting Scheme could be delivered entirely through existing youth organisations, particularly the Boys' Brigade (BB), the Church Lad's Brigade (CLB) and the Young Men's Christian Association (YMCA). His plan was that Scout Patrols could be formed in existing Brigades and Clubs and run by their officers, whilst he continued with his army career.

B-P's meeting with Pearson on January 1st 1908[10] marked however a total reassessment of the role he was to play in Scouting. Pearson agreed to fund a series of lecture tours enabling B-P to promote his new Scouting Scheme. In return Pearson was to start, under his ownership, *The Scout* magazine (See Page 58) and publish *Scouting for Boys*. It was important for Pearson to have contractual ties with Baden-Powell and his marketable new ideas. Links with organisations over which he had no control, which furthermore had their own rival publishers, were not to be part of the deal. Under Pearson's sponsorship, Baden-Powell had to become more than a mere figurehead, with other organisations hosting his creation. He had to face up to the fact that the Pearson 'package' was for a new independent movement. The Founder of the Scout Movement must have realised that the form of Scouting that he started in the 'Brother Organisations' would continue, and could be of some embarrassment to his own new independent Scout Movement

Not surprisingly, 'Brigade' Scouts found themselves slightly distanced from the new administration and at local level had to compete with B-P Scout Groups being set up, sometimes in the very churches to which they were already affiliated. B-P though was keen to play down any notions of competition and advised boys, through the pages of *The Scout,* that there was no need for them to join his organisation if they were already Scouting with another.

In his letter to Keary[11], another of Pearson's literary editors, he complains bitterly about the draft format of *The Scout* magazine that he had just received.

> *It is little more than an ordinary boys' paper – not one to bring about a great amalgamation of all boy organisations, which I had hoped for ...*

---

[10] HQ Gazette 1928 p.293/294. On January 1st 1908, an agreement was made to the effect that B-P should plan out, organise, lecture on and write up his Scout Scheme. Pearsons for their part undertook to finance the Movement for the first year and to launch *The Scout* newspaper, and also to provide a Headquarters Office from which information and instruction could go out to Scoutmasters and boys.

[11] March 12th 1908, *The Founding of the Boy Scouts as seen through the letters of Lord Baden-Powell, October 1907- October 1908.* (See page 43)

The word 'amalgamation' is very significant. It clearly shows B-P had no intention of 'competing' against the 'Brother Organisations' brand of Scouting, having a much wider vision. His Scouts, now the 'common denominator' in all these youth organisations, might be the means of their 'amalgamation'.

The Boys' Brigade

B-P made such a proposal directly to William Smith, founder of the Boys' Brigade, in a letter written on Christmas Day 1909,

> *I fully recognize that until all these* [youth] *movements are working on some system of mutual co-operation, we are only dealing with the fringe of boyhood, whereas if leagued as a 'combine', we might tackle the whole mass effectively, and really make a nation of good, God Fearing*[12], *virile citizens in the next generation. Naturally we all look to you as the leader of the boy movement .... The possibilities are enormous... but I see nothing more than very partial results if we are all working as separate organisations taking our separate lines.*

William Smith however, wisely observed that it was a false assumption to conclude that one new body might achieve more than separate organisations going about things in their own way. This refusal was, no doubt, a bitter disappointment to Baden-Powell.

Lieutenant William Smith was a Glasgow businessman, and in 1883, both a volunteer Sunday-School teacher and an officer in the Lanarkshire Volunteer Rifle Regiment. He formed the Boys' Brigade because he could see that the structure and discipline that he used with good effect with his military cadets, would also be beneficial for the youths in his bible classes. The training he devised centred on military drill, group physical exercises and religious instruction. At first the boys wore only a rosette to indicate their membership, but a uniform soon followed. Leaders were found and boys in their thousands joined, leading to the creation of a national movement.

At William Smith's suggestion, on Friday May 8th, 1903, Baden-Powell attended a Boys' Brigade display at the Royal Albert Hall, the first occasion that he had witnessed such a large assemblage of boys. The BB impressed him, and they were impressed by the Hero of Mafeking. He was created an Honorary Vice-President, a position he was pleased to fill for the rest of his life.

On Saturday April 30th, 1904, Baden-Powell was the Inspecting Officer of an Annual Review, on the occasion of the organisation's 21st anniversary in Glasgow. At the time the Boys' Brigade had a membership of 54,000 boys of which 7,000 were present at this event.

B-P informed Smith that he would be proud to lead such a wonderful body of boys and congratulated him on their turnout and drill, adding that he thought the

---

[12] B-P was careful to emphasise a religious motivation in his proposals to Smith who was a very committed Christian, maintaining a lifelong habit of bible study and prayer. Dating his letter the 25th December, might not have been the best tactic that B-P had ever devised, as almost certainly Smith would have viewed this most Holy day, as a day for worship not letter writing. This difference in the degree of religious commitment between the two great 'boy' leaders was probably the biggest obstacle to any amalgamation. Scouting was and is non-denominational. All Boys' Brigade Companies since their earliest days have to be attached to an established Christian Church.

organisation would have a wider appeal if its training was more varied. Smith agreed and instantly challenged Baden-Powell to devise such a scheme. He added that this might be done through a boys' version of B-P's army manual, *Aids to Scouting*.

B-P's report for Smith concluded,
> *I believe that if some form of scout training could be devised in the Brigade it would be very popular and could do a great deal of good.*

In 1906, Baden-Powell sent an outline of his scheme to leading public figures including William Smith, who sent it in turn to the editor of the *Boys' Brigade Gazette*. This proved to be something of dilemma. It would be a coup of course, to publish a contribution from someone so famous, but the article seemed to be opposed to many of the accepted BB practices. The problem was resolved by cutting the material to the bone and passing it off with the lukewarm comment, that it might be of interest, *... in view of our coming summer camps.* B-P's article in the *Boys' Brigade Gazette* entitled *Scouting for Boys,* was the first recorded use of one of the most famous titles ever devised and was published in June 1906.

Perhaps, because of its abbreviated form, the article had little impact at the time, but just over a year later B-P was to accept the help of Captains Robson and Green from the Bournemouth and Poole Boys' Brigades. They attended the 1907 Brownsea Island Experimental Camp along with ten of their boys. B-P's experiences at the camp featured heavily in *Scouting for Boys* published in part form in January 1908. It took the youth of the nation by storm including of course members of other 'boy organisations'.

The rise and rise of Scouting, became a concern to all established youth organisations. To retain their boys they needed to 'ride the wave' of what some saw as a 'new fad', but do it on their own terms. At the BB conference in London on April 1st 1909, the following resolution was passed unanimously:-

> *That while acknowledging the indebtedness of the Brigades to General Baden-Powell, this conference is of the opinion that the Scouting Movement should be carried on by each of the several Brigades as a branch of its own work, independently of the Boy Scouts' organisation, each Brigade adopting its own Badges, Tests, and Certificates if any.*

The Boys' Brigade had their own versions of the first and second-class badge and Scout uniform. Smith however, declined Baden-Powell's invitation to become a member of the governing body of the Scout Movement. B-P for his part was disappointed that he could not persuade the BB founder to agree to a merger which he thought, with Smith's example, would eventually include all 'boy' organisations.

BB 2nd Class Scout

We all naturally look to you as the leader of the Boy Movement. The possibilities are then enormous. I hope you can see your way to coming onto our advisory council and thus taking a hand in our policy...The Prince of Wales is in favour of such an amalgamation of aims and would, I believe, become president of such a Council if formed.

And later: *I see nothing more than very partial results if we are all working as separate organisations taking our separate lines.*

Even with such Royal inducements and the offer of overall control, Smith steadfastly refused all such offers. Despite their differences, Smith and B-P remained friends and on the BB's Leader's death in May 1914, B-P paid grateful tribute,

A smaller man would naturally have resented or been jealous of a rival organisation.

The initial enthusiasm for Scouting in the Boys' Brigade declined quite rapidly, particularly after Smith's death. The requirements for the Boys' Brigade Scout Badges were eventually incorporated into the 'Wayfarer's Award', and by 1927 virtually all traces of Scouting disappeared from their programme.

The Boys' Brigade Executive met in January of that year and the minutes note that:

It was decided to delete from the Manual the present paragraph regarding Scouting, and suggest therefore a paragraph on Open Air work in the summer which would include a reference to Scouting.

This, though, failed to materialise.

Some sources claim that the decline in Scouting within the BB was caused by increasing lack of interest from both the leadership and members. This may well be true, but fails to take account of the obvious fact that over the same period, membership of the BB declined while that of the Scout Movement rose dramatically. It seems obvious that many boys who might previously have become BB Scouts joined the Baden-Powell led Movement instead.

In 1908 the Scout Movement was dwarfed by the older organisation that initially gave it so much support. Now it is the other way round. Sir William Smith (as he became) was however quite correct to resist a merger. Freedom of choice is always an advantage. It is a pity that it is not available to every child in Britain today.

The Church Lads' Brigade

Walter Mallock Gee founded the Church Lads' Brigade on November 11th, 1891, at St Andrew's Church, Fulham when the St Andrews' Lads' Brigade, started in the July of that year, was incorporated into a new organisation, the CLB. Lord Chelmsford was the first Governor and its President was HRH The Duke of Connaught, who was later to fulfil the same role in Scouting. The CLB grew quickly and was given Royal Patronage in 1902.

It was the first uniformed organisation to take up scouting and in May 1901, Baden-Powell's Book, *Aids to Scouting* was sold through their Headquarters, with advice to CLB Officers as to how it could be adapted to suit their own training scheme. Thus B-P's ideas on Scout training were being used by a youth organisation *seven years* before the 'experimental' Brownsea Camp.

Additionally, *Hints from Baden-Powell. A book for Brigade Boys* by Rev. R L Bellamy, Vicar of Silkstone, Barnsley, was published in 1900, shortly after the Relief of Mafeking. The Rev. Bellamy, drew out moral lessons from *Aids to Scouting*, comparing the life of a lone scout in enemy territory with the dilemmas faced by a Christian boy in the 'sinful society' of the day. Members of the Boys' Brigade and Church Lads' Brigade - the intended readership of the book - were enjoined to become *Scouts in Christ's Army*.

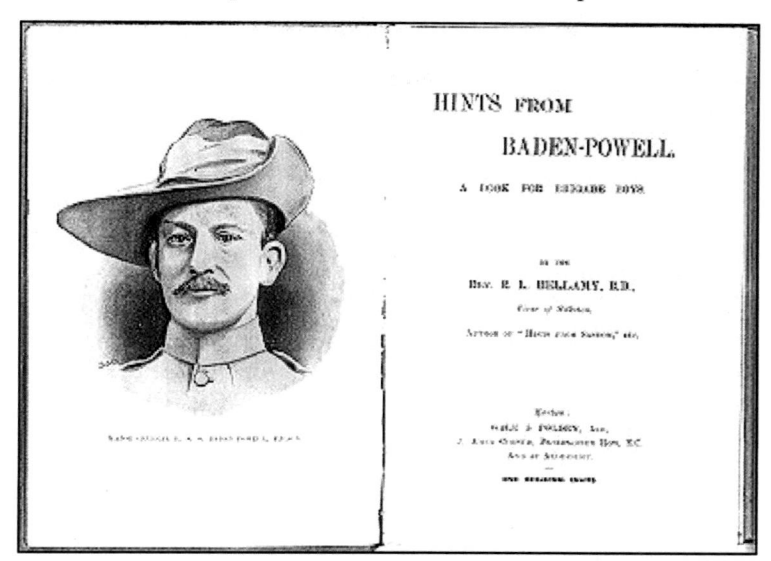

On November 1st 1906, Baden-Powell was staying with an army friend, Richard Chaloner, (later Lord Gisborough [*sic*]- see Page 74) a patron of the CLB, in Guisborough, then in North Yorkshire. His boys were the first to hear of B-P's new Boy Scouts' Scheme, which was later to be outlined in the first book for Boy Scouts, *Scouting for Boys*.

Ironically, B-P had planned for there to be some Church Lads' Brigade boys at Brownsea, but in asking local Boys' Brigade Captains Robson and Green to help him, the number of Boys' Brigade places, originally planned as six, expanded to fill all the surplus places. The Boys' Brigade Captains obviously having easier access to their own members than those of the CLB.

To legitimise the patrols of Scouts that were being formed amongst the members of the CLB in 1908, its Council formed the 'Incorporated Church Scout Patrols' (ICSP). The first committee meeting was held on March 25th, 1909, with Gee as its Secretary. On their second meeting the committee decided that their motto should be 'Watch and Pray', emphasising their central Christian allegiance and pointing up their independence from Baden-Powell. On April 21st, 1909 the ICSP was legally registered with a Certificate of Incorporation under the 1908 Companies Consolidation Act. The Certificate, numbered 102604, can still be seen at Companies House. The Boys' Brigade had declared their own brand of Scouting to be independent of B-P just three months earlier. The Articles of Association of the ICSP stated that the purpose of this new and completely separate Scout organisation was,

> ...to instruct lads in the theory and practice of scouting, tracking, and woodcraft.

The ICSP issued its own certificates, badges and medals and also had its own magazine, the *Scout Message*. In a prophetic moment, they decided to call their leaders 'Guides', two years before the birth of Scouting's sister movement, the Girl Guides. In 1913 the ICSP patrols were placed on a national basis within the Church Lads' Brigade when the junior 'Training Corps' was started and the uniform was changed to khaki, similar to that of the Boy Scouts.

Church Lads' Brigade Scout Troops (sometimes called 'Church Scouts') continued until 1936, when the Brigade was reconstituted.

The cross and lion logo with the 'Watch and Pray' motto of the ICSP.

The Young Mens' Christian Association

The YMCA was formed in London in 1844 by George Williams. By 1907 it was the oldest successful British youth organisations. Its founder had been knighted in 1894 and was laid to rest in St Paul's Cathedral in 1905.

Though primarily a Christian body, the YMCA did not have allegiance to any particular religious denomination. Their initial response to B-P's Scheme, whilst encouraging, did not propose the wholesale adoption of Scouting.

The January/February 1908 YMCA leaders' magazine *The Review* noted,

> *...Lieut.-General Baden-Powell has elaborated a scheme for boy development, along lines entitled Boy Scouts. The Committee have thoroughly investigated this scheme, and find that it is not military, and designed to develop in boys, habits of obedience, kindness, intelligence, self-reliance and usefulness. They have therefore circularised the Associations* [Local YMCA groups] *undertaking boys' work and recommended them to acquire the books giving details of the scheme, study the same, and adopt such parts of it as they may be able to utilise in their own work.*

Birkenhead YMCA first became involved with Baden-Powell on January 22nd 1906 (See Page 72). B-P later acknowledged that it was there that he first *publicly proclaimed* Scouting on Jan. 24th 1908, resulting in the immediate formation of one YMCA Scout Troop with others being formed in the days that followed.

Following the publication of the 'parts', in the first three months of 1908, there was a spontaneous explosion of Scouting activity. YMCA leaders soon realised that they ignored Scouting at their peril. Those groups that took up the Scheme increased in membership and those that did not saw 'migration' to alternative youth associations that were running the Scheme. The Central Committee bowed to the pressure and allowed the formation of YMCA sponsored Scout Groups within their existing structure. Throughout 1908 the YMCA, at both at national and local levels, were far more effectively organised than Scouting and had much to teach the emerging Movement. YMCA officials were frequently invited to sit on Local Scout Committees and their experience benefited entire districts. This contrasted somewhat with the Boys' Brigade and the Church Lads' Brigade Officers who in the main carried out their Scouting entirely within their own organisations.

Perhaps for this reason by March 1908, B-P looked to the YMCA rather than the BB or CLB as being a possible source[13] for leaders in his new Movement.

> *Y.M.C.A.-Everyone recognises the keenness and go-a-head manliness of the members of the Y.M.C.A. and Polytechnics in all parts of the kingdom, and I am convinced that if these men could see their way to do a good turn to the rising generation of their countrymen they would take it up with ardour, especially since this kind of work is becoming part of their policy. It is these gentlemen that I have specially in my eye in suggesting this scheme, as being the men who can, if they wish, get hold of practically the whole of the British boyhood by means of scouting. If every member of the Y.M.C.A. took a friend as second in command and six boys as pupils, each required to bring another recruit, and then acting as leaders and instructors to further patrols of six, there would at once be the commencement of a great 'snow ball' movement for good.*

The links between the YMCA and B-P were further strengthened when W.H. Wakefield, (See Page 127) a senior YMCA official, became one of the two Scout Association's 'travelling inspectors' during 1908, Wakefield being responsible for the northern half of the UK.

During the First World War, the YMCA organised 'Rest and Recuperation Huts' for allied forces in Northern France and in the transit camps on the South Coast of England. Baden-Powell worked closely with YMCA and through their scheme provided several Scout and Guide huts. Burchardt-Ashton, (See Page 38) a senior member of the YMCA, a member of the Legion of Frontiersmen and a Scout Commissioner was directly involved with B-P in their formation.

In large cities such as Edinburgh and Liverpool, for example, The YMCA, ran their own Scouting Districts and organised camps and competitions. Though some of the original YMCA groups later became 'unaffiliated' there are to this day still YMCA sponsored groups in many Scout Districts.

Worldwide the YMCA has 45 million members in 124 national federations. It generally caters for an older age range than the Scout Association though YMCA Scout Groups exist in most its federations. Some federations, notably in Scandinavia, have their own National YMCA Scout/Guide Association

---

[13] Robert Baden-Powell, *Scouting for Boys*. Part VI Horace Cox 1908. 26th March 1908

The Seton Influence

Ernest Thompson[14] was born in Durham in April 1860. His family was descended from the Scottish Setons, Earls of Winton, but an ancestor chose the name of Thompson, after fleeing to England. Ernest Thompson's family emigrated to Canada when he was only six.

Thompson had an abiding interest in the natural world and was a gifted artist. He won awards for his work and returned to England to study in London at The Royal Academy School of Painting and Sculpture before going on to Paris.

Back in Canada aged 21, the artist reverted to his ancestral name of Seton, becoming Ernest Thompson Seton. At this time he was appointed Naturalist for the Government of Manitoba, a title that he held until his death in 1946.

As well as increasing his knowledge of Canadian wildlife, Seton became obsessed with the folklore of the North American Indians and the way they lived in harmony with their environment. He immersed himself in their traditions and was opposed to the way the Redman was treated by the US government.

The naturalist came to hear of a 'King Wolf' that almost supernaturally seemed to be evading capture in New Mexico. A 'bounty' of $1000 had been offered and Seton decided to take up the challenge. He too had problems in trapping the wolf, which he called Lobo, but succeeded in killing its mate. The naturalist smeared her scent on a steel trap and its smell attracted the wolf. According to Seton, it realised that its mate was dead and so deliberately sprung the trap and lay down to die. Seton wrote up the story for *Scribner's Magazine*, published November of 1894.

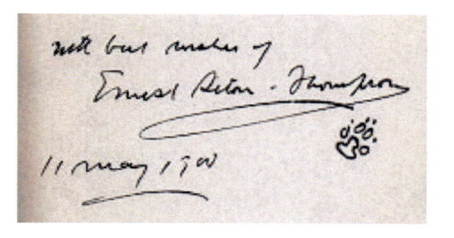

Lobo by Thompson-Seton

The incident was to be a turning point in the naturalist's life. He believed that he was possessed by the Lobo's spirit and felt that he could clearly see nature's grand design unfettered by the greed of Western 'Civilisation'. From this time on he began to sign his letters and books using a drawing of Lobo's paw print.

---

[14] All the images in this Seton sub-chapter are courtesy of the Dave Scott Collection.
See Dave Scott's two articles on Seton on the author's Scouting Milestones WebPages.

In 1901 *The Woodcraft Movement*, also known as *Ernest Thompson Seton's Boys* or *Seton's Indians*, was founded. It was based on Seton's experiences with a gang of local boys who, the previous summer, had vandalized the fence on his Connecticut estate. Seton camped with twelve of these boys to test his notion that 'Woodcraft' could be beneficial to young minds. He wrote about their experiences in a series of articles published in May 1902, in a very popular, but mainly female read, magazine *The Ladies' Home Journal*. The articles appeared under the heading *Ernest Thompson Seton's Boys*.

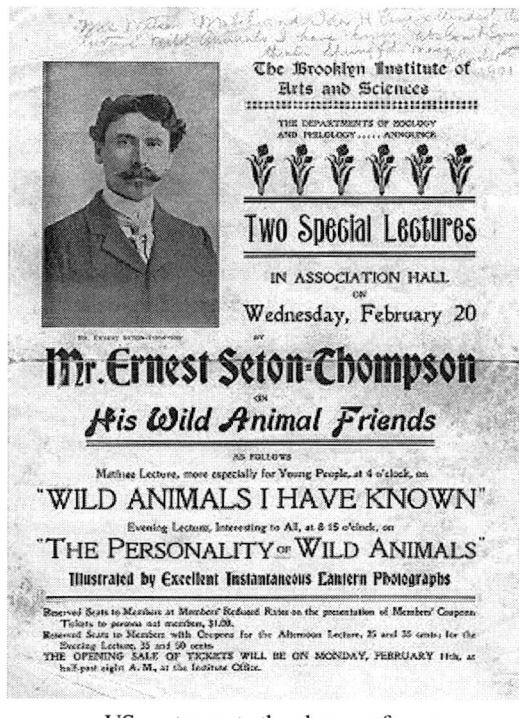

US poster, note the change of name

As was with Baden-Powell's part series *Scouting for Boys*, by the time the last article had been published, boys on their own initiative had formed their own 'tribes'. Seton formed *The Woodcraft Indians* on July 1st 1902 and began to give lectures throughout America. In 1903 he republished his original articles as a pamphlet, *How to Play Injun*.

The new youth organisation gained converts in England and Thompson Seton arrived to lecture on Woodcraft and to promote his books. He lectured on October 13th 1904, to a packed hall in London on *The Red Indian as I Knew Him* and at other venues over the next couple of months. This lead to camps being established in Eccles (Lancs.), Hove (Sussex), Hatch Kent (Kent) and New Brighton (Lancs.) All four tribes were disbanded by 1908. By the end of that year both Eccles and New Brighton had Scout Troops. (See p.152)

The Duke and Duchess of Bedford attended one of the earlier talks and through them Seton was introduced to Field Marshal Lord Roberts who had a keen interest in the possibilities of Woodcraft, having been sent, on May 6th 1906, Baden-Powell's outline plan for the *Training of Boys in Scouting*. Seton's biographer, H Alan Anderson, states that Roberts urged the naturalist to contact B-P, but as he was away from home at the time, a letter was sent to B-P's publisher C. Arthur Pearson awaiting his return. Seton's purpose in writing was to interest the General in helping him to promote his 'Woodcraft' scheme.

Once back in America, Seton led his second summer camp commencing July 5th 1906, for a new set of campers, on his Wyndygoul estate in Connecticut. A copy of *The Birch Bark Roll of the Woodcraft Indians*, based on the articles in *The Ladies' Home Journal*, was sent to Baden-Powell at this time. B-P was staggered to find that Seton's new book ran on parallel lines to his own scheme and wrote straight back suggesting a meeting. The two men began to correspond regularly.

B-P replied to Seton, August 1st 1906 thanking him for his book and promising to send him, ...*a copy of my scheme later on (it is not yet printed completely)*, inviting any comment or criticism Seton might like to make.

> *It may interest you to know that I had been drawing up a scheme, with a handbook to it for the education of boys as scouts - which curiously runs much on the lines of yours. So I need hardly say your work has a very special interest to me.*

The following day B-P sent Seton[15] the preliminary notice, which he had previously given to William Smith, founder of the Boys' Brigade. (See Page 16)

The two men eventually met at the Savoy Hotel, London on October 30th 1906. Seton asked B-P to revise and edit the content of his *Birch-Bark Roll* with a view to making future editions more appealing to younger readers while B-P obtained Seton's permission to use some of his Woodcraft ideas[16]. The following day he sent Seton a copy of *Aids to Scouting* and draft proposals for his new scheme[17].

> *You will see that our principals seem practically identical - except that mine do not necessarily make their own organisation, they are applicable to existing ones. If we can work together in the same direction I should be very pleased indeed - for I am sure that there are great possibilities...*

Letters continued to cross the Atlantic. B-P informed Seton that he *would make a point of coming to hear him speak*. Then, in June 1907 he wrote giving news of the progress on his book, *Scouting for Boys*,

> *I am now quietly working up my scheme with the most flattering encour -agement.*

In connection with his book on 24th January 1908, B-P requested,

> *I do hope that you will allow me to make frequent mention of yourself and your tribes as examples of Scouts.*

B-P sent Seton copies of the early parts of the *Scouting for Boys* series. These proved to be the cause of troubles that were to dog their relationship for years. Seton thought he had not received sufficient acknowledgment, particularly for his games. B-P apologised by return, and on the following day, March 14th wrote in his usual style hoping no doubt that all was now well.

> *The Boy Scouts are going splendidly in every part of the country without much help from me.*

Seton however was still unhappy. B-P[18] tried to placate him,

> *I enclose a request which I have ... from America regarding the publication of my book on 'Scouting for Boys' in your country, but I am unwilling to go on with it for fear of interfering with your "Woodcraft Indians" scheme.*

---

[15] B-P letter to Seton, 31 Oct 1906. BSA archives
[16] B-P letter to Seton, 1st August 1906. Dee Seton Barber Collection
[18] B-P letter to Seton, July 9th 1906. Letter in US library of Congress.

But this did not satisfy Seton. Baden-Powell felt the need to write an apology to HC Roberts[19], (English agent for Doubleday, - Seton's publishers.) In his next letter to Seton, sent on New Year's Eve 1909, B-P was still contrite.

> *I am of course glad to publish a statement, since you desire it, of my indebtedness to you for several details in Scouting for Boys.*

Seton became the first Chief Scout of the BSA in 1910, enrolling his Woodcraft Indians. He was the author of much of the original edition of the Boy Scouts of America's *Official Handbook* published in July 1910 of that year. Though this publication was meant to be all American, it had B-P's name with Seton's on the cover alongside the cover sketch from *Scouting for Boys*, with 'Old Glory' substituted for the Union Flag. (See page 52)

B-P wrote to Seton to inform him that he would be in New York on September 23rd. Seton arranged a reception for him at New York's Waldorf Astoria Hotel, with 300 leading industrialists, dignitaries and YMCA officials.

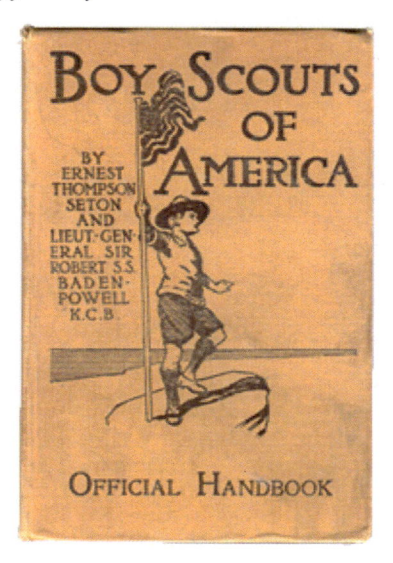

B-P's diary records:

> *New York, Took a room for the day at the Waldorf. Interview with Thompson-Seton, and Robinson, Sec of BS of Am. and Dan Beard. Interview with Roosevelt who agreed to become Vice-president. Interview with Doubleday [Publisher] Luncheon with ten men interested in Scouts at uni club. Inspected YMCA building. Addressed 250 SMs and answered questions. Interview with Murray who agreed to publish S4B like the Canadian one [5 year contract]. Reception 5.30 about 300 interested men, Seton in chair, Rockefeller Jnr on my other side. I addressed the meeting for about 1 hour.*

Famously Ernest Thompson Seton introduced B-P as the Father of Scouting. B-P responded,

> *You have made a little mistake, Mr. Seton, in your remarks to the effect that I am the Father of this idea of 'Scouting for Boys'. I may say that you are the Father of it, or that Dan Beard is the Father. There are many Fathers. I am only one of the Uncles.*
> *...I cribbed from them right and left, putting things as I found them into the book.*

Later a photograph was taken on the rooftop of the YMCA building. Seton wrote to Daniel Beard[20] on the 22nd of December 1938 recalling the event[21], complaining of the way B-P had tricked them into assuming subservient positions.

---

[19] B-P letter to HC Roberts, August 18th 1909, US Library of Congress
[20] Daniel Beard another US Scouting Pioneer had formed 'The Sons of Daniel Boone'
[21] Seton letter to Dan Beard, 22 Dec 1938, Barber Collection

The assumption was that we were equals. As we were about to pose, B-P said, 'I think I'll sit down,' and moved over to the ventilator [on the roof of the YMCA]. *You* [Dan Beard] *and I had to stand, by which trick he made us his subordinates, although he was the latest to enter the field.*

B-P however was completely unaware of any ruffled feelings and wrote[22] to Seton to thank him for his generous hospitality.

I cannot leave without telling you how very sincerely gratified I have been by the exceedingly generous reception which has been accorded to me by yourself.

Seton arrived in England again in early 1911. B-P wrote to welcome him, and followed up with an invitation to visit Scout offices,

...to see if there is anything we can do for you there.

B-P responded favourably to an invitation to preside at a Seton Lecture on the March 8th 1911. He also confirmed that he would attend when Seton addressed a group of Scouts on the 15th. B-P concluded[23]... *Meantime we would like it if you would come and dine with us.* This Seton did on March 14th. B-P sent a reminder to Seton on June 2nd, of a lunch at the Calvary Club on the 16th of that month, on a card with a hand-drawn sketch of a cowboy and followed this up with yet a further invitation,

The Committee of the Council have asked me to write ... to say how pleased they would be if you would do them the honour of lunching with them.

In themselves these event may have very little historical significance, but do show that, despite Seton's attacks on him, B-P was unfailingly respectful to the US pioneer.

Seton was totally justified in pointing to Baden-Powell's wholesale borrowings, particularly of his games, many of which were played on Brownsea Island. At that camp, Baden-Powell gave, as a prize, to at least one of the boys a copy of Seton's *Two Little Savages*. This book, dedicated in B-P's own hand, has survived (Dave Scott Collection) and is illustrated opposite.

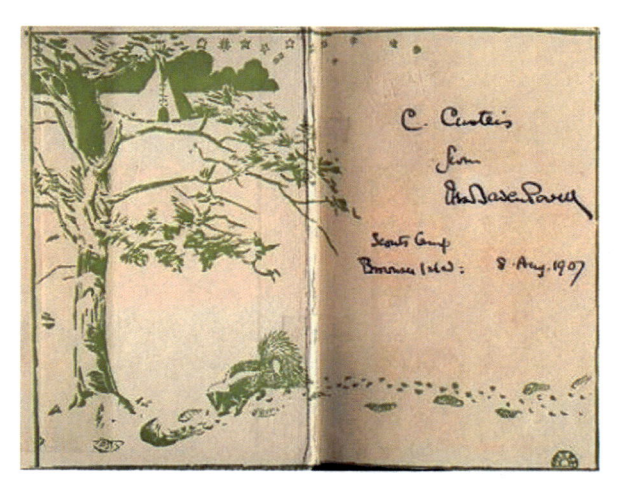

---

[22] B-P letter to Seton US Library of Congress
[23] Dave Scott Collection.

Seton claimed that B-P stole the information given to him at the meeting at the Savoy Hotel, instancing particularly B-P's use of 'proficiency awards'. This charge however seems quite bizarre. B-P had, throughout his army career, been brought up to use badges for special achievement. As a junior officer he had advocated the award of a badge to improve marksmanship where the normal pay incentives had failed. The badge, a form of public praise, let others know of the wearer's skill, improving his self-esteem. Indeed, B-P developed his own army badge for Regimental Scouts that was used in the British Army from 1885 to 1921.

B-P's army badge

As we have seen, B-P wrote to Seton to apologise for failing to acknowledge some of Seton's games described in *Scouting for Boys*[24].

> ...the truth is I had made a general statement to that effect in the introduction to the book which I afterwards cut out from the beginning and have inserted it at the end ...I had not reflected that the remarks giving the authorship of the games would not be read by the people until after the games had appeared before them. I very much regret this oversight. It is very kind of you to take it in the good-natured way in which you have.

B-P tried to make up for his error in *The Scout* magazine[25],

> I wish to take this opportunity for expressing my indebtedness to that great authority on woodcraft [Seton] for his very valuable assistance ... I got several useful hints from him personally, and from his book, for our organization.

Baden-Powell clearly did his best to appease the American pioneer, yet undeniably Seton *was* mentioned no less then ten times in the *Scouting for Boys* part series, with a further two credits to his wife.

Seton's reply dated April 30th 1910 showed that he had not seen the acknowledgments, because he had failed to read all six parts of the book.

> The rest of your letter in which you state making mention of my book on ten different pages of your own Scouting for Boy is doubtless correct (tho' I could verify only one of the pages mentioned). I appreciate the kindly spirit in which you have written, and feel sure that it is not through any ill intent that the situation has arisen.

The Scout magazine contained weekly editorials written by Baden-Powell. Seton was invited, on two separate occasions, to use the columns to address the British Boy Scouts. This very rare honour, unique amongst foreigners, was hardly the gesture of a man refusing to allow Seton his due fame.

---

[24] B-P letter to Seton March 14th 1908, in the Barber Collection
[25] *The Scout* magazine October 5th 1910

Fall out with the Boys Scouts of America

By the 1916 edition of the BSA Handbook, Seton's entire contribution had been removed. The Boy Scouts of America issued the following statement[26]:

> *Ernest Thompson Seton did not resign from the position of Chief Scout, as he alleged in a statement which he gave to the newspapers on December 4 (1915) but was dropped by the National Council at its annual meeting last February. Mr. Seton was dropped because he was not a citizen of the United States and refused to say that he would become one, and because he was not in sympathy with American customs and ideals . . .. In order that Mr. Seton might be spared the embarrassment of a public announcement of the failure of the National Council to re-elect him, it was decided to do the scout-like thing and say nothing about it.*

Seton's bitterness was not just directed at B-P. He now saw James West[27] as the architect of his problems. It was true that West preferred to work through committees he could control, rather than 'prima-donnas' like Seton. Many valid reasons could be found for Seton's departure, not least that he believed American Scouts should not be required to swear a 'pledge of allegiance'. He was not a religious man and refused to acknowledge the existence of a God, in direct contradiction to the promise all Scouts have to make.

B-P letter to Percy Everett dated the 2nd of January 1915,

> *I am much amused by Thompson Seton and his row with the American Boy Scouts - especially at his saying they were making it too material and not sufficiently spiritual. He once told me that he had explained why he put no moral teaching into his 'Woodcraft Indians' - because he had none himself.*

Seton's Legacy

Dave Scott, US Scout Historian asserts that Seton founded the 'Back-to-Nature' Movement, while B-P founded Scouting, just a part of Seton's wider achievement. Seton, Scott maintains, failed to appreciate however that it would only be through the medium of B-P's book, *Scouting for Boys*, and the worldwide Scout Movement it spawned, that his status would be assured in a way that he could never have created for himself.

B-P's travels exposed him to many cultures, but like all Victorians, he viewed the world from the perspective of the British Empire, and from the particular stance of a successful Army Officer. He had had little previous contact with young people, and no experience of running a youth organisation. He read and consulted widely, he borrowed, imitated and copied where the ideas of others supported his own philosophy. Not to do so would have been somewhat arrogant and foolish. The fact that Baden-Powell ranged widely, drawing from so many traditions gave Scouting its distinctive broad appeal and is very much to its benefit.

---

[26] *Boys' Life* magazine, January 1916
[27] Dr James E West was the US Chief Scout Executive in 1915

The Legion of Frontiersmen and the Scout Movement

In 1904 Roger Pocock, aged 39, wrote the same letter to 10 major newspapers seeking men to form an organisation of patriots[28].

It is time to enlist the legion, for good fellowship, mutual help, and possible service to the State in time of war. A few thousand men would form a sufficient army of observation, a unit of field intelligence in time of peace and war, its duties being those of scouting - to see run and tell - in case of any menace to the British peace.

Roger Pocock's biographer Geoffrey Pocock (no near relation) writes,

He was merely a minor author from a minor branch of a landed family, invalided as a humble constable from the North West Mounted Police, he had served in a most irregular band of Scouts in South Africa, leaving as a corporal.

As Geoffrey Pocock goes on to write, the early accounts of the Legion, particularly the colourful stories of its founder, are a mixture of,

Fact fed on fiction, history turned into myth...

In March 1906, Pocock advertised in *Lloyds Weekly News* and was soon able to claim[29] 5000 members for his new organisation, the Legion of Frontiersmen, (LoF). Its first chairman[30] was Sir Henry Seton-Karr MP, a noted hunter and outdoorsman. He was known to Baden-Powell and dined with him twice during the spring of 1908.

Roger Pocock in 1905

(Photo courtesy Countess Mountbatten's Own Legion of Frontiersmen photographic archive)

Professor Robert MacDonald[31] names some of the prominent people (overleaf) who supported the Legion of Frontiersmen (LoF) in 1910. There is no doubt that most of these individuals were 'supporters' rather than members of the Legion at that point. A few however were early members, (Lord Lonsdale, Earl of Meath and Cutliffe Hyne) and some of the others did join at a later date. The list however does serve to illustrate the type of person that the Legion wanted to attract and that these individuals in turn were prepared, in some way, to be associated with the 'irregular' organisation.

---

[28] 100 years of the Legion of Frontiersmen, G. A Pocock, Phillimore, 2004 (p.28)
[29] Roger Pocock, quoted p. 55 Robert H MacDonald.
[30] Geoff Pocock in correspondence with the author, - Roger Pocock noted that Seton-Karr was the first Chairman of the Legion
[31] Robert H MacDonald, Sons of the Empire, etc (pp 56- 57)

*Lord Esher,
*Sir Francis Vane
*Earl of Meath
*Earl of Onslow
*Arthur Burchardt-Ashton
  Admiral Arden Close
  Sir Gilbert Parker - Novelist
  Cutliffe Hyne - Novelist
* Lord Lonsdale - Hunter and Sportsman

  Fred Selous - African Explorer
* Sam Steele - Northwest Mounted Police
* Ernest Thompson Seton - Author Naturalist
  Rider Haggard - Author
  Conan Doyle - Author
* Arthur Pearson - Newspaper Magnate
* C.B Fry - Sportsman
  Edgar Wallace - Author

All of the people listed above would happily have sat around a dinner table at a country house party with Baden-Powell. All those starred* actually did. Some of them in later years could claim Baden-Powell as a personal friend or at least a long-standing associate. We have already recognised the central importance to Scouting of Arthur Pearson (See Page 65) and Ernest Thompson Seton. (See Page 22)

Sir Francis Vane[32], the Earl of Meath[33] and Arthur Burchardt-Ashton[34] were also early members of the Scout Association and, at different times, central to its history. Col. Sam Steele had been a senior officer in B-P's South African Constabulary and was host to his former Commanding Officer on B-P's Canadian Tour of 1910. C.B. Fry, besides his outstanding sporting prowess, was also the owner of the Training Ship TS Mercury[35] which he loaned to Baden-Powell in the summer of 1909 for the purpose of the second national Scout Camp, organised and attended by the Founder.

The Earl of Onslow was at the same fishing party in Knocklofty, Tipperary, Ireland where B-P met the Van Raaltes. With them, Lord Onslow would have been one of the first people to hear of B-P's Scouting Scheme.

Conan Doyle's creation, Sherlock Holmes is mentioned many times in the 1908 editions of *Scouting for Boys*. The author's, *Memoirs of Sherlock Holmes*, '*Adventures of Sherlock Holmes*' and *The White Company* are included as recommended reading for Scouts. Conan Doyle also wrote *The Great Boer War* which included a chapter about The Siege of Mafeking.

Lord Lonsdale, a friend of the Prince of Wales, who famously gave his name to boxing's Lonsdale Belt, accepted the honour of becoming the Legion's first President in early 1905. Despite speculation by various authors that B-P and Pocock met at a banquet held at Lord Lonsdale's home at Lowther Castle, Westmoreland on Boxing Day, 1904; the diary of neither man records their presence at Lowther on this date, or that they met at all.

Baden-Powell knew Lord Lonsdale, who had been a great 'white hunter' in his day and had in fact called on him at the castle, as recorded in his (B-P's) diary

---

[32] Sir Francis Vane recruited boys for the Legion's Cadet Yeomanry. He became an important early Scouting Commissioner in London, but in 1909 left to join the 'breakaway' organisation, The British Boys Scouts.

[33] A biography is to be found at, http://www.scouting.milestones.btinternet.co.uk/biogs.htm

[34] Burchardt-Ashton was later to become Commandant-General of the Frontiersmen, but as a member of the YMCA helped B-P to set up his 'Rest and Recuperation' Scouts' Huts in Northern France in 1916. More details of B-A's Scouting and Legion of Frontiersmen's activities are provided later in this sub-chapter.

[35] See http://www.scouting.milestones.btinternet.co.uk/beaulieu.htm

on October 27th 1904. B-P stayed but a short time and over an informal tea, no doubt heard Lord Lonsdale's news. Roger Pocock was in Russia in the latter months of 1904 and Lord Lonsdale did not become President of the LoF until early 1905. He was obviously approached by the Legion, perhaps by Seton-Karr, prior to his public appointment and so it *may* well have been over tea on October 27th that the noble Lord was able to tell B-P of his intention to join the Legion and his plans for it. (B-P's diary entry, typically does not contain any mention of the conversation, but does record the tea.)

Lord Lonsdale was later to claim that he was responsible for the Boy Scout Movement! In an interview he gave to the *Cumberland News*, published July 28th 1927, he is quoted as saying,

> *I started the Boy Scouts, Roger Pocock told me of the idea of the Boy Scouts and the Legion of Frontiersmen and I took it up at once and kept it going.*

His Lordship, born in the same year as B-P, was 70 years old at the time of his pronouncement and clearly his memory was failing, or he was overplaying his own importance to a very large degree? What he had to say however about the Legion of Frontiersmen, in this same quote, is basically correct.

In his *Boy Scouts Scheme*, (See Page 48) the purpose of which was unashamedly to persuade adults to join the Movement, Baden-Powell specifically named the Legion of Frontiersmen as amongst the *best qualified* to take up the work.

> *How to teach Scouting.*
> *The first point is to get men to take up the instruction of the boys in the art of peace-scouting. The men I have in my mind as the best qualified are schoolmasters, clergymen, and members of the YMCA, Legion of Frontiersmen ....*
> *These could all take up training of a few boys apiece...*

And later, the Legion is again identified under the cross heading,

> *LEGION OF FRONTIERSMEN*
> *The Legion includes many an old scout in its ranks who could at once take on the instruction of boys and youths and do really valuable work for the Empire, while reviving for himself many a delightful experience of camp and prairie life.*

When the first part of *Scouting for Boys* was published on January 16th 1908, under the heading, *Scouts' Work*, B-P wrote briefly about the role of *army scouts* in the time of war, concluding,

> *But, besides war scouts, there are also peace scouts, i.e. men who in peacetime carry out work which requires the same kind of abilities. These are the frontiersmen of all parts of our Empire.*

Whilst the word 'frontiersmen' was not given a capital letter which would have identified the 'peace scouts' beyond all doubt as the Legion of Frontiersmen, almost certainly B-P had this group in mind. He defined 'frontiersmen' as all kinds of explorers; trappers, hunters, missionaries, British pioneers, explorers, bushmen, drovers, the Constabulary of South Africa and the North West Mounted Police, - a fair description of the members of the LoF.

These are all, ... *men in every sense of the word and thoroughly up in scout craft*.... The Founder of the Scout Movement goes on to identify the Legion, if not in name, by a description that many people would have instantly recognised.

> *They give up everything, their personal comforts and desires, in order to get their work done. They do not do all this for their own amusement, but because it is their duty to their King ....*

B-P's admiration was reciprocated,

> *All members of the Legion are directed as far as lies in their power to assist the Boy Scouts ... Lt. Gen. Sir Robert Baden-Powell KCB, KCVO, the Chief Scout desires in connection with this regulation to state that members of the Legion of Frontiersmen are greatly respected by all Boy Scouts. The Legion is capable of exercising an immense influence for the good in this direction.*

There is no doubt whatsoever that many early Scoutmasters were members of the Legion and some, while not actually part of the Scout Association, often helped out in early camps.

Issue I, *The Scout,* April 18th 1908 carried what was seemingly the ultimate accolade. The back page, the only page in the entire magazine excepting his own contributions, that B-P was actually pleased with, was headed by the following banner.

THE LEGION OF BOY SCOUTS.
Founded by General BADEN-POWELL.
On this page every week will be found news and notes of special interest to all members of the Legion of Boy Scouts, and all other boys' organisations.

The Legion of Frontiersmen - the Legion of Boy Scouts, they sound so similar that readers could well have been forgiven for thinking that the new Movement was really the Cadet Corps of the Legion of Frontiersmen. (Indeed there was a 'Cadet Yeomanry' section under Sir Francis Vane)

This impression is heightened by the fact that one of the first contributing writers to *The Scout* was Roger Pocock with a whole page article entitled *The Tightest Corner I Was Ever In*. Pocock described not one, but five life-threatening experiences in detail and another twelve similar adventures were alluded to that occurred at sea, in America and Canada. Pocock had lain before the first Boy Scouts his credentials as a 'British Adventuring Hero,' endorsed by no less a person than Lieut.-Gen. Baden-Powell.

This 'patronage' was even more apparent when the announcement, illustrated on the following page, appeared in May 2nd 1908. It must have appeared that Pocock was very close indeed to the Scout Movement as his topic was The Work of To-day's Scouts, In the words of the advert, *To-day's Scouts were the Hunter, the Cowboy, the Explorer, the Railway Builder, and the strong men of the Empire.* The list, it will be observed, contains no reference to any of the armed forces. It had been deliberately tailored to exclude references to conflict. These men were the models for Baden-Powell's Boy Scouts, they were citizen Peace Scouts.

The Scout's very patriotic notice with Pocock in B-P hat. Scouts are told he writes 'true stuff'.

When the two-page article appeared, the header proclaimed,

> *In this series Mr Roger Pocock, who knows his subject from actual personal experience, will deal with different pioneer types, and tell you how they work and live.*

The following week *(May 10th)* another article in the series appeared entitled, *The Life of a Cowboy*. This time the introduction informed Scouts that they were in the hands of *a real cowboy*,

> *No man knows better* [about the life of a cowboy] *than Mr Roger Pocock, who has followed their trails and lived their hard lives.*

In the following weeks two more articles[36] appeared in the same series, *Hunters and Trappers*, (May 23rd) and then *The Railway Builders (May 30th)*.

Pocock contributed three major features to *The Scout* within its first two months, not merely the 'Penny Dreadful' style fictitious adventures, of which B-P did not approve, but apparently 'real-life' accounts. (Pocock was not beyond exaggeration, he lived by selling entertaining yarns.) The Founder of

---

[36] Pocock was not the only Frontiersman to write articles for *The Scout*. LoF member John Mackie, described in the magazine as an explorer, pioneer, and gold digger who had served in the North West Mounted Police and the South African War, contributed seven articles during the first six months of the magazine's existence.

the LoF and the leader of the emerging Boy Scout Movement looked set to bask in mutual adoration, but it was to be very short-lived.

The same day as Baden-Powell received his first copy of the new magazine, just prior to its publishing date on April 18th, he dashed off a letter to Pearson's publishing agent Peter Keary expressing his frustration over what he had just read. It was as though he could not believe his eyes. After making general criticisms, (See Page 58) B-P concludes,

> *The word Legion Page 20 will damn the scheme with most of the big organizations ... you may remember we agreed to delete 'Legion' when it appeared before in a proof.*

The following week the back page of *The Scout* had a new header (compare with that on Page 32). The title *Legion of Boys Scouts* had been dropped, never to be used again, no doubt as a direct response to B-P's criticism.

BRITAIN'S BOY SCOUTS.
Founded by General BADEN-POWELL.
On this page every week will be found news and notes of special interest to all members of the Boy Scouts, and all other boys' organisations.

Why was it then that, on the one hand, B-P should be casting his net to find future Scout Leaders from amongst Frontiersmen, yet at the same time be so seemingly 'down' on the organisation. He was not directly criticising the Legion himself, but seemed certain that most of the *big organisations* would not tolerate any association with it. Pocock's biographer believes the answer is complex, but lies mainly with that of founding Frontiersman's own background. There were many in the Legion itself who believed fervently in its aims but were 'uncomfortable' that their leader was from a different social class, particularly that he had never been an Officer. Baden-Powell himself came from an 'upwardly-aspiring' family, his widowed mother lived above her means, but had the ear of the 'great and the good'. We know that B-P used every social situation he encountered to further the promotion of his Scouting Scheme, so it is possible that he felt that, whilst the Legion itself contained men of 'the right stuff', its leader did not have the qualities that would endear him to the upper classes, who were so necessary in the promotion of his own Movement.

Whilst this point of view is entirely rational, it flies in the face of what we know about B-P and his endorsements of Pocock in The Scout. During the 217 days Siege of Mafeking, for example, he was forced into the closest proximity with all ranks of 'colonial' soldiers and the entire civilian population of the town[37]. He was the leader, and all looked to him for salvation. B-P had to bring the best out of each and every one. It is perfectly true that he did not suffer fools gladly and there is well-documented evidence, for example, that he relieved his Principal Medical Officer William Hayes of his command, because he lacked confidence in him and some of his own officers were locked up in the town jail for drunkenness. Yet after a study of over twenty published and unpublished

---

[37] In Mafeking Baden-Powell commanded 774 men, mainly from the two regiments that he raised in British Bechuanaland to form his 'Frontier Forces', including a few Imperial Officers that he brought out from England with him. A further 300 men (and their families) who lived in Mafeking or who had arrived as refugees in the days before the town was besieged were also B-P's direct responsibility.

siege diaries, numerous letters written during the siege, and the town's newspaper *The Mafeking Mail Siege Slips* ('Published Daily shells Permitting') there is hardly one word of criticism to be found about the 'Gallant Colonel' in a situation where 'grousing' was endemic. The reason for this, it would appear, was that he took men at their face value and inspired their loyalty.

There was never a hint throughout his entire life that B-P was 'a snob'. (see *Laws for me when I am old*, p. 54.) In his explanation of the fourth Scout law B-P wrote,

> *A Scout must never be a SNOB. A snob is someone who looks down upon another because he is poorer... a scout accepts the other man as he finds him, and makes the best of him.*

Pocock had many of the attributes that B-P admired. Above all they shared a common love of Empire. Pocock had been a member of the Canadian North West Mounted Police, an organisation regarded as an elite by Baden-Powell. As a newly appointed Constable, Pocock had lost toes through frostbite and had been lucky to escape with his life after undertaking a march over snow in sub-zero temperatures in his leather riding boots[38] without the necessary insulation, a case of culpable negligence, - but B-P would not have known this. Even if he had, he could have hardly have attached too much blame to Pocock, as early in his own army career, he had accidentally shot himself in the leg[39] 'playing with his pistol', whilst stationed at Korkoran, India, in 1876.

Both men had served during the Boer War, B-P as an Imperial Officer, Pocock as a volunteer rising to the rank of corporal in, what his biographer describes as, *... a most irregular band of scouts.* Not much is known of Pocock's time in South Africa but his status as a volunteer would have been readily understood and approved of by the Hero of Mafeking. B-P had enlisted many such gentlemen, who had come out to Africa at their own expense, specifically to fight with his 'Frontier Forces'.

Both B-P and Pocock sold articles to magazines and both had written books. Pocock's father was ordained in the Church of England as was B-P's. Both recognised that Rudyard Kipling's sentiments were useful to their cause. B-P knew Kipling both in India and in South Africa but whilst using the story of Kim in *Scouting for Boys* did quote from it directly. He asked permission to use The Jungle Book to promote Wolf Cubs in 1913 and this was given by return. Pocock on the other hand was unknown to Kipling[40] but in his book *The Rules of the Game* which Pocock published in 1895, he quoted directly from Kipling's poem,

The Lost Legion

There's a legion that was never listed,
That carries no colours or crest,
But, split in a thousand detachments is breaking the road for the rest.

---

[38] Later to be called 'Strathcona boots' by the 'Mounties' of the RCMP
[39] Jeal p.65
[40] Kipling and Pocock did meet later, but even then their conversation, as reported by Pocock in his article for the *Lloyds Weekly News*paper in 1903, contained no reference to the poem.

Like Scouting's founder, Pocock's choice of Kipling's work was inspirational. He felt moved by its words and used them in 1904 to promote his new organisation. Members of the public could be forgiven for assuming that Kipling had written about the Legion of Frontiersmen, rather than the Founder of the Legion choosing a Kipling poem written nine years previously.

Both B-P and Pocock saw the necessity for Britain to have access to intelligence about foreign countries which were intent on bringing harm to the Empire[41]. They thought that Englishmen abroad could/should do their country great service by indulging in private espionage. Baden-Powell wrote a book about his experiences in this capacity entitled *My Adventures as a Spy*, which was published in 1915 (at a time, it should be remembered, when the country was in the midst of the First World War). In it, he proclaimed that he had no time for 'traitor spies' who sell their country's secrets for money. *The best spies, he maintained, are unpaid men who are doing it for the love of the thing, and as a really effective step to gaining something valuable for their country or their side.*

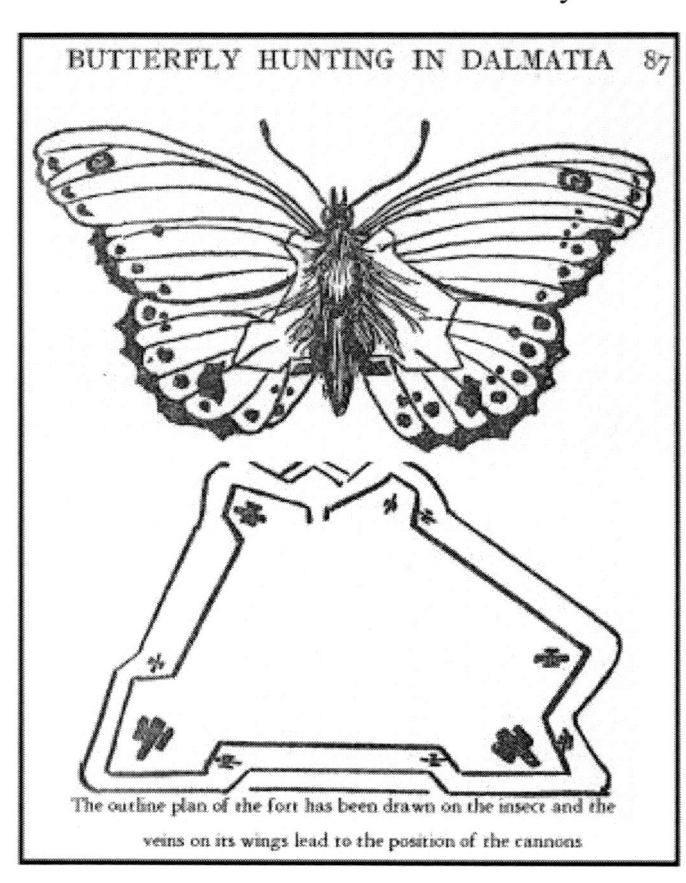

BUTTERFLY HUNTING IN DALMATIA 87

The outline plan of the fort has been drawn on the insect and the veins on its wings lead to the position of the cannons

Baden-Powell could not be described in such terms. He was a career soldier with a professional interest in gathering intelligence. In 1891 he was appointed Intelligence Officer for Mediterranean Countries. In his book, B-P described the 'ruses' he adopted to get himself close to military installations. On one occasion, dressed as an eccentric British entomologist he chased butterflies across forts and then recorded the position of the turrets and gun positions within a drawing of the butterfly's wings. The watching guards could only laugh at his stupidity.

In 1904 Pocock was working as a steward on board a ship at the time of the Russian-Japanese War of *1904-5*. When he docked at Sebastopol, a strategically placed port with many military installations, Pocock dressed in his steward's uniform, set off to find adventure. Arriving at a coastal fort the amateur spy

---

[41] Both B-P and Pocock rightly warned against the danger of the German Menace. B-P did so in what he thought was a private meeting in Newcastle on May 2nd 1908, and as a result was criticised in the House of Commons.

attempted to survey its defences. His hobby was geology, so he made great play of examining the composition of the rock-hewn floor closest to the gun emplacements, (pre-empting almost to the letter B-P's advice for would-be spies in his 1915 book about the value of being stupid).

Pocock was able to compile a report on the fortifications which he sent to Prince Louis of Battenberg resulting in the Prince joining the Legion. (The Prince became First Sea Lord in 1912 and changed his name to Mountbatten when he was ennobled as the Marquess of Milford Haven in 1917.)

Like B-P, Pocock recommended that Englishmen abroad should follow his example of collecting useful 'intelligence', whenever the opportunity arose.

> *All that was needed,* he wrote, *was an organisation to collect and collate these trifles.*

Pocock, in 1904, though he may not have known it, was very closely following B-P's example, and what is more, was an amateur doing it for *the love of the thing*. One cannot but think that Baden-Powell, when he came to learn of Pocock's exploit, would have very much approved

An Adventure too far

On the face of it, Roger Pocock would appear to have possessed all the attributes of the citizen 'Peace Scout' that the Founder of the Scout Movement was forever extolling. Pocock demonstrated his love of the Empire, selfless service and, when needs must, was not content to sit at home and pay others '*to do his fighting and dying for him*'.

Accepting that Baden-Powell was not a snob, why then did he distance himself from the founder of an almost parallel movement that he so much admired?

In 1897 Pocock advertised in *The Times* for investors to join him in a money-making expedition to the Klondike. From 43 replies he chose eight adventurers. One of these was a 40-year-old Baronet, Sir Arthur Curtis. The following year when the party was navigating the Caribou Trail in British Columbia, they found the track had been turned into a quagmire caused by the thousands who had passed that way previously in search of gold. A dispute grew up between Curtis and the expedition leader, 'a storm in a teacup', totally normal for people thrown together in exasperating conditions for long periods of time. Curtis took himself off, and was never seen again. Every attempt was made to find the missing man, but in the end Pocock left the expedition to tell Curtis's wife back in Britain the bad news. She contacted the authorities in Canada and fresh trackers were hired but with the same result.

Geoffrey Pocock writes[42]:

> *Accusations flew around, mainly directed at Pocock that he had murdered Curtis for his money belt. The mud that was hurled in Pocock's direction and the stigma remained throughout his life.*

---

[42] Geoffrey Pocock, 100 years of The Legion of Frontiersmen, p. 26.

No charges were ever brought. The grieving widow, as soon as she was able, had her husband declared dead and re-married. Pocock's biographer feels the 'Klondike' incident was at least partly responsible for many of his misfortunes, including the fact that the Legion, which he created, dispensed with his services as Commandant-General on October 15th 1909.

Earlier that year Roger Pocock produced *The Frontiersman's Pocket-book* on behalf of the LoF which, even today, can be described as a useful guide to survival in wild places and/or behind the enemy lines. Amongst the 70 contributors was Lt General RSS Baden-Powell, though his contribution was merely a single paragraph on horses. Another contributor was Ernest Thompson Seton. (See Page 22)

B-P recommended *The Frontiersman's Pocket Book* to his Boy Scout readers in the 1909 edition of *Scouting for Boys* under the heading *Books to Read,* even though it cost 5s (25p.) At the same time, *Aids to Scouting* - admittedly nine years old, cost only one shilling (5 pence), and the soft cover edition of *Scouting For Boys* was also the same low price. Their cheapness of course made B-P's books accessible to boys, something on which the Founder absolutely insisted.

There is no record of the Legion's involvement at the 1907 Brownsea Island Camp. In 1908 however, one of the Humshaugh Camp diarists, Lawrence Humphreys, (See Page 131) records that WB Wakefield, one of the six full-time Scoutmasters at this camp, was a member of the Legion of Frontiersmen. Wakefield was a 'gentleman of means' who may well have worn his Frontiersman's uniform at the camp. He had worked voluntarily for the YMCA in a senior capacity and in October 1908 became (still as a volunteer) one of the first two Inspectors of Scouting, having responsibility for North of England, Scotland and Ireland.

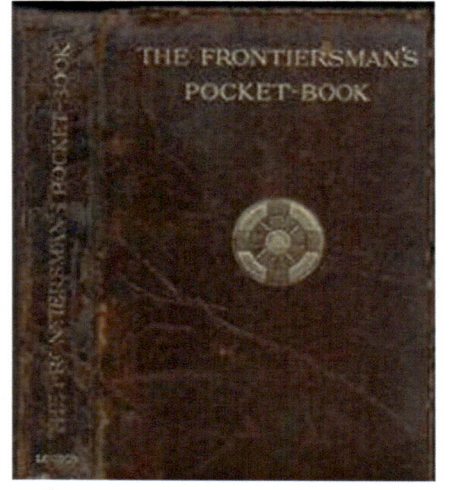

1st Edition Frontiersman's Pocket Book
Image: Countess of Mountbatten's Own, LoF Photo Archives.

Arthur Burchardt-Ashton, a Scout Commissioner for West Wales was another respected Frontiersman in the ranks of the Scout Association who had also been a high official within the YMCA. (See Page 21) He had worked closely with B-P during the First World War and Chief Scout had a high opinion of him.

Burchardt-Ashton   *Photograph courtesy of Countess Mountbatten's Own Legion of Frontiersmen Photo Archives.*

B-P was to wrote[43] of him,

> He is a man of great experience with Colonials and as fearless as they are made, and keen to make the Legion to be of service to this country as it proved in the war.

In 1930 Baden-Powell received an invitation from Burchardt-Ashton, who by then was Commandant–General of the Legion, to join its Grand Council. B-P wrote that though he was flattered to receive the invite he felt he must decline. He revealed that in the past he previously been asked to join the Legion, but had also declined at that time because he felt, *...he was in a difficult position as head of the Boy Scout Movement.* On January 9th 1926, B-P wrote again to Burchardt-Ashton to thank him for a recent pamphlet on the Legion,

> *The old volunteer Corps always kept up their wonderful spirit so long as they were not subsidised by the Government and the Legion is apparently the only Corps of that kind now existing, showing the true spirit of unpaid patriotic service.*

Photograph courtesy of Countess Mountbatten's Own Legion of Frontiersmen Photo Archives

B-P's letters show his admiration for Frontiersmen and their ideals, but he was still unwilling to be officially associated with them. What was the cause of this love/hate relationship that seemed to start off so promisingly in 1908? Snobbery? The whispers about Pocock's alleged involvement in the disappearance of Curtis? We may never know the answer, but the above photograph, taken in Regents Park, London in July 1906, may indicate the great Peace Scout's problem – guns and gung-ho!

The photograph shows a band of patriots, an irregular force of men who were prepared to go at any time, at their own expense, to lay down their lives if necessary in the defence of the Empire. They wear their military uniforms with pride and even, in the peaceful surrounds of a London park, they all appear to be armed.

---

[43] B-P letter, Aug. 26th 1926, Legion of Frontiersmen UK Archives.

Here then was B-P's dilemma. Though he had attempted to 'sell' Roger Pocock and the Legion as Peace Scouts, the same banner under which the Boy Scouts were formed, they clearly were men of action. Though intellectually there can be an academic debate about the maxim, 'if you want peace, you prepare for war', the Legion of Frontiersmen were irregular *soldiers*. The one criticism that the Founder of the Scout Movement consistently felt the need to stamp down on, and at times stamp very hard indeed, was that as a career Colonel he was now training his young Peace Scouts for a war with Germany, which he himself thought was inevitable.

In August 1914, at the outbreak of the First World War, the Legion's strength was claimed as being in excess of 17,500. Just prior to Britain's entry into what became the First World War, a number of eager Manchester Legion volunteers, some of whom had been deemed too old to serve in the British Forces, had been given passes to enable them to join the Belgium Army. They became the first Britons to see action, and were congratulated by Albert, King of Belgium. Their position was regularised when they were transferred into the British Army in February 1915.

Though now fewer in number, the Legion of Frontiersmen continue as a voluntary organisation, both in the United Kingdom and in some of the former dominions of the Empire, particularly in Canada. United Kingdom. Frontiersmen were awarded the distinction of being officially named Legion of Frontiersmen (Countess Mountbatten's Own) in 2002 and celebrated their centenary in 2004-5.

Many Frontiersmen have been Scouts and some, in a private capacity, are still active within the Scout Associations of Commonwealth, and former Commonwealth, countries.

Photograph courtesy of Countess Mountbatten's Own Legion of Frontiersmen Photo Archives

Chapter 3

1908 Publications

The writing of a best seller

William Smith, Founder of the Boys' Brigade, it will be remembered, (See Page 17) challenged B-P to come up with a scheme for training boys based on *Aids to Scouting*. In response, B-P sent him a paper outlining his ideas on 6th May 1906. The Boys' Brigade published a synopsis of his submission in the 1st June edition of the *Boys' Brigade Gazette*, under the heading *Scouting for Boys*.

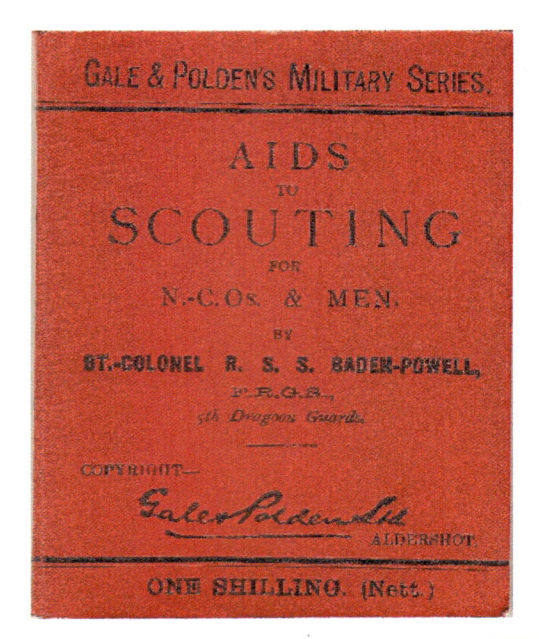

Aids to Scouting was published whilst B-P was besieged in Mafeking in 1899. It became an instant best seller and although aimed at Army personnel, some educators, including the Church Lads' Brigade began to incorporate training aids that B-P advocated in their programmes. The book was serialised in *Boys of the Empire*, a new 'up-market' comic, published October 27th 1900 bringing B-P, for the first time, to the immediate attention of young people. Interestingly the editor chose '*The Boy Scout*' as the caption for the extracts. (See images below.)

© Walker 2008

Exactly one year after the BB article, on May 6th 1907, B-P's term of office as Inspector General of Calvary came to an end and he determined to 'fill the gap in his life' with his new scheme. Just the night before, he had given a lecture to the Sheffield BB about his 'Peace Scouting' ideas.

The story of Arthur Pearson's connection with Scouting is fully explored elsewhere in this book. (See Page 65) It was after their initial meeting in July 1906, no doubt spurred on by Pearson's promise of financial support, that B-P began his writing of *Scouting for Boys* in earnest. On June 15th, 1907, six weeks before the Brownsea camp, B-P set out with his tin dispatch box, bursting with notes and cuttings, to the Izaak Walton Hotel in Dovedale, near Ashbourne, Derbyshire.

There is no doubt that B-P, an enthusiastic fly fisherman, had chosen the venue with a view to at least spending some of his time fishing. The River Dove was after all one of the best trout streams in the land. Perhaps writing was to be the wet weather alternative, as B-P's diary records that it was not until June 19th that he began a major assault on the task he had set himself. He spent 9 hours writing that day but the river was not to be totally denied, as he wrote in his diary, *...fished for a short time, got nothing...*. That same day B-P wrote to Captain Robson of the Bournemouth BB... *I am thinking of having a camp...* so initiating the Brownsea Island experiment.

The Izaak Walton Hotel, Dovedale 2007

On his return to London, work on the book continued spasmodically. A shorthand typist visited B-P's home on June 24th, but all writing activity was interrupted by the Brownsea Camp, which occupied B-P from July 26th to August 9th. This however was time very well spent. The camp confirmed that many of the ideas he had 'borrowed' from others or drawn from his army experience worked well with young people of Scout age. They were noted down and of course, provided material for the book.

By mid-October 1907, Pearson and Baden-Powell came to an agreement - as yet not contractual, that B-P would provide his manuscript for publishing as cheaply as possible in fortnightly parts, and then at a later date as a complete volume.

It became clear that Baden-Powell, and his emerging 'Movement', required much better facilities than the bachelor ex-soldier could provide from his mother's home. Pearson, as part of the 'arrangements', had included the provision of an office.

The newspaper magnate wrote to B-P on October 22nd 1907,

> *It will be best I think to arrange your office in Henrietta Street. The place I have in mind here is quite empty.... If you will communicate with Keary he will fix you up with an office and a stenographer[44] at once.*

---

[44] One skilled in the art of taking down Pitman's shorthand for typing.

> The previous quotation and most of the others used in this chapter come from a booklet entitled *The Founding of the Boy Scouts as seen through the letters of Lord Baden-Powell, October 1907- October 1908*. This treasure house of information came into the public domain when, in 1973, a New England Scout Troop (USA) was on an exchange visit with a London Church Scout Group. During this time a collection of 60 Baden-Powell related letters from Scouting's first crucial year came up for auction. Paul C Richards, a Manuscript Dealer and Collector attached to the Group, had the vision to purchase the collection with a view to opening a Scout Museum in his hometown, East Bridgewater, Massachusetts. A purpose built annex to an existing museum was created and the above-mentioned booklet was published. Richards reportedly *broke with the Church and Scout Group* in 1976. He died in March 1993. Extensive enquiries have recently revealed that some of the letters at least are held by the Howard Gotlieb Archival Research Centre, part of Boston University.

Peter Keary, a published author, was one of Pearson's editors assigned to assist B-P in the creation of *Scouting for Boys*. Baden-Powell had submitted a draft of 'Part I', as an appeal for adults to become leaders in his new Movement. While this initially appeared to meet the approval of the publishers, Pearson's letter of October 22nd dropped the first bombshell in their relationship.

> *I do not think you ought to publish as a pamphlet your Part One... You see we want the parts to come out and secure a large sale before they are published in Book form. In order to secure a large sale they must appear in regular and short intervals, and must be well boomed*[45].

B-P's logic seems faultless, before you create a group needing leadership, you recruit and then train leaders. To a marketing man, especially a 'hustler' such as Pearson, the boot was on the other foot, his instinct was to go immediately for the mass market, the boys. He offered Baden-Powell a compromise,

> *...so what I think ought to be done is for you to bring out a small pamphlet, about ten pages, magazine-size with a cover, just giving a general boil-down of the scheme which can be used as ground work, and put on the bookstalls at a penny a copy; this will answer every purpose required perfectly well.*

This 'new direction' should perhaps have forewarned B-P that the price of accepting Pearson's financial backing was going to involve swallowing a very bitter pill. B-P was not going to have it all his own way. The following sentence must have felt a little like a trap closing,

> *If you have no time to boil down Part One for this purpose, Shaw*[46] *will be able to manage it for you.*

The Hero of Mafeking had met his match. Either he transposed his *Part I* into a penny pamphlet, or Pearson would get somebody to do it for him. The final round however in this 'good/bad/good news sandwich' had yet to be announced. Pearson concluded his letter,

---

[45] Boomed = loudly advertised.
[46] Herbert Shaw, yet another of Pearson's editors, became Editor of the Scout. He had been with Everett on the last day of the Brownsea Camp, and may have taken the only known photographs of the camp.

I think the idea of your brother coming as manager is quite a sound one from every point of view. We agreed, did we not, that the manager should receive a salary of not more than £300 per year.

The brother B-P had in mind was Major Baden Baden-Powell who had also served in the Boer War and was an expert in ballooning and early aviation. In the event he did not take up the position, which was then offered to B-P's long-term regimental friend Kenneth (The Boy) McLaren who was his Assistant Scoutmaster at the Brownsea Experimental Camp in 1907.

The office in Henrietta Street belonged to Pearsons. B-P, a man who was acutely aware of coincidence, would have been immediately struck by the fact that the street bore his mother's name and would have seen this as a lucky omen. Pearson made a point of telling B-P that though the office stood empty at the moment, to allow him use of it would attract rates of ...*150 pounds a year, which is rather a consideration.*

B-P wrote as instructed the following day to Keary, to confirm the arrangement,

I may not be able to get to you today: but I could come tomorrow about 11.30 and get the use of a room and a shorthand writer. I could dictate the whole matter for the pamphlet, which is to be issued as a preliminary in place of Part I as originally proposed.

Throughout the rest of October and November 1907, B-P worked spasmodically on his handbook. His diary shows that he only returned to the Boy Scouts Office once, on November 12th. For the remainder of the time, he was 'out of town', either a guest at country house shoots or giving lectures to support the scheme. He was however stung into action on November 17th when he received a copy of a proposed agreement from Pearson's solicitor. He replied to Keary,

I don't much care for the proposed agreement as drawn up by your solicitor: it rather alters our mutual relations as originally proposed by Mr Pearson. So I am writing to him for his wishes on the subject.
I certainly can't work with a committee ....

> *A camel is a horse put together by a committee!*
> In the army of course, 'orders is orders', no committees involved! In his Scouting career however, B-P had to work with many committees. He was never afraid to surround himself with the best of men and women, who were often challenging, but he would not submit himself to the democratic vote. To have done so would run the risk, as is the case in all democracies, of being over-ruled. Roger Pocock, of the Legion of Frontiersmen, discovered this to his cost when the organisation that he had founded voted him out in 1909. B-P's legacy survives to this day, as although Scouting is led by leaders who work through supporting committees, they (the leaders) are appointed rather than elected.

Writing from Burton Constable, Yorkshire,[47] B-P informed Keary that another publisher, Alston Rivers, had offered better terms. Baden-Powell wanted the book to be as cheap as possible so boys could afford to buy it and Rivers had quoted 3d each for 'The Parts' and 1/- for the complete edition. B-P's response to Pearsons can be seen as a tactic. He had signed nothing yet and was not going

---

[47] On 24th November 1907

to sell the rights to his scheme indefinitely for a 'mess of pottage'. The main sticking point was, what was to happen at the end of the first year of operation[48],

> *As regards the concluding clause. I am very sorry but I cannot bind my self or my scheme to Pearsons for an indefinite time...*

He insisted that either side must have the right to opt out.

> *... by which both of us have our wants supplied, i.e. Pearsons get their newspaper started, I my Boy Scouts* [with Pearson's £1000].

B-P followed this up with another letter on November 30th 1907 where, equally passionately but in more considered terms, he stated that an 'opt out clause' after the first year *must* be a part of the final agreement *...in the interests of both parties*. B-P found the response was acceptable because on December 6th, he wrote to Alston Rivers *...declining them as publishers*.

December 8th 1907 found B-P at yet another Country House shoot, at Battle Abbey in Sussex. His diary records that there was a gale and so, as a 'wet weather alternative', the *Boy Scout Scheme* was finally finished.

> *Shoot Battle Abbey, gale- did a lot of work, posted pamphlet to printer.*

B-P was still smarting over Pearsons' attempt to tie him to their coat tails for the foreseeable future, so on 17th December 1908 he wrote to Keary again.

> *I have shown the agreement to two different lawyers and their first remark in each case was "But there is no dissolving clause...." I must have some means of getting free.... There ought to be some clause to enable us to divorce: so I have added one, but less abrupt than the former one, in the hope that it may suit you too.*

B-P informed Keary that the pamphlet would be ready by Christmas and the first of the 'Parts' by January 15th 1908. (The subsequent five parts were to be issued every other Wednesday.)

Back to work

After a hectic three weeks, which saw B-P giving talks in Exeter and Scotland, he found himself on December 22nd at the Cleveland Arms in Middleton in Teesdale, where he again applied himself to his manuscript. He wrote to Keary that the only thing still required to complete Part I, was a map of the British Empire, could Keary help? B-P suggested that *McLaren could see to this* if Keary could not. Major Kenneth McLaren, been taken on as the first Manager of the Scout Association and not his brother Baden as he had hoped. (See Page 44) McLaren, who suffered ill health, was to remain in post over a year. In this same letter to his publisher's agent, B-P revealed that though behind schedule, his time was not completely devoted writing. The outdoorsman needed the outdoors.

---

[48] Letter to Keary 29th November 1907

Worked all morning on 'Scouting for Boys', walked 5 miles of Teesdale, to High Force waterfall. Hotel managed by ex servant to Lord Ainslie. (There for three days).

High Force Waterfall in the Upper Tees Valley is, after rain, considered the most stunning in England though at 20m, it is not the highest. Many Scouts must have visited these majestic falls as they lay on the route of the Pennine Way.

Photo by StoatBringer

© CWalker 2008

This burst of activity was prompted by the looming deadline for Part I of *Scouting for Boys* which was to hit the news-stands on 15th January 1908. B-P must have been painfully aware that at his present rate of progress the impending deadlines would not be met. He needed the seemingly impossible, a place remote enough to write without interruption, preferably in the countryside he loved, yet at the same time close his publishers.

On December 26th 1907, Baden-Powell took up residence in a cottage under the Windmill on Wimbledon Common belonging to a Mrs Fetherstonhaugh[49] whom B-P had met during his service in Malta. Though the cottage was empty, B-P's mother[50] thought this arrangement very improper and insisted he contacted *the cantankerous Mr Fetherstonhaugh*. B-P did so and was able to tell his mother, *...that Mr F. had written, wishing me a good time, so it's all right.*

Keary lived in Wimbledon, and Everett also found it convenient to visit the windmill cottage. Everett was much impressed with Baden-Powell's handwritten manuscript, illustrated directly with his own sketches.

> *It was fascinating to watch him writing and sketching, now with his right hand, now with his left ... I can still see him at Wimbledon, surrounded by a mass of papers, sketches, notes and all sorts of cuttings and letters.*

---

[49] Fetherstonhaugh –'Fan-shaw', is the most common of five different pronunciations.
[50] Jeal p.383

Scouting for Boys: B-P's Original Manuscript

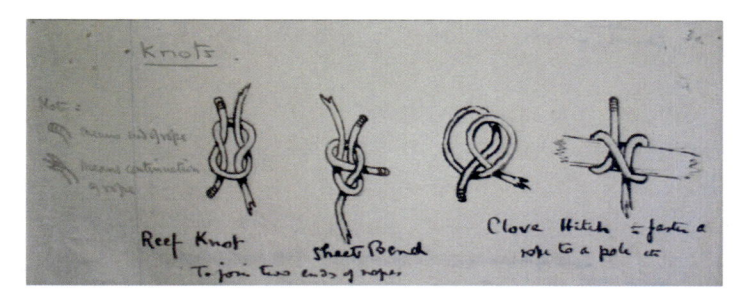

Much of the manuscript of *Scouting for Boys* is held in the UK Scout Archives at Gilwell Park London, by whose kind permission these images appear.

Below: The original MS was written on all manner of paper. This example is on Savoy Hotel letter heading.

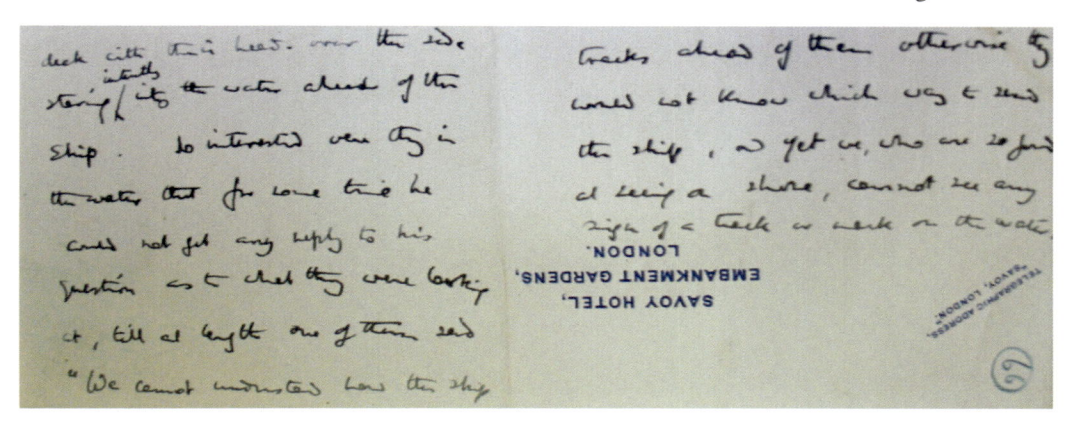

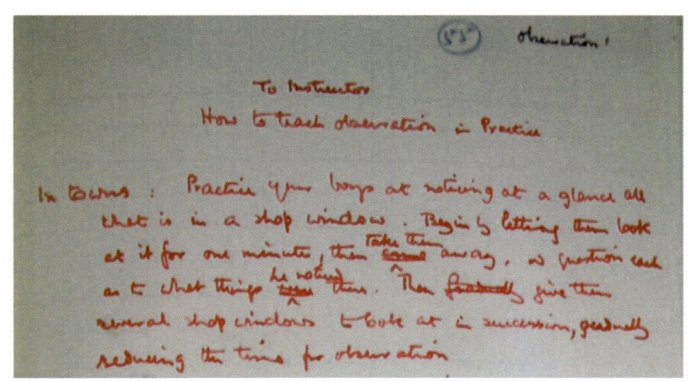

The use of different types of paper and the number of crossings out and amendments make it appear that there was very little system to the work. B-P however coded parts of it in different colours so it could not get mixed up. Red ink was for the Instructors' Section.

Below: The 4th Scout Law
Capital letters spell out the law itself, followed by explanatory text in lower-case handwriting.

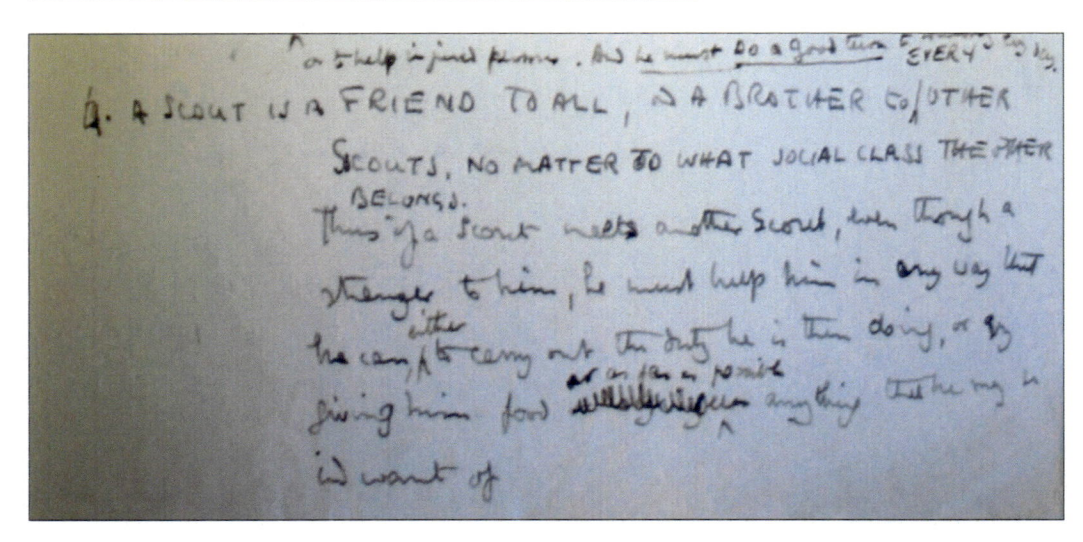

The first draft of the 4th Scout Law, Baden-Powell's greatest achievement.

The process of proof reading was made much easier by the way that B-P quickly returned all correspondence, writing directly on the copy sent to him.

New Year's Day 1908 was significant. Following a flurry of mail, Baden-Powell had finally agreed conditions and so contracts were exchanged. B-P did not mark the occasion in his diary but, once having signed the contract, he was demanding the advertising campaign that Pearson had promised and, on January 2nd, sent his own review to leading editors and also excerpts from the book for Keary to use in its promotion. The Founder, still shaken by the previous omissions from his text, asked to see the proofs before they were used.

Having completed Parts I and II, B-P left the solitary confinement of the Wimbledon Mill cottage for his family home in London. The *Boy Scout Scheme* was published on January 10th, only six days before Part I of *Scouting for Boys*. The same day B-P wrote to editors promoting the scheme:

> *Any proceeds that may come from the handbook will be devoted* [to] *the expenses of the organization.*

The *Boy Scouts Scheme*

As the 'Scheme', was really meant to be part of *Scouting for Boys*, it is not out of place to consider its implications at this point.

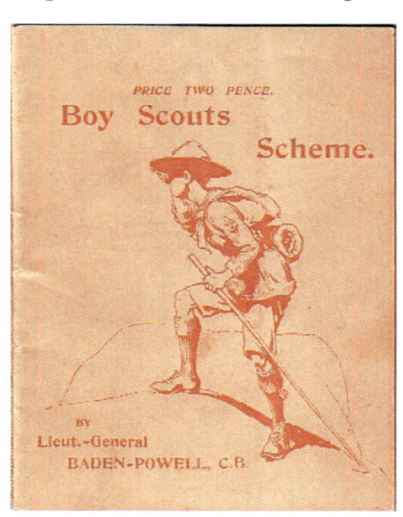

The booklet has a foreword printed in red on its inner cover, *A suggestion which may help any man who desires to do a good turn to his country, his neighbour and himself.*

There then followed a series of *hints* sometimes three to a page, in which B-P puts forward the case for *Peace Scouting* as a remedy to hooliganism. A list of *men who are the best qualified*, to run such a scheme follows:

Schoolmasters; clergymen; members of the YMCA; Legion of Frontiersmen; officers of the Cadet Corps; Boys' and Church Lads' Brigades; Rifle Clubs; country squires; telegraph-masters, etc.

These adults were encouraged to begin work with a patrol of six to eight *smart lads*. The handbook *Scouting for Boys* was promised in the near future to assist them. Baden-Powell was careful not to *teach my grandmother to suck eggs*, addressing his *hints* just to those who had not had previous experience in teaching boys.

The success of the experimental camp on Brownsea Island was described with advice on how to acquire and maintain a *club room* which would need to have a *bright fire* in winter. The provision of a coffee bar, B-P wrote, would help develop a regular income to offset costs. There followed advice on religion and discipline. The pamphlet concluded with a further exhortation to the reader to *train half a dozen boys*.

> *Play the Game: Don't look on.... The British Empire wants your help.*

Clearly the long-term future of the Movement required adults to assist the rising tide of boy-initiated patrols that had been inspired by the first issues of *Scouting for Boys*. The words in *The Scheme* were meant to ensure the supply of leaders, but with its restricted circulation, it could only have had limited benefit.

When *Part I* appeared on January 15th, it was priced at 4d not the 3d that B-P had hoped for. On February 1st 1908, B-P wrote to Everett to thank him for sending out copies to key people. He added somewhat bizarrely that he thought that *Part II* was the most important one for them to see because ... *if the people like it they can then order Part I*.... Revealingly he still had no idea as to whether or not the publication would be a success.

> *I cannot tell how they will go....*

B-P spent February promoting the book, mainly at YMCA organised meetings in;

> Chester (1200), Leeds (900), Newcastle upon Tyne (600), Oxford (300), Nottingham (? Keary present), Sheffield(?), Sunderland(?) and Wakefield (1600).

These promotional lectures were to be the last for some time, as B-P returned to Army life on April 1st 1908 as the Commanding Officer of the Northumbrian Territorial Army. Most of March was spent sorting his remaining commitments, including the final parts of *Scouting for Boys*

On March 12th, following the publication of *Part V*, B-P wrote to Keary from Wroxall Abbey Estate, Warwickshire. He had, he felt, been betrayed,

> *Part V of 'Scouting for Boys' just out is a bit of a fiasco. The corrections of the proofs which I sent in have been completely ignored....*

> *All mention of Continence has been omitted and I should be glad to know who is responsible for this. I can see no excuse for omitting what I sent for publication unless I am consulted and give authority for its omission.*

> *... the promotion of continence is one of the main reasons for starting the scheme... It is a grand blunder to have omitted reference to it in Part V and it will have to go in Part VI - but rather out of its place.*

And another mail on the same subject on 30 March 17th,

> *I have rewritten 'Continence' and I think that as it now stands there can be no objection to its going in its proper place.* [In the complete edition]

> *I don't think it can now shock anybody's susceptibilities, and cannot possibly do any harm to girls, I have taken my mothers opinion on it.*

> *In its present form the paragraph can't do any harm as one of the Hints to Instructors.*

['Continence' and its significance to Baden-Powell is explained overleaf.]

> **Continence and Smoking.**
>
> In 1908, one of the meanings of 'continence', taken from its association with chastity, was 'self abuse' or, as we call it today, masturbation. B-P's view was that this activity *... brings with it weakness of heart and head and if persisted in idiocy and lunacy.* So of course he was anxious to warn his Scouts against this *vice*.
>
> His words however were omitted from *Part V*. Keary blamed Cox, the printers, but they were under Pearson's control. Baden-Powell was not pleased but re-wrote the offending piece, with advice from his mother and others, forcing the above quotation to be included in *Part VI* and then the Complete Editions.
>
> In hindsight B-P was wrong, and his publishers were right to try to remove this subject from the book. Over the last century the 'continence' topic has been used more frequently than any other to deride B-P and his teachings. Though the advice is now acknowledged as unhelpful, it seems perverse to criticise the man and his teachings for what was then a widely held view, supported by medical opinion and the Church, that persisted until the 1950's.
>
> B-P had much other sound health-related advice to offer boys. He was, for example, before his time in his opposition to smoking, when few were opposed to the habit. Baden-Powell had promoted anti-smoking organisations before he wrote *Scouting for Boys*, and he was emphatic,
>
> **A Scout does not smoke.**

B-P wrote to poet Henry Newbolt, asking for permission to quote his poem, *Play up and Play the Game* (properly entitled *Vitaï Lampadas*. Play up! Play up! and play the game! is (see opposite) a repeated line. He enclosed a one-guinea fee which Newbolt returned with his permission to use the work. The poem was included with directions as to how it could be performed on stage, each of the verses being set as a 'tableau'.

By March 13th 1908, it was done. B-P had finished his great work. He wrote to Keary apologising for his previous 'fierceness' over the matter of 'continence' and again one day later to ask if the publicity for the bound edition could contain,

> *...as little reference to me, or to Mafeking, please!*

*There's a breathless hush in the Close to-night
Ten to make and the match to win
A bumping pitch and a blinding light,
An hour to play and the last man in.
And it's not for the sake of a ribboned coat,
Or the selfish hope of a season's fame,
But his Captain's hand on his shoulder smote
"Play up! play up! and play the game!"*

*The sand of the desert is sodden red,
Red with the wreck of a square that broke;
The Gatling's jammed and the colonel dead,
And the regiment blind with dust and smoke.
The river of death has brimmed his banks,
And England's far, and Honour a name,
But the voice of schoolboy rallies the ranks,
"Play up! play up! and play the game!"*

*This is the word that year by year
While in her place the School is set
Every one of her sons must hear,
And none that hears it dare forget.
This they all with a joyful mind
Bear through life like a torch in flame,
And falling fling to the host behind
"Play up! play up! and play the game!"*

An interesting insight into a man who is often cited as a self-publicist.

On March 25th, B-P had made a final attempt at trying to persuade his publishers to keep the price down, *with a view of it getting into proper hands ....*

> *I am certain that anything over 1/6 will be no use for sales purposes – and I can't see why it cannot be got down to 6d in the end, if those printers hadn't been such owls.*

On April 1st 1908, Baden-Powell returned to Army life as the Commanding Officer of the Northumbrian Territorial Army, based at Richmond, North Yorkshire. The TA had only recently been set up by RB Haldane, Secretary of State for war, who had often been at the same house parties as Baden-Powell, and had spent time discussing military matters with him. This appointment severely curtailed B-P's speaking engagements, but did not prevent him from going ahead with publishing the complete edition of *Scouting for Boys*, which was issued on May 1st 1908. Its author must have obtained a special dispensation from the Army, as serving Officers at that time were not permitted to publish books etc. without permission.

Though naturally occupied with his new command, B-P's brain was still in overdrive as to how the book could be better promoted, not to mention the advent of the Scout Magazine (April 13th 1908- see later this chapter) and the preparations for his first National Scout Camp at Humshaugh. (See Page 110)

In his continuing correspondence with Keary, B-P asks,

> *Do you think we could get some presentation copies bound nicely, to send to the two Princes and the Duchess of Connaught?*
> *How would it be to advertise them to schoolmasters as good school prizes to give to boys?*
> ...
> *I have heard of one or two regiments having taken up 'Scouting for Boys' as a handbook for training their recruits.*
> *How would it do to suggest this to the Commanding Officers by circular, or by postcard?*
> ...
> *Have received the four beautifully bound copies. I am sending to each of the following:*
> *Duchess of Connaught, Prince Edward of Wales, Prince Albert of Wales, President Roosevelt.*
> [B-P dedicated *Scouting for Boys* to the two Princes.]

The President of America wrote back to B-P on August 1st 1908 to thank him for his presentation copy, stating that he already had the ordinary version and that he agreed with much of its contents,

> *I most cordially sympathise not only with the methods of the book, but perhaps even more with its purpose ... the lessons which it teaches are as applicable to and as necessary for young Americans as to young Englishmen.*

It should not be assumed however that Baden-Powell was 'over the moon' with his new creation. He complained again to Keary about the over-use of his name.

> *...the last page of the letter press [sic] and mentions my wretched name every other line and makes me pray that nobody will read it.*

The Content

The cover, with its drawing by John Hassall, a friend of B-P's and a member of the London Sketch Club, was first used for *Part V*. It was used for the complete edition, perhaps because the strong image best promoted the spirit of adventure and the widening of horizons. The cover of the Boy Scouts of America 1910 handbook also portrayed the image though the 'Old Glory' replaced the Union Flag. The image continued to be used in the UK until the 1940's.

The chief purpose of the book was to provide boys with a means of finding out about Scouting. There was no other way to discover what a Scout was or, more importantly, how to become one. The answers were all there.

You join a patrol, or ... raise a patrol yourself by getting five other boys to join...

The book was necessarily a 'do it yourself' guide. Thanks to Pearson, B-P's planned plea to help provide the leadership for the new Movement had been relegated to a poorly publicised hardly-read pamphlet. It was not until *Part V*, in April 1908, that adults were addressed in the *Hints to Instructors* section.

Scouting for Boys has been compared to the *Reader's Digest*, an assorted collection of seemingly un-related articles. In his, *Camp Fire Yarns,* B-P his usual anecdotal style, displays a gift for engaging the reader on a personal basis. There are extracts from *Kim* by Rudyard Kipling[51] and a play by B-P about his ancestor Captain John Smith and Pocahontas. It was a rich and varied kaleidoscope that could not fail to attract the adventurous boy.

One hundred years on, having grown up with Scouting as an existing phenomenon, it is difficult to gauge what impact S*couting for Boys* must have had when it was first published. A war hero found he had something to say to the youth of the nation, and he said it directly. To paraphrase the message,

You have enjoyed the campfire yarns and my description of Scouting activities and so now you want to become a Scout yourself. All you have to do is find four or five other boys join in the game and that's it. - You're Scouts! If you have problems that you cannot sort out with the help of this book, ask an adult to help.

B-P felt that Scouters should be like older brothers and act as advisors, not authority figures. He hated the term 'Scoutmaster'.

It must have all been very exciting, if not revolutionary at the time.

---

[51] Baden-Powell had a long friendship with Kipling, detailed on the *Scouting Milestones* website, www.scouting.milestones.btinternet.co.uk/kipling.htm

War or Peace?

The sub-title of *Scouting for Boys* is *A Handbook for Instruction and Good Citizenship*. The very first *Yarn* however is about the Mafeking Cadets and how they helped their country in a time of war. A few pages later, B-P goes on to make a distinction between *War Scouts* and *Peace Scouts*. Army Scouts and the Mafeking Cadets had, in a time of war, already shown what a valuable contribution they could make. *Peace Scouting,* B-P wrote, *involves Scoutcraft that can be put into practice at home.*

There is no doubt that B-P played-up the idea of patriotism. He was one of the first to foresee the growing strength of Germany as a cause for future conflict and had spoken publicly about the necessity of being ready for such an eventuality. The motto *Be Prepared* clearly included being ready to cope in all situations, including that of war. In the final part of the fortnightly issues, Baden-Powell rebuffs those who had criticised the early parts of S*couting for Boys* as being 'militaristic' in outlook;

> *I can only fear that these gentlemen have not read the handbooks very carefully, or I have expressed myself very badly. Even if I had advocated training the lads in a Military way, (which I have not done) I find no harm in it...*
> *The whole intention of the Boy Scouts' Training is for peaceful citizenship.*

Yet in this same issue he encouraged his would-be Scouts to learn to shoot.

> *So make yourselves good scouts and good rifle shots in order to protect the women and children of your country should it become necessary.*

B-P's recurring theme can perhaps be best expressed by the age-old saying, *if you want peace you must prepare for war*. B-P did not believe he was training soldiers, but making future citizens aware of their responsibilities.

He was to some extent however the architect of his own misfortunes. In *Part V*, for example, there is a B-P line drawing entitled, *Two of my Boy Scouts at Mafeking*. What was B-P doing? He was acutely conscious of the charge of 'militarism' and he, above all others, would know that the Mafeking Cadets were not permitted to bear arms and that they were not *Boy Scouts*. So why introduce rifles totally unnecessarily? The mystery deepens because these boys were not from Mafeking at all! The original drawing is to be found in B-P's book, *Sketches in Mafeking & East Africa,* published in 1907, where it is entitled, *The Boys of Bulawayo.*

Scouting for Boys was published less than six years after the Boer war and so we should not be surprised that its pages featured stories from this conflict. Young boys then would be as excited by them, as all generations have been by war stories. From the perspective of nearly 40 years of world peace, author

Michael Rosenthal in his 1984 thesis, *The Character Factory,* uses this material to assert that B-P designed the Movement to serve the existing order and indoctrinate the young of the nation to become the gun-fodder for the next war. Such attacks have sold books and become the basis for TV documentaries, but of course their authors tend to ignore anything that does not support their contention. In a lifetime of Scouting I like most other Scouts, have never seen a weapon of any kind, and our annual St George's Day attempts to 'march', would have brought tears to the eyes of any Sergeant Major. There are still however some blinkered academic sociologists who are happy to lump all 'uniformed organisations' under one military hat.

Left or Right?

As a leading public figure, just how subversive was B-P being, when he told his immense readership of susceptible young minds not to believe all a politician says?

> *The thing is to listen to them all, and don't be persuaded by any particular one, for they all tell fibs, and they each want to get into power.*

Baden-Powell was careful to balance his criticism and praise of the major political parties, but was true to his *Laws for me when I am old,* written when he was just eight years of age in which he stated ...*I will have the poor people to be as rich as we are....* In *Scouting for Boys,* under, *Our Government.* In *Scouting for Boys* he wrote,

> *The Socialists are right in wanting to get money more evenly distributed so there would be no millionaires and no paupers ....*

The balancing viewpoint is contained in the 2nd Scout Law, A Scout has to promise loyalty to his employers and ...*be against anyone who is their enemy or even speaks badly of them.*

B-P's most revolutionary statement however comes from the set of nine Scout Laws[52], in *Part I* of *Scouting for Boys*, that all Boy Scouts were expected to live by. They have been amended over time but still remain central to the concept of what a Scout is. I refer particularly to the original fourth Scout Law:

> *A Scout is a friend to all, and a brother to every other Scout; no matter what social class the other belongs. (Original MS on page 47.)*

Anything more against the established order of things could hardly be imagined in class-conscious Edwardian Britain. The full implications of the statements were perhaps not recognised until Scouting had spread across the globe creating Scouts of every possible colour and creed. It was not just 'classism' that was under attack, but racism too. To make it perfectly clear that B-P was insisting that a Scout should be a friend to *every* other Scout, the final phrase was changed to,

> ...*no matter what colour, class or creed the other may belong.*

---

[52] The original nine laws were extended to ten in 1911. Today the UK Scout Association has seven Scout Laws, the third of which reads, *A Scout is friendly and considerate.*

B-P's great idea was that 'Scoutcraft' was the 'vehicle' by which Peace Scouting could be delivered. The 'craft' most evident in *Scouting for Boys* is that of Camping. To misquote an old 'Scoutism', the 'out' B-P put in 'Scout' refers to the 'outdoors'. In the year 2000, the Scout Association commissioned a major survey amongst young people both in and out of the Movement. Their overwhelming response, when asked about their expectations on joining the Scouts, was that they wanted to go camping. Of those who had left the Movement prematurely, the overwhelming majority said that they had left because their section did not go camping enough. It is true that even though a privileged majority holiday further from home than ever before, most young people would still benefit immensely from being part of an organisation that properly introduced them to the skills of outdoor living. Indeed, it seems perverse that today's youngsters are educated to know more about environmental issues than any other generation but, unless they become Scouts, or have enlightened parents, they are likely to have even less experience of the countryside than that of their grandfathers.

The Success of the Book

Just measure the success of *Scouting for Boys* in terms of sales, is a little like trying to equate the importance of Shakespeare to literature from merely knowing how many people went to see his plays whilst he was alive. However, the statistics are in themselves impressive;

May 1st 1908, published in book form, cloth-bound by Horace Cox at 2s. and in paperback 1/-. It ran to four reprints in the first year. By 1927 the book was in print in 27 countries as well as those of the British Empire. In 1948, 500,000 copies were sold in Britain alone. E E Reynolds, B-P biographer and Scout historian, tells us in his *Boy Scout Jubilee* that the book was still a bestseller between 1946 and 1954.

B-P biographer, Tim Jeal, not one of Baden-Powell's staunchest supporters, wrote in 1989, that *Scouting for Boys* had probably sold more copies than any other title in the 20th century, with the exception of the Bible. Most people however would also include other religious tracts and Chairman Mao's Little Red Book in the 'most published' list.

Pearsons published a 'Centennial Edition' in 1957 marking the 100th anniversary of B-P's birth. Only in 1967 did they admit that sales were declining, but a new centennial edition has ensured its continuing presence in bookshops and on the Internet.

Of the newspapers that reviewed the work at the time of its publication, the *Daily Graphi*c was the most prophetic,

> *All can help ... This is a kind of snowball to which nobody could object.*

The snowball was rolling, and it has never stopped. The millions of former and present members of the Scout Association worldwide are the true 'success indicators' of the book.

Some modern commentators[53], instead of looking at B-P the Victorian soldier, and asking what it was in his 1907/8 writings that inspired today's 29 million member Movement, seem to delight in pointing out how 'non P.C.' (Politically Correct) B-P's early writings were. Given that they were written over a century ago, ought that really to be a surprise? There might be some point in the criticism if Scouts were still using the same handbook, word for word, today. That however is not the case. All that is relevant, and much is, has been utilised and added to vibrant modern handbooks. The Association has moved on.

Baden-Powell's reputation, and Scouting, have nothing to fear from honest historical research and analysis at whatever depth. Commentary based on the aspirations of 'political commentators', without any attempt to understand just how revolutionary B-P's proposals were to the world in which he lived, is simply misguided.

The Latest 'Review'

A milestone was achieved on BBC Television on Thursday May 14th 2007, when Ian Hislop presented his hour long documentary on *Scouting for Boys*. Hislop, veteran of many a libel case, is well known as a witty but acerbic denunciator of 'the establishment'. Many in the Scouting fraternity must have trembled at the treatment he was likely to hand out to possibly the most lampooned book in the world, and its misunderstood author, particularly as some of the previous BBC documentaries in the Centennial Year had proved to be carping and at times very derogatory towards the Founder of the Scout Movement.

Right from the start Hislop, in a quite endearing way, made his viewers aware of all of the 'baggage' usually associated with the nearly 100 year old book and its famous author. He then clearly spelt out what the pundits, and even the Scout Association itself, have consistently failed to do, elaborating on just why the book was a world best seller with themes that are still very pertinent today. Hislop quoted B-P's concern with disaffected youth, his attempt to inculcate 'Citizenship' (now a Government aim), the provision of role models etc. And all this was done with a cheery admission that though he himself was not a Scout, he had found the book fascinating and rather surprised to be agreeing with much of its central message.

The programme then used a series of 'experts' to provide the 'balance' so beloved of documentary makers. Paul Moynihan, the Association's archivist, guided Hislop through the actual handwritten manuscript of the book. The greatest advocate for Scouting however was B-P himself, through the inclusion of footage of the great man. This included the never to be forgotten sequence where B-P appeared to address Hislop referring to him as, *You - the ugly one in the corner over there.*

---

[53] See the Foreword, *Scouting for Boys* published 2004 published as a collector's edition.

Inevitably one of B-P's greatest 'character assassins', Tim Jeal, was allowed to have his say and came up with his same tired non-proven, largely irrelevant, 'insights' into B-P's sexuality[54].

The editor of the most recent edition of *Scouting for Boys* thankfully refused to comment on B-P's 'sexuality', no doubt still conscious of the comprehensive howl of disapproval over her recent very long and 'politically correct' analysis in her introduction to B-P's book. She however still managed to convey her misguided allegation that B-P was fixated on 'orifices'.

Such was Hislop's good-natured and even admiring treatment that the detractors' views were, for a change, placed in the context of a positive appreciation of B-P and his works. Hislop actually stated that there were in fact historians who disagreed with Jeal. His refreshing approach was such that I find it difficult to be critical of him. Well almost! Towards the end of the transmission, we find him standing outside a newsagents and turning directly to the camera makes the most outrageous suggestion of the broadcast,

> *If Baden-Powell were alive to day, he might not be allowed to be a Scout Leader.*

What? The message was further rammed home on a prominent placard which read *B-P Perv*. This really was not at all in keeping with the rest of the programme - it was a cheap jibe and not at all funny - especially to parents of the 29 million children in the world who entrust their offspring to B-P's memory. These millions of present-day Scouts would, I am sure, add a final criticism - they received no mention. Their vast numbers, diversity and the modern programme of training they receive, all inspired by the book (*Scouting for Boys*) the programme was meant to be about, was sadly lacking.

In the main however Hislop's programme was a breath of fresh air. It was simply the best programme on the history of Scouting made in recent years. At least two and half cheers.

The Scout Magazine

Whilst the chronology of *The Scout* magazine, runs parallel to that of *Scouting for Boys*, these publications need to be considered separately. The book was Baden-Powell's creation and was, in essence, an expression of his belief that boys could be turned into useful citizens. *The Scout* magazine was meant to be a continuing means of communication. Under the control of its publishers however, it was, as B-P himself said, little more than *an ordinary boys' magazine.*

Baden-Powell had had very high aspirations for the new journal. He detailed them in a letter to Peter Keary, sent March 1st 1908,

---

[54] See Scouting Milestones review of Jeal's book *Baden-Powell* for many examples of the way he provides, erroneous at worst, skewed at best, evidence that allows you to come to 'your own conclusion' that B-P was a repressed homosexual, a stance that he seems to be dropping by the day in favour of a straight charge of homosexuality.

> *With regard to the 'Scout' I should like to suggest as one of its chief aims it should make for bringing all organizations for Boys together - to act as a bond between them all such as; Boys' Brigade, Church Lads' Brigades, YMCA Junior Branch, Cadet Corps, Rifle Clubs, Working Boys Clubs, the Public Schools, Choirs, Cricket and Football Clubs, etc.*
>
> *The existing Gazettes of the Boys' Brigade, YMCA, CLB, etc. are addressed to the officers and not to the boys of those Corps; where as the 'Scout' could be made to appeal to both.*

The second paragraph was really a very astute observation. *The Scout* could, if properly targeted, have become the one magazine for all youth organizations. B-P was hoping that the already-formed Scout Patrols within the 'brother organisations', would read, and be influenced by 'his' magazine, allowing him to exercise some influence over a wider membership. Whether or not the leaders of the other organisations would have allowed this to happen is another matter.

B-P voiced these same concerns to Keary on March 13th and added that he hoped that the paper would be mainly for boys but partly for instructors. This was sound logic, but there was little precedent for a publication appealing to such a wide age-span, and who was going to write to such an audience? Under its first editor H Shaw, the publication date[55] was set for Tuesday April 14th. B-P had hoped it might be earlier, as his Army duties re-commenced on April 1st. He feared that regulations would restrict his name from appearing on the cover, but permission must have been granted, as all future issues displayed the legend, *Founded by Gen. Baden-Powell*.

On being provided with a mock-up of the first issue, B-P wrote to Keary,

> *I think the stories for the 'Scout' are good. But I hope that there will be a lot of improving stuff too, like model making, career making, sample lives of self-made men etc.*

This attempt to improve the Scouting content of the magazine did not succeed. Costing only one penny, *The Scout*, typically had 22 pages. B-P provided a weekly page and most probably was the author of another, entitled *Round the Campfire*. Two further pages, not written by B-P, *What All Scouts Should Know* were targeted directly at Scouts. The last page entitled *Britain's Boy Scouts* was, B-P thought, the most important of all. A further page was devoted to the *Great Race* i.e. the Humshaugh Scout Camp competition which, as we have seen, Baden-Powell hated. The other 17 pages contained up to six boys' stories, only the first of which, such as *The Boys of the Otter Patrol,* had a Scout theme. The other stories drew on the exciting experiences of guest writers such as Legion of Frontiersmen, Roger Pocock and John Mackie. (See p.33)

On March 29th 1908 B-P voiced his strong disapproval over *The Scout* competition as it appeared in the mock-up;

---

[55] This was achieved, though the date on the masthead was April 18th 1908. The following week was the 'St George's Day Issue'. Would it have been better to have launched the magazine on this day, announcing that St George was to be the patron saint of Scouts? Besides being England's national saint, St George was also the patron saint of B-P's Calvary Regiments.

*That sheet in the 'Scout' advertising the camp has been recurring to my mind in a rather unsatisfactory way. There is something in it, which I fear will put off readers of the better sort. The fact that it touts for subscribers is to my mind the weak point: it looks like we feared not to succeed on our merits; and this is an obvious puff [sic] not to spread it afar (as **my** policy would be) but to get subscription.*

These criticisms did not stop the Founder of the Scout Movement sending out press releases dated 29th March. B-P was loud in its praises, not so much applauding *The Scout* as it was, but what he wanted it to be.

I venture to send out for your favourable consideration a copy of a newspaper, 'The Scout' which Arthur Pearson Ltd are bringing out for me as a penny weekly, with the following objects.

To further, in an interesting form, the aims of Peace Scouting for Boys: to bring the various existing organisations for boys into closer mutual touch, through the medium of Scouting, and to supply ideas and suggestions for instructors and officers of such organisations in their great work of improving the rising generation in character and good citizenship.

When B-P saw the first issue on April 14th, he was devastated,

'The Scout' reached me - but I'm afraid I'm not enthusiastic over it. ...It is to the outsider little more than an ordinary boys' paper - not one to bring about great amalgamation of all boys' organisations which is what I had hoped for - and which opens up a virgin field and a big prospect.

In his letter, B-P lamented that the back page of the paper *…is almost the one that ought to be at the front…*and reminded Keary that they had agreed that they would not use the word 'Legion' *as it would …damn the scheme with most of the big organisations'.* (See page 34) In short The Founder must have realised his earlier protests had been to no avail and he had very little, if any, control over this magazine that had been created in his name.

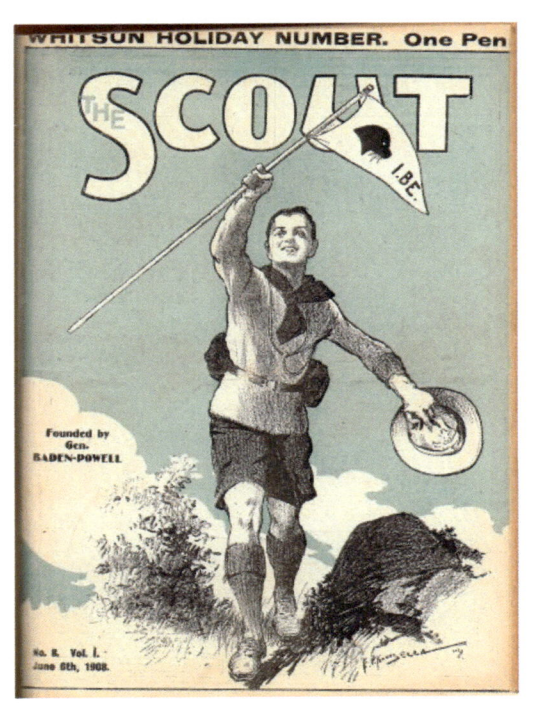

The first issue of *The Scout* magazine had, at B-P's insistence, the very striking cover used as the main feature in the cover design for this book. It is an adaptation in colour of the black and white drawing that was used for *Part I* of *Scouting for Boys*. The following covers however were in black and white. B-P told Keary of complaints he had about this and forwarded them to him, adding;

I agree with this man re the Cover of the 'Scout'. - The present get up does not show at all on a bookstall. (I passed it over myself when actually looking for it) - and it is not nearly so attractive say as even the 'Boys Herald' in appearance. Would the cover add very much to the expense? If so why not have really good frontispiece on the front page instead- to catch the eye.

59

B-P's suggestion was taken on board and the cover of the Whitsuntide issue, June 6th 1908, was again in colour. Baden-Powell was so full of admiration that he asked if he could have the original artwork.

The love/hate relationship with *The Scout* was to continue for the rest of B-P's life. The Founder did his best to try to 'bring it into line', but he never could. In a letter to Keary, July 11th 1908, the Founder wrote,

> *I received samples of the Boy Scouts Post Cards but find my name printed all over them. It really is too bad. I shall be forced to give up the whole thing if there is any more of it. One evidently cannot trust to the discretion of the staff....*

A consequence of B-Ps dislike of the content, and distrust of the managers of *The Scout,* was that he realised none to soon, that his adult leadership could not be expected to read the *penny dreadful*, and needed a proper 'Gazette' of their own. Once the initial contract period, he had so wisely insisted on, had expired, the Scout Association was, in July 1909, able to publish the *Headquarters Gazette*, an 'all-Scouting' monthly for Scouters. Though it has had a variety of names the magazine continues to be published under the title *Scouting*.

There was, according to B-P's diary, a chance that the magazine might yet be salvaged and appear in the Scouting style that the Founder so craved. On February 2nd 1909, Baden-Powell volunteered to edit *The Scout*, ... *but Pearson's financing did not suit.* The salary offered was clearly too low. The question is, was it deliberately made to be unacceptable?

The Scout survived until September 24th 1966, when it became uneconomic to produce. It has never been resurrected, though in this age of free mass communication it is hard to see why a similar work could not appear 'on-line'. Many Scout Groups and Districts do offer on-line magazines, and the author's own website[56] contains many articles on Scout History, which used to be, on occasion, a feature of *The Scout*. Technology continues to advance and Scouting continues its tradition of keeping up with the times. Today, 'pod casts' are available to Scouts worldwide via *Scouting Radio.*

The station[57], staffed totally by volunteers from across the globe, would surely have raised a smile on the face of the Founder who, in 1908, was desperate to find a way of communicating with his emerging worldwide Movement.

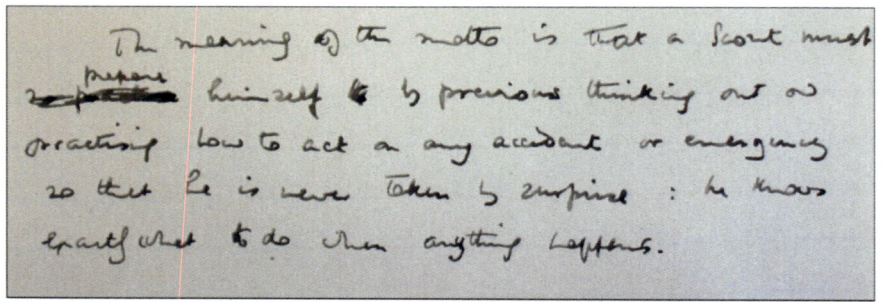

The original manuscript explanation of the Scout Motto, *Be Prepared*. Courtesy UK Scout Archives

---

[56] www.scouting.milestones.btinternet.co.uk
[57] www.scoutingradio.com/

Chapter 4

The First Troops

Throughout its history, the Scout Association has always declined to nominate the first ever Scout Troop. Since 1957 however they have maintained, and have now published on their website,[58] a list of troops which claim to have been started during 1908. The 1957 register had 55 troops, while 99 are currently listed.

It is important to recognise from the outset that the central organisation would have no knowledge of emerging groups until such time as they registered. The first opportunity for this to have occurred was after the opening of the Scout Office[59] in Groschen Buildings, 37 Henrietta Street, WC2 in January 1908. As we shall see, there are many reasons why groups did not send in forms with the necessary registration fee for some months or even years[60] after their inauguration. Even when groups were registered, some records over the years have been lost[61], making it impossible to provide a chronological list of the earliest group registrations. Clearly the history of a group will not begin with its registration. Though this formal stage in the life of a founding troop is certainly of great interest, other evidence must be found to establish the actual start date.

The date of registration depended on the efficiency of both the local officials and the willingness of the patrol/group to be 'organised' and pay the cost of affiliation which was decided locally. In Birmingham for example it cost one shilling (5p) to register a single patrol of eight Scouts, five shillings (25p) for a troop. This was a considerable amount of money[62] in 1908. If the patrol/group already belonged to one of the 'brother organisations', which already had an effective means of support at local and national level, registration with the Scout Office would not have been necessary.

The Founder would of course have been aware of some of the earliest groups and in his later life, particularly at Scouting anniversaries, he was asked for his opinion. His response was to throw questioners completely off the scent by denying that he had had anything to do with it. He would affirm that Scouting was a Movement, not an organisation[63], stating,

> *As a matter of fact I didn't actually see the start of the Boy Scout movement because the blooming thing started itself unseen.*
> *Before many parts of the book had been published I began to get letters from boys who had taken up the game themselves, boys not belonging to the Boys' Brigade or any other association telling me how they had started*

---

[58] http://www.scoutbase.org.uk/library/hqdocs/facts/pdfs/fs295303.pdf
[59] The Office was owned by B-P's publisher Pearson. (Page 15 footnote 10)
[60] See Percy Everett and the 1st Elstree account in this chapter.
[61] EE Reynolds, The Scout Movement p. 56
[62] Five Shillings in 1908 (25 pence) equates to about £25 in today's values
[63] B-P distinguished between *a Movement that moves, and an Organisation which bogs itself down in red tape.* (Scouting in London, *PB Nevill, p.124*)

patrols and Troops and had got men to come and act as their Scoutmasters.

There are many well-documented examples that prove B-P's case. Having read the early editions of the part series, boys went with their friends into the fields and woods of Britain (sometimes with permission!) to practise the great game of Scouting. To give them respectability, but more often than not in the hope that they might be provided with a place to meet, they sometimes sought out a sympathetic adult whom they thought could be persuaded to take up the role of Scoutmaster. These first patrols were, as B-P decreed, given a patrol name and either the oldest boy, or the instigator of the idea, became the Patrol Leader. The P.L. would then nominate his 'Corporal' or, as we would say today, Assistant Patrol Leader.

These patrols, with or without adult guidance, were usually the first evidence of Scouting in any district. Two or three patrols might link together for activities and still not think of themselves as a Scout Group. They were precluded from Group status until there were at least three patrols[64] meeting in the one place, by which time an adult would have become involved. Registration did not usually occur until the group, with its Scoutmaster, was recognised by a Local Committee under its Secretary. Local Committees were not by any means as fast in forming as Scout Patrols. Many large areas of the country were still without local committees by January 1909, though good progress had been made in the cities and most towns.

B-P's publisher and sponsor, Arthur Pearson, diverted the Founder's original intention of writing the first part of *Scouting for Boys* specifically for would-be leaders, placing this information in a smaller unpublicised pamphlet, the *Boy Scouts Scheme*. (See page 48) This may have been the correct commercial decision, as without the boys there would be no need for Scoutmasters and of course far more copies would be sold to boys than to adults. The guidance available to the adult leadership was then initially restricted to a brief two-page 'introduction' in *Part 1*, issued on January 15th 1908. Further help was not to come until *Part VI* some three months later. The consequence of this was that there were many patrols in the early months of 1908 without adult involvement.

For brave souls who had volunteered, or had been press-ganged by eager children, into the role of Scoutmaster, there was very little information to assist them in this new 'game' that they had taken on. It was not until July 1909 when the monthly *Headquarters Gazette*, a magazine specifically for adult leaders, was launched that a regular means of communication was established. Unlike *The Scout*, this publication was directly under B-P's control and its contents were totally about Scouting. Though mainly instructional, it was occasionally, thanks to its letters pages, a dialogue between Scouters and Headquarters. It was exactly what was required, but unfortunately one and half years too late.

Baden-Powell realised from the start that the 'Movement', formed by the youth of Britain or not, required structure and organisation if it was going to survive. His 1907-8 lecture tours (See Page 7) had a dual purpose. As well as 'spreading the word', Baden-Powell set out specifically to identify key personnel for future

---

[64] *Scouting for Boys* Part 1, January 1908, *Camp Fire Yarn 3*, under *A Scoutmaster*.

Local Committees, noting in his diary the name of any prominent person who might become District Secretary when the scheme was launched.

The duties of Local Committees were spelled out in a circular B-P sent to all interested parties on September 28th 1908[65], the prime requirement being,

> *To bring into touch with themselves all Patrols and Troops of Boy Scouts in their districts and register them.*

Once formed, committees found it difficult to cope with boy-led patrols without any form of adult supervision. These 'ad hoc' units strengthened or dissolved as their members grew older. Middle and upper class boys went off to school while the lower classes often had to leave home to find employment. They were sometimes referred to, perhaps a little unkindly, as *'monkey patrols'*.

There was no official census of Scouts at any point in 1908, but by the end of that year however, Liverpool is known to have had 3000, and other large centres of population in excess of a thousand. A conservative estimate of the number of Scouts in the United Kingdom at the start of 1909 has been placed at 55,000[66] If the average number of boys per group/patrol is taken as 25 (some Scouts would still be in single patrols), there must have been at least 2200 groups/patrols.

Very little is known about most of these and only a fraction, the 99 troops on the Scout Association list, can claim to have been in existence since 1908 and are still active today. These troops may well have a different name however from that of the founding troop as a result of reorganisations and amalgamations. The Appendix contains a listing of troops that can be proven to have existed in 1908, those still in existence are indicated with an asterisk.

The Snowball begins to roll

The 1908 groups were just the first signs of a gathering momentum that started with just 22 boys[67] on Brownsea Island in August 1907 to the 39 million[68] Scouts and Guides of today. The following group histories have been selected from those that are available, because they have had a significant role to play in the history of Scouting, or offer a particular insight into its development.

Arthur Primmer and the 'Washhouse Patrol'

Fifteen-year-old Arthur Primmer was already a Junior Clerk for Trevannians, a firm of Poole Solicitors, when he was selected by his Boys' Brigade Captain, George Green, to attend Baden-Powell's Experimental Camp. Out the of ten BB boys selected to attend the camp, just three, including Arthur, came from Poole, one of the ferry ports for Brownsea Island, less than a couple of miles across the water from the historic campsite.

---

[65] EE Reynolds, The Scout Movement, p.50
[66] S Harris, Legalised Mischief Vol. 1, Graph p,145
[67] 21 participants plus B-P's nephew Donald. See *Brownsea: B-P's Acorn* Ch. 6
[68] Statistics from the UK Scout Association and World Association of Girl Guides.

Primmer, who lived to be 91, told a newspaper reporter[69] that after returning from the camp he formed the world's first Scout Patrol in a disused washhouse at the back of a cottage in Chapel Lane, Poole. (Chapel Lane still exists today less than half a mile from Poole Quay, but most of its original buildings were demolished after bomb damage in World War II.)

> *We took the example from Baden-Powell's 'Scouting for Boys' fortnightly magazine, formed our patrols, and forced adults to help us rather then the other way round*
>
> *I was seventeen when a large troop was formed in Broadstone* [a district of Poole]. *I dropped out and the lads moved into that one.*
> [Arthur was 17 on February 3rd 1909]

A local Broadstone publication[70] has recently documented Primmer's involvement in the 1st Broadstone. It records that Primmer went to Bournemouth to see his friend Victor Watkin (the first ever King's Scout). Together they approached the local vicar, Rear Admiral Thring (retired) to discuss the founding of a troop, …and by the following week there were eight interested boys. The Broadstone group thrives to this day.

Arthur Primmer and the Washhouse Patrol?

There is one piece of strong, but unfortunately non-conclusive, evidence that supports Arthur Primmer's claim. The author, when researching his *Brownsea: B-P's Acorn* book, had the privilege of being able to scan the photograph above from Arthur Primmer's own Scouting photographic album. The image is also to be found in *Bare Knee Days*, by F. Haydn Dimmock (A former editor of *The Scout*). Dimmock claims the image was taken in 1907 on Brownsea. For reasons fully explained in *Brownsea: B-P's Acorn* this is not the case. We are looking at a 1908 patrol.

---

[69] Scouts Honour 'Grand Old Man, The Times Herald Series, February 14th 1981
[70] The New History of Broadstone, Margaret Roebuck and Julie Wenham

For the photograph to be included in Primmer's album, it is reasonable to assume that he was on it. As few other people could have had as much Scouting experience, he was most likely the Patrol Leader (with the patrol pennant). Arthur Primmer daughter's Wanda, who inherited the album, said her father always maintained that it was his patrol.

King Scout Alfred Watkin

If Primmer's reference to the fortnightly parts of *Scouting for Boys* is taken as an indication that his patrol was formed after their publication, then his was just one of many patrols that started at this time. However if he was referring generally to Scouting in 1908, as seems very likely by his use of the word 'patrols', then this is not contradictory to the clear assertion that his was the first patrol. Arthur Primmer was certainly aware of the formation of the other 1908 patrols/troops in his locality. As he had achieved what some would see as the supreme accolade of being with B-P, at the 1907 Brownsea Camp there is no reason to disbelieve his story of the creation of the 'washhouse patrol', particularly as it confirms other accounts of the formation of the Broadstone group with Alfred Watkin.

Whether 'first ever', or just very early may now be difficult to prove, but without doubt Brownsea pioneer Arthur Primmer and his early Scouting friends deserve a far wider recognition than they have been so been accorded.

Percy Everett and 1st Elstree Group

Everett's association with Baden-Powell began when he was invited to a dinner party at the Surrey home of his employer, publisher and philanthropist Sir Arthur Pearson in July 1906. Everett worked as one of Pearson's literary editors and, like everybody else of his generation, looked forward to meeting 'The Hero of Mafeking'.

Pearson had a considerable publishing empire, including the *Daily Express* which he founded in 1900, and a record of supporting worthy causes, not least his own 'Fresh Air Fund'[71] for taking blind children to the seaside, or into open country, often with the assistance of London taxi cab drivers.

After the meal, B-P was asked to talk about his Mafeking experiences and the success of his book *Aids to Scouting* which had been serialised in a boys'

---

[71] The charity renamed Pearsons' Holiday Fund is still operative today.

magazine, (See Page 41) *The Boys of The Empire*[72]. The Hero of Mafeking had of course been asked similar questions many times before at the numerous 'house parties' he had been invited to attend since his return from South Africa in March 1903. Pearson however was a man he wanted to impress, a man with ideals as well as ideas and the means to enable B-P to achieve his latest ambitions, the pro-motion of his Scouting Scheme. So, once having satisfactorily fielded his host's questions, B-P departed from his usual 'script', and went straight to the point,

> *There are,* he said, *one and a quarter million boys in the country at present, mostly drifting towards hooliganism, for the want of a helping hand.*

Of course Pearson and the other guests wanted to know just what the Lieut.-General was suggesting and so B-P was able to unveil his scheme that he had been formulating since 1904, that utilised his scouting/woodcraft skills as a vehicle to help produce better citizens of the Empire. He referred to his idea as 'Peace Scouting'.

Pearson was, as history demonstrates, sufficiently impressed to volunteer his support B-P's scheme financially in return for publishing rights but, in the context of this chapter, it is Everett's reaction which is under consideration. The literary editor was later to write[73]

> *I always look back on the little incident* [the dinner party] *as one of the great landmarks in Scouting in this country; also with much personal pleasure, as it was the cause of me joining the movement in its initial stages....*

Everett was privileged, as Pearson's representative, to visit and report on B-Ps experimental Scout Camp on Brownsea in August 1907. His role, and the profound effect the experience had upon him, is thoroughly documented in the companion volume to this work. Suffice it to say that he came away from the camp inspired by B-P and his methods.

The following year on February 20th 1908, Percy Everett recorded in his diary,

> *...five or six Elstree boys approached me with a view to forming a troop.*

This was something of a life-changing moment because, although he was involved in B-P's plans to promote Scouting, he had never considered that he might himself become directly involved as a Scoutmaster. Some years later he wrote[74],

> *No idea had ever crossed my mind of running a Troop. I felt much too humble to imagine that I could make any sort of success of the job, but what do you do when six boys from your village come and say in chorus, 'Please, sir, will you be our Scoutmaster?'*

These boys had learned about Scouting through reading the early editions of the fortnightly *Scouting for Boys*. Everett of course succumbed, and the inaugural

---

[72] *The Boys of the Empire*, 'The Boy Scout' articles occur between Nov 3rd 1900-Jan 26th 1901
[73] Frank Brittain, *The History of Hertfordshire Scouting*.
[74] Sir Percy Everett, *The First Ten Years*, p.30.

meeting of the 1st Elstree Troop took place on March 13th 1908. Everett noted down the names of 16 boys whom he formed into the Otter and Eagle patrols, including his daughter Winn (aged 6) whom Everett maintained was the first ever Girl Scout. Winn was to remain in her father's troop until she went away to school, probably when she was eleven. Unlike most Girl Scouts (see Page 78) she had the privilege of knowing the Founder.

> *Baden-Powell was a wonderful person, I just thought that he was my friend. I used to think that when he came here, he had come just to see me, not to see anybody else[75].*

One of Everett's 1908 founding Scouts visited the Elstree Scout hut[76] in 1952 when a memorial was unveiled to Sir Percy, (as he became). Mr A. Bailey recalled that he and five other boys had formed a patrol and called on Mr Everett to be their Scoutmaster. The boys met in his stable and were 'afforded unfailing courtesies and patience'. Percy Everett's tolerance must have been sorely tried however when on one troop night, fighting broke out amongst the boys. Order was soon restored, but the Elstree's Scoutmaster did not make a fuss, ... *he simply told us that we were wrong. This quiet approach having a better effect than shouting.*

It was not however, until May 9th 1909 that, despite his very central position, Percy Everett received his warrant as the Scoutmaster of the Elstree Troop. Take away the famous name, and this same scenario was repeated hundreds of times all over country. The two most common elements of the 1st Elstree story are that the inspiration came from the boys (and in this case one girl) and that official recognition in the form of a warrant or registration document could, for whatever reason, be a long time coming. The Elstree records prove beyond doubt that any contemporary official (1908) listing is not going to record all groups that were in existence, even those that were properly constituted and led by responsible adults with close connections to the Founder.

Sir Percy Everett, whom B-P often referred to as his 'right hand', became Deputy Chief Scout. He was awarded a 6 bead Wood Badge, the only other being the one B-P himself wore. Everett was one of three men charged with the administration of the Scout Movement in March 1940, when during a crucial stage of the war, the then Chief Scout, Lord Somers, went to the Middle East to supervise the Red Cross.

The 1st Glasgow

The 1st Glasgow Scout Troop was formed by Captain Robert E Young of the Glasgow Army Training Corps. The boys, members of his corps, attended Glasgow Academy, Kelvinside Academy and Glasgow and Hillhead High Schools. In 1907 a section of the Army Training Corps, called the Cadets Winter Training Club, began to meet separately in their adjutant's house. 'Boss' Young met B-P, most probably on December 18th 1907, when the Founder lectured in Glasgow before 2500 people. On January 15th 1908, the Cadets' Club was disbanded and the 1st Glasgow was formed. The new group came to

---

[75] Wynn Everett's Story p 20, Avril Chick, courtesy Frank Brittain Hertfordshire Scout Archives.
[76] Undated newspaper report held in Hertfordshire Scout Archives.

the attention of *The Scout* magazine on 25th July, when it was reported that they had three patrols, and again on August 22nd with the news that the troop now had 15 patrols of eight boys and could boast a library of 150-200 volumes. On Nov. 28th *The Scout* again carried news of the group, commenting that it (*The Scout*) had a 'rival', as the 1st Glasgow was producing '*a Scouting Journal*'.

> *It is a very well got up magazine typed and bound by members of the troop, with an artistic cover, also drawn and lithographed by one of the Scouts.*

Scoutmaster 'Boss' Young continued to run the troop until his death in 1940. The group are still working to capacity to this day, with some of its members coming from the same schools as those of the 1908 founding boys.

The certificate on the following page is believed by many to be the earliest known registration document, dated 26th January 1908. Whilst there is no doubt that the group was in existence at this time and that the certificate is genuine, it is doubtful that it was signed and dated in the same year as the group was formed.

One might expect that the very first Scout Groups would have a certificate signed by Baden-Powell. The 1st Glasgow example is however signed by Archibald J Kyle[77]. Kyle himself received what may have been the first Scoutmaster Warrant on October 6th 1908, for a London troop, an appointment which was not sufficiently senior to have involved him in the registration of Scout groups, particularly those in Scotland. He was however appointed Manager of the Scout Association in April 1909, a role in which he would have been expected to sign such documents. The registration document itself is of the 1909 pattern.

EE Reynolds in his book *The Scout Movement* describes the registration document of the 1st Newport Old Guard, also formed in the early days of 1908.

> *... by the end of January [1908] the 1st Newport troop was in being. It was registered at the provisional Headquarters in London, and on Saturday 8th February, the certificate of enrolment was received. Unfortunately, though the small registration card was carefully preserved for many years, it was lost during one of the frequent removals to new headquarters.*

Reynolds described the Newport document as *a small registration card*. The stunning 1st Glasgow certificate could never be described in that way.

The inescapable conclusion is that the Glasgow registration document was kindly backdated by Secretary J Archibald Kyle in 1909 to a date provided by the group. Both 1st Glasgow and 1st Newport can be proved to have been offering good Scouting in early 1908. The honour though of the earliest known registration on the above evidence must go to the 1st Newport. Their history is to be found on the next text page.

---

[77] Kyle was also known by the short-lived term, 'Hon. Chief Scoutmaster'. Reynolds. *The Scout Movement* p. 64.

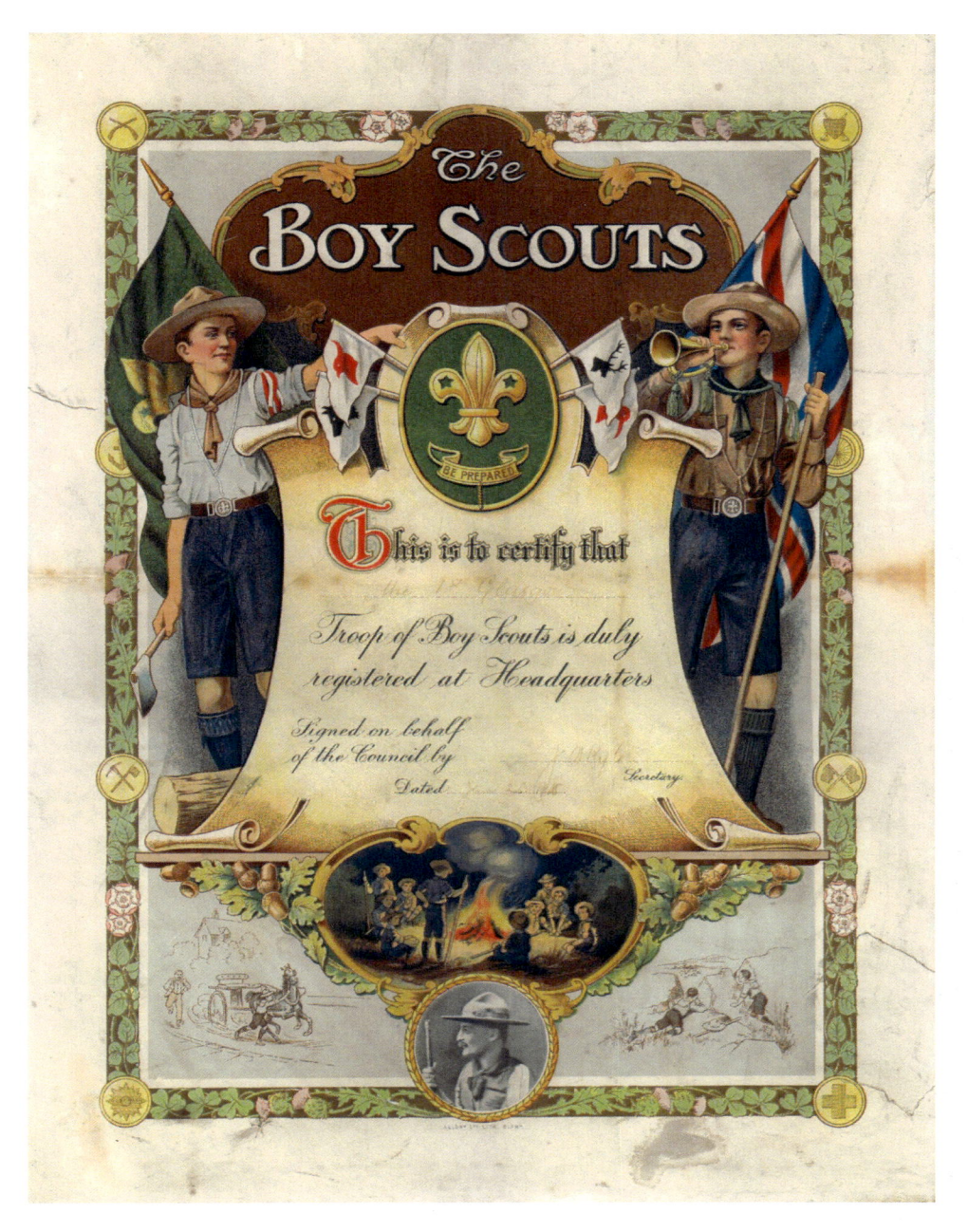

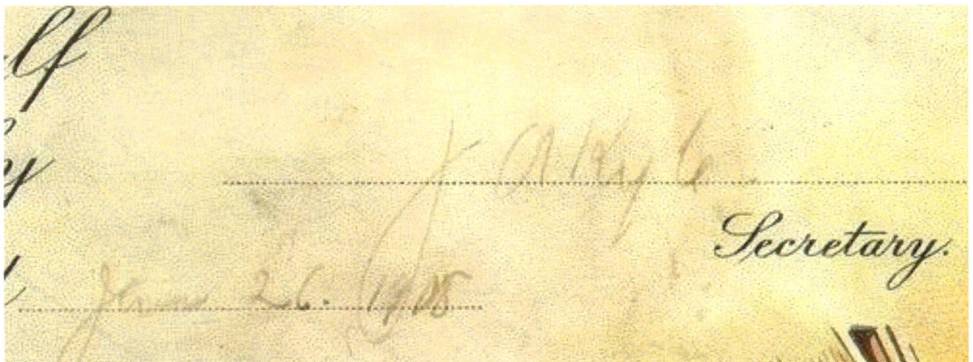

1stst Glasgow registration certificate

The 1ˢᵗ Newport (Old Guard) Isle of Wight Group

Sgt Burgess of the Isle of Wight Territorial Army had, by late 1907, already started his own youth group called Vectis Juvenile Scouts[78]. He had been a keen reader of B-P's 1899 book *Aids to Scouting* and was no doubt also influenced by reports of the camp on Brownsea Island. In January 1908 however he read the first issue of the fortnightly *Scouting for Boys* and decided to become part of B-P's scheme. The first recruit to his new group was his brother. The inaugural meeting was held by the end of January with four patrols being established, Hounds, Pewitts, Tigers and Wolves. The group attempted to comply with B-P's pronouncements on uniform and purchased a quantity of hats from Gamages' Department Store in London, however no two were of the same design! The group, as already stated, were registered on February 8ᵗʰ 1908 and by the end of March every Scout had his own membership card.

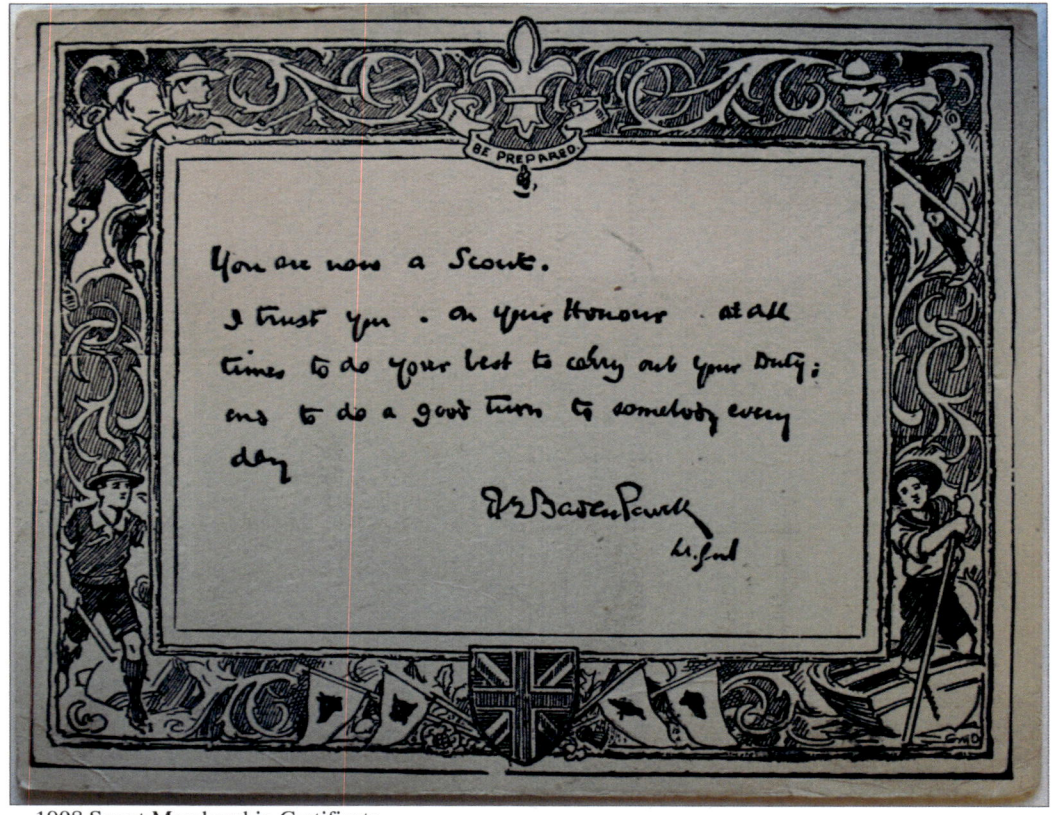

1908 Scout Membership Certificate

The Scout magazine of July 4ᵗʰ 1908 proclaimed that the 1ˢᵗ Newport now had five patrols with 70% of its Scouts having gained their First Class Badge. The group was one of the earliest to have a trek cart. It was emblazoned with the slogan, *General Baden-Powell's League of Scouts.* The use of the word 'league' in relation to B-P's Scouts was employed in the first edition of *The Scout* magazine of April 19ᵗʰ 1908, (See Page 32) before it was dropped as identifying too closely with the League of Frontiersmen. This terminology then is an indicator of the date the cart was sign-written.

---

[78] EE Reynolds, The Scout Movement p. 56-69

'The Old Guard' was incorporated into the group's name in 1914. By that time the Isle of Wight had Scout Troops in most of its towns and villages and the name was used to indicate Newport's seniority. The group have had a long proud history and flourish to this day.

John 'Wilkie' Wilkinson and the 1st Blackpool Scout Group

'Wilkie' – a grand old Scout aged 100!

John Frederick Wilkinson was born on June 10th 1897, in Oldham, Lancashire. He was two when his Mother died and so he and his brother Ted were sent to live with aunts in Blackpool.

One day in January 1908, Wilkinson, aged 10, had been fishing with friends in Garstang. Returning on their bicycles, they called at a newsagent's shop in Blackpool, owned by a Mr Frank Raynor to ask him to weigh their catch. Raynor showed Wilkinson a copy of the first fortnightly part of *Scouting for Boys*, which the boy bought. Once home as he started to read the book, he became fascinated by the '*Camp Fire Yarns*' and was sufficiently motivated to laboriously copy out sections of it by hand which, the next day, he gave to his friends. He asked them to attend a meeting to discuss the extracts. So started the Lion Patrol that was to become the 1st Blackpool Boy Scout Troop. Later the boys returned to Frank Raynor's shop and encouraged him to become their Scoutmaster, the first in Blackpool.

John Wilkinson led his patrol with great enthusiasm in many activities, involving them in signalling, radio, fishing, searching for signs of smugglers and attaining Scout badges. 'Wilkie' had to leave the troop when he moved to Stockport aged thirteen[79].

The example of the Lion Patrol illustrates just how successfully B-P had targeted the imagination of boys. That a ten-year-old should go to such lengths to persuade his friends to join him in the great game of Scouting is, you might think, exceptional. By comparison, the adult role of the good Mr Raynor seems almost insignificant.

---

[79] After his move from Blackpool 'Wilkie' went on to become a Kings Scout, Scoutmaster and Assistant District Commissioner. He was a member of the first-ever Wood Badge Course (Leader Training) at Gilwell in 1918 and the first person ever to run a Wood Badge course outside Gilwell. He gained his Silver Wolf in 1999 and remained in Scouting until he died aged 102. (The above photo was taken on his 100th birthday). This note is only a glimpse of the Scouting career of a truly remarkable man. His biography can be read on the Scouting Milestones Website: *www.Scouting.Milestones.btinternet.co.uk/biogs*

The 1st Birkenhead (YMCA)

On October 28th 1907, B-P wrote to 50 town clerks and YMCA secretaries offering free 'lantern slide talks'. This was part of a systematic campaign funded by publisher Pearson's £1000 'sponsorship', to bring B-P's Scheme to the attention of invited audiences and the wider public.

Not surprisingly there is a high correlation between the places Baden-Powell on his lecture tour and the incidence of early troops. Perhaps the best-known example is that of Birkenhead where B-P first gave a lecture in the YMCA Hall on January 22nd 1906. The Secretary of the YMCA was overwhelmed with applications and many had to be disappointed. The talk was about Peace Scouting and, although B-P was in full army uniform, he played down '*soldiering*'.

The *Birkenhead News* carried a lengthy report of the proceedings of which the following extract describing the arrival of B-P into the hall is only a part.

> *The boys, from the front and from behind, sprang to their feet in an ecstasy of delight. To say that they cheered the General would be to put it very mildly indeed. They shouted most fiercely, they waved their hats, handkerchiefs, and anything else that would lend itself to the purpose.... At last the boys sat down, but it was from sheer exhaustion; they had no voice left. Then they commenced to clap, and did this too with an (extraordinary) energy. General Baden-Powell, on the right of the Mayor, stood, smiling placidly and bowing his acknowledgments to the audience.*

B-P returned to Birkenhead on January 24th 1908 to speak to the Junior Department of the YMCA. A handbill advertising the event gave a brief description of the talk entitled, *Scouting and Good Citizenship*.

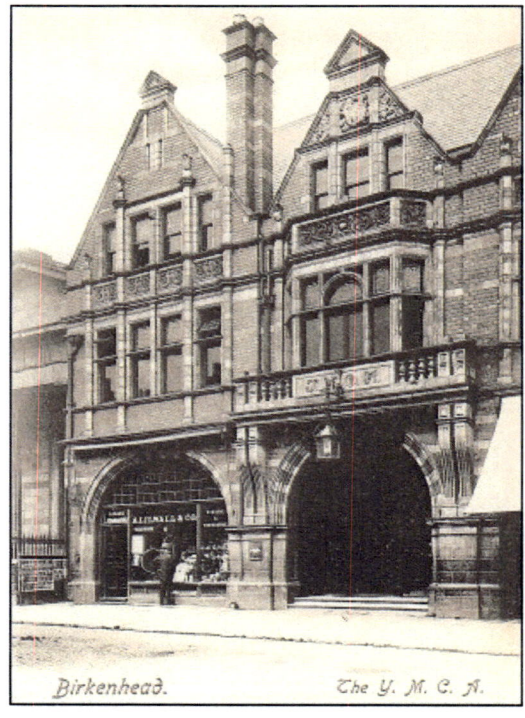

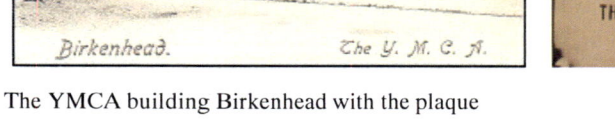

The YMCA building Birkenhead with the plaque

The talk, the handbill explained, was to be an ... *explanation of the Scheme for instructing boys in Scouting, and an appeal to men to help carry out the same in Birkenhead.*

Again the meeting was an overwhelming success. During the interval, Mr Clinch, a Junior YMCA leader, announced his intention of forming a Scout Troop, the 1st Birkenhead (Duke of Westminster's Own[80]). Their members had already been meeting throughout 1907 as St Paul's Rambling Club, using B-P's book *Aids to Scouting* as a training manual. Under their leader James Johnston they had camped on Hilbre Island near Birkenhead as early as March 1907. The 2nd Birkenhead, which still operates, was also formed as a result of this same meeting. Both troops were registered in February1908.

B-P wrote to Mr Ralston YMCA secretary,
I do hope that Birkenhead will make a real step in advance in starting the movement, because it was in Birkenhead that I first mooted the idea in public and received such encouraging response.

The 1st Birkenhead's Bass Drum, as displayed at the Birkenhead Centennial Exhibition, January 2008.

B-P returned to the town on April 25th 1910 where, as the Founder of a now well-established Movement, he unveiled the plaque[81] commemorating his earlier visit, (see previous page) proclaiming that the Scout Movement was *publicly inaugurated* in the building on January 24th 1908.

Harold Price and the 1st Chiswick West London Troop

In 1908, as now, finding a suitable meeting place was very difficult. Community Centres did not exist as such, but Church Halls and Chapel Rooms were a feature of every parish.

Harold Price of Chiswick, West London, was fourteen years old when he formed a patrol from amongst his friends and approached his Church organist Tom Foley for help in finding a meeting place. Together they asked the Vicar for the use of the Church Hall. The cleric was happy to agree, but only if all the members were church attenders. Some of Harold's friends however were of different religious persuasions, or none at all, and so neither Price nor Foley found the conditions acceptable. The patrol then found less restrictive, though much smaller premises, in a shop basement and began meeting in September 1908, leading to the formation of the 1st Chiswick Scout Group.[82]

Harold declared that the troop must always be open to people of all faiths, or none. This continued to be a guiding principal until the group ceased to function in 2003, when it was integrated into the neighbouring 3rd Chiswick, which celebrates its 100th anniversary in 2009.

---

[80] This title was in place by July 1908. The Duke of Westminster's family was, and still is, very influential both in Birkenhead and throughout the region.
[81] The plaque stored in the YMCA archives for many years was put on public view in 2008.
[82] Shaun M J Johnson ex SM 1st Chiswick on http://www.secularism.org.uk/38060.html

The 1st Chiswick Scout Group was a testament to one 14-year-old boy's very firm idea of morality. As Harold Price demonstrated it was, and still is, non-conditional for a Scout Troop to be affiliated to a church, though many of the very earliest troops certainly fell into this category. Thankfully most modern churches have more liberal views, though 'sponsored groups' are still entitled to restrict their membership.

The 1st Sunderland and the 1st Hampstead

On February 22nd 1908, his 51st Birthday, B-P was able to make his first visit to a working Scout Troop.

His entry reads: *Inspected Boy Scouts at Sunderland* (Col Vaux).

Colonel Ernest Vaux DSO, ten years younger than B-P, was an army colleague who had served with distinction in the Boer War. He was a member of the famous North East brewing family, and had an estate at Grindon near Sunderland (Teeside).

B-P met his old acquaintance at a shooting party at Chillingham Castle, in Northumberland, one of the homes of Saxton Noble, who was so central to the success of the experimental Brownsea Island camp. Saxton Noble had invited a number of guests including B-P and Colonel[83] Vaux to the castle on September 10th 1907, just a month after the camp. The events on Brownsea were surely a major topic of conversation, especially as one of the 'guns' was Brownsea boy, 15-year-old Humphrey Noble.

The following year, on February 13th 1908, B-P stayed with the Vaux's and was again a guest at their Grindon estate when he addressed a meeting in Sunderland on May 3rd to promote his Scouting Scheme. He wrote in his diary that there were 300 enthusiasts present at his talk and mentioned Col. Vaux's involvement in a letter[84] to Peter Keary,

> *Maj. Vaux of Sunderland has 20 Scouts in training, and from these he will select the best eight for the second exhibition patrol ....*

Only two weeks later, B-P records inspecting Vaux's Boy Scouts in Sunderland. Though this appears to have been an impossibly short period of time to have prepared a troop from scratch, Vaux had known about B-P's proposals since their meeting at Chillingham. The Colonel was a patron of The Sunderland Waif's Rescue Agency and Street Vendors Club[85], (later called Lambton Street Boys Fellowship). It is possible that Vaux had also attended a meeting addressed by B-P at Guisborough (N. Yorks) on November 1st 1907, chaired by his friend Richard Chaloner[86], later Baron Gisborough[*sic*] who would in, any event, have kept him abreast of B-P's latest proposals.

Vaux acted swiftly. From his existing 'reservoir' of local boys, he enrolled his first patrol, the Pewitts. The new troop was called Lambton Street Troop,

---

[83] B-P wrote of Vaux as both Major and Colonel.
[84] The Founding of the Boy Scouts etc. P. Richard Ed 1973
[85] Twenty-one Years of Scouting. E.K. Wade, The 'street vendors' sold newspapers.
[86] Richard Chaloner, had also served in the Boer War with B-P and Col. Vaux. In November 1907, he invited B-P to address 300 CLB lads at Guisborough. They were one of the first audiences to hear from the Founder's lips of the success of the Brownsea Camp.

(Vaux's Own) led by Capt. Webb and Mr Fred Wood, who actually trained the boys.

As the title of the club suggests, the boys concerned were from poor families who depended on their sons' income as 'Newspaper Boys'. When meetings had to be called that clashed with the selling of that evening's papers, Colonel Vaux solved the problem by buying the entire stock.

The history of the Sunderland Troop is closely entwined with that of the 1st Hampstead (known as the 'The Firsts'). B-P had encountered their leader, Captain Colbron Pearce, who must have impressed him greatly as he arranged for a demonstration patrol from his troop, the Kangaroos, to give public demonstrations and to camp with Colonel Vaux's boys on Grindon Estate farm.

On May 3rd in the previously mentioned letter to Keary, B-P concludes with the information that Col Vaux will ...*select the best eight to form the second exhibition patrol to work with Pearse's* [Captain Colbron Pearse].

> *We will settle on the exact displays for each of them to practise before they come together.*

Things began to happen very quickly. On May 15th 1908 B-P visited Keary at his home in Wimbledon, and together they observed a competition on Wimbledon Common between Colbron-Pearse's Hampstead boys and the Putney Troops. (This surely must have been one of the first inter-troop competitions.) The meeting, with B-P's comments, was reported in the May 30th edition of *The Scout*, and generally the Founder was fulsome in his praise.

> *The drill and discipline in all the patrols was very smart and good....*
> *The fire laying-lighting was very good indeed especially when one considers it had been raining very hard the previous day and scouts were not allowed to use any material other than that they could find in the woods there.*
> *The meat was excellently cooked, and I did enjoy my kabob.* [sic]

> Axemanship though good, was not beyond criticism,
> ...*there was too much hitting the tree all over the place with the axe.*

One wonders if the Scouts had permission to go round cutting trees down on Wimbledon Common?

Stronger criticism was yet to come,

> **'Silence is Golden'**
> *In one patrol- I won't say which one, but I leave its guilty conscience to tell – there was too much talking, only the voice of the Patrol Leader should be heard when work is being done....*

A camp loom, as made at the Brownsea Island camp, was demonstrated. The postcard photograph on the following page was taken by Walter P Adams, a Scoutmaster from Putney and depicts the exact loom being used at the Wimbledon Common event on May 15th. The evidence for this supposition is that the image shows a number of seemingly well-regulated spectators consistent with a public display. The photograph was part of a number of photographs that were issued as part of a set of six postcards and also gave rise to a series of Magic Lantern slides. These were brought to the attention of the readers of *The Scout* on July 11th as being available for loan with lecture notes.

Adams contributed to the May 3rd edition of *The Scout* where he outlined that *in a rash moment,* he had undertaken to give a magic lantern talk on Scouting, and so had some of his boys, *fitted out as Scouts to train them sufficiently for me to take photographs of them at work.*

Lieut.-General Baden-Powell's Boy Scouts at Work and Play.   No. 5.

This postcard was used to advertise the series, '*Official Postcard of Boys Scouts at Work and Play*', in the July 18th issue of *The Scout*. Note the Kangaroos white jerseys to provide greater photographic contrast.

B-P was so enthralled with the competition, and the *work* being demonstrated that, as he writes in his letter to Keary, he left the competition much later than he had anticipated and, in consequence,

I only just got back in time for the Mafeking Dinner[87].

Only twelve days later on May 27th, B-P was to meet up with the Hampstead Kangaroos again, 275 miles further north.

B-P wrote in his diary,
> *Paid a casual visit to Vaux's Camp at Sunderland, (Lampton Street Club plus Hampstead demonstration patrol) – and was delighted with the smartness shown by the lads.*

The camp was to last for 10 days and involved 12 boys from Sunderland, the Pewitts, and a similar number of the Kangaroos from Hampstead. Baden-Powell's visit to the camp, though in a 'casual' capacity, was significant, it being the first 'proper' Scout camp he had ever seen.

---

[87] Mafeking was relieved on May 17th 1900 and from the Siege onwards B-P always celebrated it with other members of the garrison and the Relief Columns. It was a major event in his year and for the Hero of Mafeking, to be late for it, would have been unthinkable.

By contrast with the 'Brownsea Boys', the Scouts of Sunderland and Hampstead had taken their 'law and promise', wore Scout Uniform and came from recognised Scout Groups.

The Scout of July 4th carried a report of B-P's visit, again with his comments.

> *The spot was an ideal one for a camp, concealed from view and weather, in the scooped-out side of a hill – on sandy soil below the turf, so that after the heaviest rain the ground was quickly dry again.*
> *Both patrols looked smart and seemed to have a good time in camp, and they worked quickly and cleverly, each Scout looking out for what was required of him.*

There was still more than a hint of criticism which, disappointingly for Baden-Powell, targeted the very same fault he had tried to advise against after the competition on Wimbledon Common.

> *In one patrol there was just a little talking at times amongst the Scouts; this should not be allowed - Scouts must, the moment they get their orders, carry them out at once, silently and smilingly; tenderfeet talk, Scouts smile and start to work.*

The two patrols went back to their respective groups but were active giving demonstrations of Scouting across the country. The Hampstead Kangaroos claimed they were the first Boy Scouts to be seen in Cornwell. Col. Vaux's troop had expanded to over 250 boys by September and they had '*quite outgrown their clubroom*'.

Author's note.
B-P's greatest achievement was bringing together boys from varied social backgrounds. He was determined that Scouting should be inclusive and so the sons of lords and tradesmen shared the same tents at the Brownsea camp. The camp at Grindon, may not have been graced by nobility, but the social and language difficulties between the very poorest children from Sunderland and the boys from Hampstead would have been equally problematic.

Readers should not assume from this, that I am in anyway casting aspersions on the boys from the North. They came from a culture that I know and love and so appreciate just how hard it would be for a 'southerner' to understand their dialect – which must never be called 'Geordie' though Newcastle is only 12 miles away. The Sunderland 'Mackem' dialect may be similar to 'foreign' ears, but is as distinctive from 'Geordie' as 'Cockney' would be to Kentish people.

What Two Girls Did? The Henfield Troop of Scouts.

The Scout, June 13th 1908 carried this astounding letter,

On reading an article on Scouting (writes SM and ADW of the Henfield Troop of Scouts*), *we two girls wrote to headquarters for necessary information for starting a troop, and obtained the six books on 'Scouting for Boys'. We then called a meeting of 18 sporting boys known to us, who at once expressed a wish* *to become Scouts and gave us names of other boys. Our next move was to procure an old disused carpenter's building for a clubroom, which we whitewashed, painted, and cleaned; collected subscriptions, games, and rough furniture and now have a troop of five patrols sworn in and in working order- and hear that others are still wishing to join.*

*SM's and ADW's full names were not revealed in The Scout, The group's present GSL Keith Jennings confirms that 'ADW' was the sister of Major AG Wade MC[88], a senior early employee of the Scout Association who was to become its joint 'Managing Secretary'.

The distinction between the sexes in 1908 was, in reality, a larger gulf than that which existed between the classes. Boys and girls, by and large, were not educated in the same schools if their parents could afford it. Even in mixed council-funded schools children played in different playgrounds and went into the building through doorways marked Boys or Girls.

It would be difficult to imagine a situation where boys might run any sort of scheme for girls, but it was even less likely that girls might 'command' boys, but then the Scout Movement was a social revolution.

The troop made the news again in the September 5th edition of *The Scout*. On this occasion though, three females were given the credit for founding and managing the troop. We discover that the *sporting boys* were between 10 and 16 years old. Most of the elder ones having already won their Second Class badge.

Girl Scout 'Scrap' 1909

Stalking and tracking is showing great improvement and several boys are getting on with semaphore signalling.

The Henfield Group still prospers to this day.

Girl Scouts

While no official registration of an all-girls group in 1908 exists, there is no doubt that there were some all-girl patrols. Unsurprisingly, the female equivalent of a Boy Scout was a Girl Scout[89], though there will be many who will have never encountered this term in British Scouting as it is not generally realised however that these girls were an official part of the Movement. The term *Girl Scout* was as legitimate as its male counterpart. Not only were girls permitted – their presence was encouraged.

---

[88] Captain Wade worked for the Scout Association as an 'Organising Secretary' from 1912. In 1920 he married Eileen Nugent, one of his typists, who became B-P's 'confidential secretary' for 27 years, She wrote several well-regarded books on B-P and the Movement, but surprisingly never mentioned the achievements of her sister-in-law.

[89] Girl Scouts are to this day the mainstream female branch of Scouting in the USA. The British term for Scouting's sister movement, 'Girl Guides', was not taken up.

The first mention of Girl Scouts in *The Scout* magazine came just one month[90] after its first issue, in a contribution from Baden-Powell himself, under the heading,

Can Girls Be Scouts

The Founder said that he had several letters asking,

> *...whether scouting would be a good thing if girls were Scouts...and ...whether there was any chance of their being sufficiently plucky enough to make good scouts.*
>
> *I have replied that girls can get just as much healthy fun and as much value out of scouting as boys can.*
>
> *Some who have taken it up have proved themselves good scouts in a very short time. As for pluck, women and girls can be just as brave as men, and have over and over again proved it in times of danger.*

B-P then went on to give examples of heroines including Grace Darling, the 22-year-old daughter of a Northumbrian lighthouse keeper. With just her father, they set off in an open boat to take off shipwrecked survivors from rocks off the Farne Islands during a terrible storm in 1838.

Some of the girls, lucky enough to have had access to the magazine, were as B-P intended, suitably inspired to become Girl Scouts.

Two weeks later, *The Scout* described the competition on Wimbledon Common attended by B-P, between Putney and Hampstead Scouts, as detailed earlier in this chapter. The competition had visitors from the Wolf Patrol of Fulham and also *several Girl Scouts wearing their badges*. These badge-earning females were justification enough for B-P's assertion that girls could make good Scouts.

In *The Scout* magazine of July 25th 1908, an unnamed writer, but most probably B-P himself, answered readers' questions,

> *Let us tell Mary, Isobel and Mr Ferguson that there are already many Girl Scouts and successful ones too. They enter all the games and practices with zest, and exhibit as much intelligence, courage and reliability in performing their work as any of their masculine companions.*

A modern day feminist could really want for little more. Girl Scouts were being praised by the Founder, who it must be remembered, was a product of the Victorian era. He had spent nearly all of his life in the army or at public school in an all male environment. His views on female equality, as far as Scouting was concerned, like his views on social class were revolutionary. Because of his upbringing however, he could perhaps be forgiven for his follow-up comment,

> *A patrol of Girl Scouts should extend a beneficial interest in the troop and inspire the boys associated with them with high ideals. Sometimes when boys get together their play is apt to border on roughness.*

---

[90] *May 16th 1908,*

There is little wrong with the psychology, which even today is often given to justify co-education. Implicit in the Founder's comment is that he was keen to admit girls because of the benefit they bring to the boys. The message however was clear, girls were to be encouraged.

Elizabeth de Beaumont[91] formed a patrol with her brother and her governess.

> We got our precious copy of 'Scouting for Boys' by the Chief Scout and read all we could lay our hands on about Scoutcraft. We had Scout hats and poles and scarves and belts. We were the Seal patrol and desperately in earnest about it. It was a wonderful game, so full of something that was lacking in any other!

Miss Elsie Lee is thought to be the first Girl Scout in Newcastle. The Fleur de Lys on Elsie's hat has the two five-pointed stars that were added to the Scout Badge in July 1909, (see page109) so the photograph could not have been taken before them.

At first glance Elsie's image seems so well photographed and not unlike coloured postcards of the era, that she could perhaps have been a photographer's model. Her shirt however has correct patrol ribbons and her Scout salute is immaculate.

Marguerite de Beaumont, surely a relative of Elizabeth, was another Girl Scout who went on to become a personal friend of the Founder and also author of a B-P biography, *The Wolf that Never Sleeps*. In her book, she states that she became the proud Patrol Leader of the Wolves Patrol and reveals that they had a secret password, *Impeesa - The Wolf that never Sleeps*,[92] which allegedly was the name given to Baden-Powell by African tribesmen.

Marguerite was one of the girls who turned up at the Crystal Palace Rally on September 4th 1909, with her patrol dressed in what they thought a Girl Scout should wear. (See postcard images on following page) She recounts how, on her first meeting with the Founder, she was asked who she was. She replied,

> ...PL of the Wolves Patrol of the Girl Scouts and we want to do Scouting just like the boys.

And Scout she did. In 1944 when *The Wolf that Never Sleeps* was published, the author described herself as a Scoutmaster as well as Guider. With many male Scouters fighting in the Armed Forces, some ladies were inspired to become 'Scoutmasters', but few if any could have had such a history.

---

[91] The Leaders Opinions, Vol. VI April/May 1921, as quoted in *On My Honour*, Tammy M Proctor.

[92] Wolves are not native to Africa. The tribesmen in fact described B-P as a Hyena, an animal thought by Europeans to have little charm or courage. No wonder the name was changed!

THE BOY SCOUTS. A Girl Scout Comrade.

GIRL SCOUTS. INSPECTION OF GIRL SCOUT BRIGADE BY GENERAL SIR R. BADEN POWELL.

Marguerite de Beaumont may well have been one of the girls pictured above. B-P is clearly speaking to the Girl Scout holding the patrol pennant though it does not appear to have the Wolf Patrol symbol.

The Chief Scout made mention of Girls Scouts in the September 12th 1908 edition of the *The Scout*,

> *I have had several pathetic letters from little girls asking me if they may not share the delights of a Scouting life with the boys. But of course they may. I am always glad of Girls' Patrols being formed. ... There is no reason why girls should not study Scoutcraft and earn their badges just as boys do, and the more the merrier.*

In the 2nd Edition of *Scouting for Boys*, 1909, B-P suggested that Girl Scouts might wear the Scout blue, khaki or Grey shirt with blue skirt and knickers.

Allison Cargill and the Cuckoo Patrol of Girl Scouts, Glasgow

Image Courtesy Girlguiding Scotland

The first patrol of Girl Scouts ever to be registered was the Cuckoos. Its Patrol Leader Allison Cargill formed her patrol of Girl Scouts amongst her school friends in Glasgow. They met in a stable loft, which could only be gained by climbing up a ladder, adding considerably to the fun. The girls tested the security of their knots by lowering themselves out of an access door down to the stable floor below.

In 1909, this patrol became attached to the 1st Glasgow Troop. (See Page 67) One of the Scoutmasters attended the Girl Scouts' weekly meetings, to examine and pass them when they had earned their badges, setting them challenges and competitions for their next meeting.

This association with a 'proper' Scout Group, enabled them to be registered and to 'parade' with the boys. The patrol's proudest moment came when they were allowed to march with the Boy Scouts behind a bugle band, to a wood on the outskirts of Glasgow to practise their 'Scoutcraft'. They lit their own fire, made tea in billycans, and joined with the boys in Scouting games.

In 1910, the patrol was advised that they could no longer remain in the Scout Movement but should join the new Girl Guide Association. Reluctantly the patrol was renamed the Thistle Patrol of the Girl Guides. *They* [Allison and her friends] *felt that Girl Guiding could never be as much fun*[93]. Allison went away to school in the autumn of 1910 and the Guide patrol lapsed unregistered.

In 1930 Allison Cargill became County Commissioner for Midlothian and later in 1953 the President of the Scottish Girl Guides Association. The Scottish Association, now called Girlguiding Scotland, have buildings and campsites named in honour of the Girl Scout they regard as their first member.

The End of Girl Scouting in Great Britain

Miss Mildred Thomlinson of Clifton near Brighouse wrote to *The Scout* to ask for advice and her letter was printed in the 1908 September 19th edition. Miss Thomlinson stated that she was a P.L. of a Girl Scouts Patrol and asked if boys could become members of her patrol. She was advised that boys could join, but should be placed in an all boys patrol within the same group. There was after all a limit to the 'integration of the sexes'.

That limit was however soon to be replaced by a barrier. The 'ahead of his time' attempts by the Chief Scout to strike a blow for female emancipation was short

---

[93] The quote comes from Girlguiding Scotland's website. (See Bibliography)

lived. His lead in this area of Scouting at least, was not supported by Scouting's main sponsoring bodies, the churches and the affiliated 'brother organisations'; such as the BB, CLB and the YMCA. Indeed, Edwardian society in general, never did ready itself for such a radical proposition.

Violet Markham, a committee member of the newly formed 'Anti-Suffrage League', was to write to the influential *Spectator* magazine,

> *Girls are not boys and the training that develops manly qualities in one may lead to the negation of womanliness in the other.*

Her main motivation for opposing Girl Scouts however, was surely bound up in her opposition to female emancipation. These stave-carrying, broad-hatted girls were being treated in total equality with their brothers. They were, Mrs Markham must have thought, unlikely when older to agree to be subservient to them on the issue of the right to vote. Boy and Girl Scouts maintained Miss Markham,

> *...roam the countryside together, arriving home late and doing who knows what.*

This 'over the top' allegation, (just how did Miss Markham know they had arrived home late?) was designed to appeal to the worst fears of the readers, but it was given the oxygen of publicity and the Spectator's editorial approval.

Girl Scouts from *Boy Scout Life Book* James Brown & Sons Glasgow, 1909

As always B-P consulted his mother who, not surprisingly for a Victorian lady, thought that if Scouting was to include girls it should be practised well away from the boys. B-P reluctantly asked his sister Agnes to help him form the Girl Guide Movement, which was launched in 1910. Agnes Baden-Powell's handbook, *How Girls Can Help Build the Empire* came out belatedly in 1912. B-P was not over impressed, calling it, *'the little blue muddly'*.

Females could then only join Scouting as adult helpers or Akelas in Cub packs, but with advent of the World War I (1914-18), with many of the Scoutmasters at the front, some like Marguerite de Beaumont became Scout Leaders. B-P's brave attempt at equality was over. The rules of the 1st Kilmarnock Guide Company by 1910 stated,

1909 Girl Scout Fiction

> *Guides while in uniform will only associate with members of their own sex.*

In 1908 however, as now, Scouting was for girls as well as boys.

83

Social Scouting in 'the missions', Charterhouse and Toynbee Hall

The difference between the 'haves and the have-nots' in 1908 was more pronounced than it is today, there being little in the way of state organised benefits to support those below the 'poverty line'. In the large industrial cities, such as Newcastle, Liverpool and Birmingham, large numbers of people lived in slum conditions and this was also the case in the nation's capital. The lack of direction for youngsters in these circumstances was often given by B-P as his reason for founding the Scout Movement, but he was far from being the only public figure with a social conscience. It was fashionable for many 'upper-class' organisations, such as public schools and universities, to support the work of 'missions' and 'settlements' in the worst of the slum areas. Other well-heeled private individuals up and down the country, such as Colonel Vaux were, as we have seen, not slow to include Scouting into their existing structure for the benefit of their charges.

In the very first edition of *The Scout*[94], we read that B-P's old school Charterhouse, had a 'mission' in the East End. The school had long links with London, B-P having first been enrolled there before it moved to Godalming in 1872. One of the 'moving spirits' of the mission[95], Mr Hume Pollock, wrote to B-P, with the suggestion that Scout clubrooms should have upright mirrors affixed to its walls so boys can check how they look 'before they go out on parade'. His thoughts were published in the first issue of *The Scout* and *Scouting for Boys*. Clearly Scouting was alive within the mission.

One of the most influential of the early London Scouters was Dr T S Lukis of St Bartholomew's Hospital, who was associated with the Toynbee Hall residential 'settlement' that had been opened in 1884. Students from Oxford and Cambridge universities came to work amongst the poor of London's East End to attempt to affect and improve social conditions. Many of the early 20th century reforming politicians such as Clement Atlee, Alfred Milner and William Beveridge were associated with the Settlement.

On Wednesday May 27th 1908, the Wood Pigeon patrol of the 1st Hoxton, was inaugurated in Toynbee Hall. Six 12-14 year old boys from Scrutton St. Primary Council School had been selected to form a patrol. Preference being given to *…boys of spirit… not excluding those 'roguishly inclined*[96].

The patrol proved a handful but were eventually won over,

B-P Nevill, in *Scouting in London*, quotes Lukis himself describing how he used to take his scouts out from London's grime to the delights of the countryside

From Chingford we marched through the glorious sunshine across the Golf Links to the border of the Forest….
[Epping Forest, on the very edges of the present day Gilwell Park.]

---

[94] April 18th 1908.
[95] The Charterhouse Mission receives no further mention in *The Scout'*.
[96] PB Nevill, Scouting in London, p.125.

The troop prospered and was selected by Baden-Powell as the most efficient of those present at the Earls Court Rally in 1909. At the outbreak of war in 1914, Lukis (a doctor who could have easily remained at home) placed himself at the head of a column of 80 East London Senior Scouts, 'Old Scouts', and Scoutmasters, to march to the nearest recruiting office where he enlisted with them as a private in the London Regiment. He was sent to France and killed near Neuve Chapelle in March 1915 aged 29.

Schools
Many schools and colleges formed their own Scout Groups, schoolteachers with clerics being the most common professions amongst Scoutmasters.

The 1st Wigan (Grammar School) Troop was formed on January 28th 1908, the day after B-P lectured to the YMCA in the town and so was, after the Birkenhead Groups, one of the earliest ever to be formed. The Headteacher RC Chambres was the Scoutmaster and remained so until he retired in 1926. The group folded in the early 1960s. (From Wigan GS school records)

Port Talbot County School, Totnes Grammar School, Lowestoft School and College, and Watford Grammar School Troop were all also formed in 1908.

Works Groups.
As the School Leaving Age in 1908 was 14, many large employers had a significant number of employees of Scout age. Some set out deliberately to employ Scouts recognising that any boy who could adhere to the 1908 *nine* Scout Laws, especially the 2nd, would made a model employee,

> *A SCOUT IS LOYAL to the King, and to his officers, and to his country,* **and to his employers** [author's emphasis]. *He must stick to them through thick and thin against anyone who is their enemy, or even talks badly of them.*

It is not surprising then that by 1909, many employers either sponsored Scout Groups directly or were actively promoting Scouting within groups or districts. One of the first 'Works Sponsored' Groups was that of the Constable Works of Edinburgh, which probably belonged to the Edinburgh publishers of that name. Pilkington's Glass Works in St Helens Lancashire also had their own group, Baden-Powell visited the factory on 28th January 1908.

Cycle Patrols

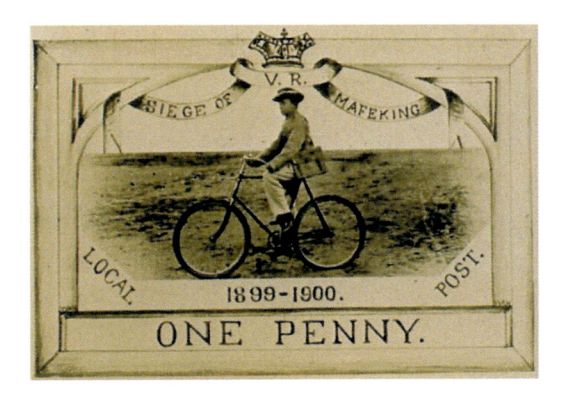

The bicycle was every bit as much of a social revolution as Scouting itself. Mobility, stretching beyond bus or train routes, became available to the masses. Women, once they had jettisoned the encumbrances of the Victorian/Edwardian dress code, could also enjoy the freedom of the open road. Cycling clubs proliferated and every boy's ambition was to own a 'bike'.

A 'trial' (not used) for a Mafeking Siege stamp with Mafeking Cadet, Sgt Major Goodyear, on his cycle.

Military Cycle Patrols were commonplace during the Boer War and B-P, unlike some Cavalry offices, was an advocate of them. The Mafeking Cadets, whom the Founder claimed in Camp Fire Yarn No. I of *Scouting for Boys,* were his main inspiration in forming the Scout Movement, were first mounted on horses, but when these had to be eaten to fend off starvation, they used cycles.

The book, *Cycle Scouts Training,* written *by a B-P Scout,* was initially published prior to 1910. Its first chapter, *The organisation of a Cycle Patrol* carries the sensible advice that a Cycle Patrol Leader should look to the quality of the boy, not that of his cycle.

The first such patrol may have been formed in Sunderland as Baden-Powell noted in his diary that on May 22nd 1908, he inspected 'B-P Cyclists'. The 1st Dublin Cycles, mentioned in the pages of *The Scout* as being formed prior to December 1908, seemed to have formed around the cycle, in the way Sea Scouts are dedicated to boats.

A CYCLIST SCOUT IN MARCHING ORDER.

BOY SCOUTS.
X CYCLIST SCOUT.

The image on the left of a 'Cyclist Scout in Marching Order' is from the book *Cyclist's Scouts Training for Boy Scouts,* 2nd Edition 1910. The coloured picture is from a postcard. At first glance it would appear that the coloured image, though 'artist enhanced', is faithful to the black and white original. A closer examination reveals that whilst the cycles in both images have a signal flag attached to the crossbar, only in the black and white photo is there a rifle (mounted along the diagonal part of the frame that runs from the handlebar to the pedals). The removal of the rifle was part of a campaign to 'de-militarise' Scouting's public image.

CHAPTER 5

1908, Lieut.-General Baden-Powell, Chief Scout of the World

The above heading, in conjunction with its 1908 dateline, will have an unfamiliar ring to most Scouts. Those who are interested in Scout History may well recall that the title 'Chief Scout of the World' was conferred on Baden-Powell by those Scouts present at the end of the first World Jamboree at Olympia in 1920. However, the title 'Chief Scout' had been in existance since 1908, as the quote below from *Scouting for Boys, Part I* proves,

> *Officers: The head officer of all the boy scouts*[97] [sic] *in the world is called the Chief Scout.*

The question might well be asked: When the above statement was published in January 1908, were there any Scouts in other parts of the world? The answer is probably not, but within a few weeks there certainly were.

Gibraltar

The Cobra Patrol of Gibraltar under Scoutmaster Mr H Rigby was mentioned in the July 11th 1908 edition of *The Scout*. News of the patrol's formation might have taken some time to come to the attention of the editor, as the patrol was the basis of the 1st Gibraltar Troop, who claim they were in operation by March 27th 1908. Gibraltar had a unique status in 1908, a British Territory of 25,000 people governed by a Military Governor, an Admiral and a Colonial Secretary. Its early Scout Troops (of which at one point there were five, including Sea Scouts) probably gave rise to more Scouts per head of population than most UK mainland towns.

1908 Gibraltarian Scout

Present day Gibraltarian Scouts claim to have the honour of being *the first recognized* [chartered] *overseas unit in a country controlled by the United Kingdom.* The word 'unit' nicely dodges the issue as to whether this was a patrol or group.

The 'founding troop' has since amalgamated with the 4th Gibraltar Scout Troop, becoming the 1st/4th Gibraltar (Marquess of Milford Haven's Own) Scout Troop. In 1910 the then Prince Louis of Battenberg conferred his patronage on the 1st Troop. He changed his name to Mountbatten when he was ennobled Marquess of Milford Haven in 1917 the patronage was re-confirmed and has continued ever since. Keen readers may recall that the British arm of the Legion of Frontiersmen have been granted the honour to call themselves *Countess Mountbatten's Own.* Countess Mountbatten is the daughter of Prince Louis of Battenburg who became First Sea Lord in 1912. He had been a

---
[97] B-P usually used capital letters i.e. Boy Scouts to refer to the Scout Movements, reference to scouts before 1907 would be with a small 's'.

member of the Legion of Frontiersmen since May 1905, and therefore, in assisting the 1st Gibraltar, was merely following Legion Regulations of December 1909. Regulation 77. (See Page 37)

Scouting still thrives on the rock and, to this day, is still organised as a branch of the United Kingdom Scout Association.

Malta

The Malta Scout Association formally applied to become a member of the British Movement on November 9th 1908 and was officially recognised a year later. Captain RF Lock R.A. was appointed Scout Commissioner. Prior to the official recognition, Scouting in Malta was organised under the auspices of the 'Malta Command District Committee'.

The Association then consisted of five Scoutmasters and 338 Scouts. It is not surprising that Malta should have had such an early start, as B-P had strong connections with the island. He was stationed there as Assistant Military Secretary to his uncle, General Sir Henry Smyth, between March 1st 1890 and April 1893, and so naturally had many friends, some of whom were still resident on the island in 1908.

The 1st Sliema Scout Group was formed in 1909 under the leadership of Mr. Dutton with Mr. Grech as his assistant.

The group was registered on Oct. 12th 1910 at Scout H.Q. in London. Their certificate, similar to that of the 1st Glasgow[98]. (See Page 69), still hangs on the wall of the group's HQ.

There must have been Scouts[99] on Malta in 1908 to support the Maltese application of that year. The 12-month delay in recognition may have been purely administrative, or because only Scout Troops of three or more patrols could be registered. By 1909 however there were several sufficiently large operational troops, one of which was admonished for training on Sundays. The 1st Sliema Troop[100] were granted the title 'Bernard's Own' in 1933 in memory of Sir Edgar Bernard, a former Island Scout Commissioner.

---

[98] Interestingly in 1909 the Malta Boy Scout Association received a letter of encouragement from the 1st Glasgow Scout Troop. (See Page 67

[99] Mizzi JA, Scouting in Malta, Progress Press, Valletta, 1989

[100] http://www.sliemascouts.net/

Canada

On May 30th 1908, B-P wrote a letter to Peter Keary (Pearson's Literary Agent) enclosing *...a prospectus of a camp which is run in Canada for boys* ....The details of the camp had clearly impressed B-P as he went on to write that he hoped that his forthcoming Humshaugh Camp could be run on similar lines, if only he could find *the right place* and the *right men.*

> *I have sent the Canadian Camp a copy of 'Scouting for Boys', parts 1-III and a copy of 'The Scout'. And have told him* [the organiser of the camp?] *of my hope to get Scouts all over the Empire to be started and to get into letter correspondence with each other.*

This communication with the unnamed organiser(s)of the Canadian Boys' Camp (who could not have been Scouts) is the first record of *Scouting for Boys* arriving in the Dominion. As the copies were sent by B-P himself, with his express hope that they be used to introduce Scouting into Canada, it may well be that one or more of the early Canadian Scout groups had some connection with the camp. It has to be said however that there is no evidence has been found so far to support any such claim.

Three 'First' Scout troops were established in Canada in 1908, in Merrickville – Ottawa; Port Morien - Cape Breton Island Nova Scotia and St. Catharines - Ontario. All three troops believe they were not just the first in Canada[101], but in all of North America. (See Page 95, USA)

Merrickville, Ottawa

The 1st Merrickville troop was founded by a Methodist pastor Rev. Ernest Thomas, who had learned about Boy Scouts while on holiday in England. There were about 30 boys in the troop, according to Joe Hutton[102] one of the three original members still residing in the area in 1982. Two of the other 1908 Scouts were Harold Hutton and Carman Knapp.

> *Activities then were much the same as now, with Mr Thomas giving instruction in knot-tying, outdoor survival, fire-building, and the host of other endeavours for which the Boy Scouts have become famous.*

Port Morien, Cape Breton Island, Nova Scotia

In 1908 William Glover, a coal company official in Port Morien, founded a troop of 10 young boys. Some of the original members were, Alex MacDonald, Dave McArrel, Charlie MacLeod, Bobby Orr, James Meigher and George McArell.[*sic*] The last surviving member was James Meigher who died in 1991.

In 1983 the Glace Bay District Scout Council constructed a monument marking the troop's 75th anniversary[103]. The image on the following page depicting some of the boys and their leader is from a plaque placed on the monument

---

[101] A Century of Scouting, James Careless, November/December 2007
[102] 75 Years of Scouting in Canada, which Scouts Canada published in 1982.
[103] Information taken from Port Morien, Pages from the Past, page 112 by Ken MacDonald

Port Morion Scout Troop.
Note the boys have tunics and some sort of uniform belt, but no Scout hat or neckerchief.

St.Catherines, Ontario

According to a 1955 letter, written by a former troop member Merrick O'Laughlin, St. Catharines Boy Scout Troop first met in a henhouse in Harris Neelon's backyard in 1908,

> *Harris got the gang together and it was Harris who wrote to Baden-Powell and got permission to form the Scouts.*

Scouts Canada maintain a website which has a timeline indicating that the first Canadian Scout Troop was formed in 1907! Correspondence reveals that Scouts Canada are in possession of a 'charter' dated November 1907 in relation to the St Catherine's Scout Troop. Logical arguments such as the Scout Law and Promise were not published prior to January 1908, and that it is these elements that define the term 'Scout', have had no affect on their assertion that Scouting in Canada began with the St Catherine's troop in 1907.

When Baden-Powell first arrived in Canada in 1910, on his World Tour, he was met by Scouts in every town and city that he visited. There were an estimated 5,000 Scouts throughout Canada by that time.

Australia

New South Wales.

Mr T H Roydhouse edited the Sydney *Sunday Times*. He had been impressed with the way that Baden-Powell had organised the defence of Mafeking during the famous siege, (Oct 1899 to May 1900) so through his newspaper, he initiated an appeal to raise funds to present B-P with a fitting tribute. The sum of two thousand pounds was collected, a massive amount in those days. Some of this was utilised to present B-P, in South Africa, with two cavalry chargers and their equipment. This still left £600 and so Mr Roydhouse commissioned a gold-mounted cavalry sword and scabbard which he took to England to present to B-P in 1903.

The two men struck up a friendship and corresponded from that time, so it was natural that Roydhouse should be aware of B-P's Scheme and have had early copies of the part-series *Scouting for Boys* sent to him. The proof of this association is contained in a letter B-P sent to Peter Keary, on September 9th 1908.

> *We might begin to get the scheme going in the Colonies - and I expect the Australian 'Sunday Times' would be useful in helping us. They got up a 1/- subscription during the war and provided me with 2 chargers and saddling, etc.*

Roydhouse collected together a number of boys of scout-age and gave them the part editions of *Scouting for Boys* to read. These boys, possibly the first in Australia to read B-P's book, were like boys everywhere 'infected with the bug' and wanting, in the Australian idiom, *"to give it a go"*. The first meeting of the new patrol was on 31st March 1908, in Bon Accord, New South Wales when Jack Summerville was made Patrol Leader.

By the end of 1908 there were 1200 Scouts in New South Wales including troops in Mosman, Summer Hill and Petersham.

The 1st Mosman NSW Scout Group was mentioned in *The Scout* on September 5th 1908. It was formed in May 1908 after Charles Hope bought a copy of one of the first six parts of *Scouting for Boys* from his local bookshop. He formed the Kangaroo Patrol[104] which met in stables. They began to wear the all black neckerchief which the group still wear to this day.

1st Toongabbie Scout Group in the western suburbs of Sydney was also founded in 1908 and is still operating.

Victoria

Taarooga Road State School, Caulfield, Melbourne was home to the first Scout Patrol in Victoria. Schoolboy Roy McIndoe had a friend in England, who reputedly had been one of the Brownsea Campers in 1907. This Brownsea pioneer sent his Australian friend some published information about Scouting, most probably the early parts of *Scouting for Boys,* or perhaps newspaper reports of the Brownsea Camp. Regrettably just which of the Brownsea boys was involved is not known. McIndoe showed the information to his friends who formed themselves into a patrol, dressing up in red shirts and their fathers' old felt hats and '*whooped around the place like Red Indians*'. Their enthusiasm was infectious because another patrol was formed in the same district under the supervision of Mr J Lister. Mr DJ Chandler, who was also involved, wrote[105] that this patrol expanded into the first Scout Troop in Victoria known as the 1st Caulfield Troop, which was also the first in Victoria to go to camp.

Scouting quickly spread to other Melbourne districts, usually, as elsewhere, in the form of patrols that later became fully-fledged Scout Groups. The 1st Northcote was formed from a Scout Patrol in 1908 and is still operating (after a name change) as the 5th Northcote Scout Group.

---

[104] Information from Group Website. www.mosman.scouts.org.au/
[105] Those Boys Scouts, *A Story of Scouting In Victoria* AR (Dick) Milne and CB (Bo) Herward.

A patrol of Scouts was started at Ivanhoe under its patrol leader J Bowe. 'Skipper' Wilson became its Scoutmaster in January 1909. The troop eventually converted to Sea Scouting and is still operating today.

The Cuckoo patrol of South Malvern, Melbourne, started by P.L. Reuben Thompson, became the 1st Malvern (8km SW of Central Melbourne) under SM Mr L Farie, in June 1908, though like so many others the groups were not warranted until 1909. Other 1908 troops in Melbourne included 1st Albert Park, previously a boys' athletic club that, under its leader Mr I. Ray, switched to Scouting in 1908.

Western Australia

Scouting began in Western Australia in 1908 when eighteen year old Frank Roche from Spearwood, Perth, established the first Scout Patrol in the Town Hall building. They had to make their own uniforms with only copies of *Scouting for Boys* for guidence. By the end of the following year there were 416 Scouts in Western Australia so Roche, then only 19 years old, called a meeting of fellow Scoutmasters to establish the Western Australia Executive Boy Scouts Council in Subiaco, Perth.

South Africa

Cape Town in late 1907 was in Cape Colony, predating the Union of South Africa. Two brothers. Fred and Charles Stern, attended Claremont Public School in the city and via a copy of *Pearson's Weekly* they had learnt of the impending publication of Baden-Powell's new book *Scouting for Boys*. Once they could get their hands on the first part of the new series, around the end of February 1908, they became enthralled with its contents, particularly as so many of the stories were based in their native land.

The brothers joined with their friends and asked their headmaster, Mr George French to become the Scoutmaster of their Troop, which first met on March 3rd 1908, - the first Scout Troop in the whole of Africa. George French's son Cyril became Assistant Scoutmaster, and later took over running the Troop. Frederick Stern aged 16 was the first Patrol Leader, and later Troop Leader. His fourteen-year-old brother Charles was his 'Corporal'.

George French

The rest of the world learnt of the formation of the first South African troop when *The Scout* magazine, on July 18th 1908, announced that the troop had two patrols under the leadership of George French. The troop records show a weekend camp took place in 1908 where tenderfoot and cooking tests were passed at Cotton's Farm. A later 'standing holiday camp' was held at Harringay, Cape Flats in June/July 1908.

Fred and Charles Stern were introduced to the Chief Scout[106] in 1912 as the first Scouts in South Africa. Fred had written a letter and poem welcoming B-P to the country. On this same African visit, B-P was to present a flag to a Scout Troop in Mafeking, the town that made him famous.

Fred Stern[107], a Baptist minister, emigrated to America in 1924, and started a troop on Long Island, New York. His brother Charles, also a minister, later moved to England after being the senior chaplain to the SA armed forces during the Second World War.

Later in 1908 other troops sprang up in Cape Town, Johannesburg and Natal, but like many much closer to Scout Headquarters London, their registrations did not arrive until after July 1909. *The Scout* of August 22nd 1908 records that the Lads' Guild of East London (West); and later that a new group, the 1st Inanda had been formed in Red Hill Durban.

Not much remains of the First Claremont's 1908 White Ensign.

New Zealand

Lieut.-Colonel David Cosgrove served in South Africa during the Boer War from 1901/02 and it was there that he met Baden-Powell. After the hostilities he returned home to resume his teaching career and, on June 1st 1908, wrote to his old comrade expressing his appreciation of B-P's Boy Scout Scheme, asking for further information. B-P replied inviting Cosgrove to promote the scheme in New Zealand as others were doing in Canada and South Africa.

The first issues of *Scouting for Boys,* had by this time already arrived in NZ, though one of the early consignments had to be brought ashore from a shipwreck. Once copies were in the hands of the boys, as we have seen elsewhere, patrols were formed spontaneously though it would appear that at the time of his letter to B-P, Cosgrove was unaware of any Scout activity.

The first NZ patrol was formed in Kaiapoi[108], near Christchurch South Island, by Mr T Mallasch, a former member of the German navy. It consisted of four boys including the Scoutmaster's son. The precise start date is not known, but the Patrol had been in existence for some weeks at least before it was 'sworn in' by Major Cosgrove on July 3rd 1908.

---

[106] www.scouting.org.za/groups/1stclaremont/history/stern.html - author Ian Webb
[107] A description of the group's activities is contained in the July 18th 1908 edition of *The Scout*
[108] New Zealand Scouting, The First 50 Years, SG Culliford DSO, 1958, BSA of NZ

Cosgrove wrote to leading newspapers in each province in New Zealand, setting out the basics of Baden-Powell's scheme and asking interested parties to contact him. As a result, he received numerous requests for further information. Thirty-six troops were started before the end of 1908, mainly in the South Island, with Christchurch as the centre.

The first NZ Scout Patrol 1908 under Mr Mallasch.

A meeting of Scoutmasters was held at Papanui at the end of December 1908 when Cosgrove was elected as 'Dominion Chief Scout', the first Chief Scout in the world other than Baden-Powell himself. This speaks highly of the way Cosgrove had set out his plan for the introduction of Scouting in New Zealand, which some say was organisationally in advance of that in the U.K. In early 1909 the *Dominion Boy Scouts Handbook* appeared containing the approved constitution of the Movement in New Zealand and by the end of that year, 500 Scout groups had been formed in the North and South Islands amongst New Zealand's, mainly rural, one million population.

The only 1908 group mentioned in *The Scout* was the 1st Auckland, run by HH Lowe of the NZ Garrison Artillery, which had 45 boys by September 1908.

Smyrna Asia Minor

The most unlikely outpost of Scouting in 1908 was to be found at the International College in Smyrnia, now called Izmir, Turkey's third largest city. The college, an American Foundation was founded in 1891 by Scotsman Alexander Bladder MacLachland with his wife Rose.

In 1896, the school became The American Collegiate Institute for Boys and, in 1902, was incorporated into the American Board of Foreign Missions. Its graduates were admitted to the Universities of Geneva and Chicago and to the Massachusetts Institute of Technology without examinations. All of the above serves only to establish that the school was indeed an American institution.

Its Scouting credentials were estabished for all time in the November 14th 1908 issue of *The Scout*:

> *The Boy Scouts are breaking out in a new place. A troop has just been started in Smyrnia , Asia Minor , by Mr A Hichens, We wish them every success.*

An Internet history [109] records that the college was the first, in what is now Turkey, to have electric lighting. It produced the first seismograph, had the first observatory *and the first Scout Troop.* This troop must then be one of the earliest manifestations of American Scouting. (See the following page.)

---

[109] http://maviboncuk.blogspot.com/2006_06_01_archive.html

United States of America

The Boys Scouts of America were formed in 1910 and do not recognise any US troops that may have been formed before this time. The small town of Burnside in Kentucky however had a Scout troop[110] that pre-dated the BSA by two years. Mrs Myra Greeno Bass visited England in early 1908 and returned to her home town with a copy of *Scouting for Boys*. She set about organising the Eagle Troop with her husband William. The 15 boys had no official uniform but wore a red neckerchief. Horace Smith was the first Troop Leader, but Mrs Bass herself led the Scouts in hiking and camping activities.

William Bass introduced the Scouts to the new American game of Basketball, which was responsible for the troops demise some five years later when the boys pursued the game rather than Scouting. The town of Burnside, population 675, now has roadside markers which state that it is the 'Birthplace of the Boy Scouts of America'.

Germany

Dr Lion in 1919*

Scout Groups were not formed in Germany[111] until September 1909, however the 1908 contact between Baden-Powell and the German father of Scouting, Dr Alexander Lion, clearly shows that the origins of German Scouting date from this year. Dr Lion was a Staff Surgeon in German South West Africa who, like B-P, was interested in the skills of reconaissance. Lion became a leader in 'The Wandervogel', a youth organisation based on the outdoors, which had been formed in November 1901. In May 1908, having read *Scouting for Boys*, Dr Lion wrote to B-P with a pamphlet of his own about 'Scouting'. The two men corresponded and B-P entertained Dr Lion in London on September 29th 1908 and again on 2nd October when the Founder may have taken his German friend to see the Scouts 'camping' in Gamages Store. (See Page 112)

In March 1909, a Pfadfinder Society (Scout) was formed in Berlin but, though this club gave its name to German Scouting, it was merely a society, not a Scout Group. Dr Lion, with a military friend, Hauptmann Maximilian Bayer, translated *Scouting for Boys* which was published with B-P's consent in May 1909. Over Easter of the same year, Archibald Kyle (See Page 68) took a group of Scouts to Germany where they were entertained by the Wandervogel and in July/August 1909, a group of the Wandervogel visited England. Though they were referred to by Baden-Powell as 'Scouts', the first German Scouts were not enrolled until September 1909, when Scout Troops were founded in Berlin, München, Bamberg, Metz and Beslau. Dr Lion died in Bavaria aged 93 in 1962.

---

[110] *Old Burnside,* Harriette Simpson Arnow, Uni. of Kentucky, 1996. Page 28.
[111] Information from Dr Stephan Schrölkamp of Berlin including the image* copyright Archiv der deutschen Jugendbewegung, Burg Ludwigstein, 37214 Witzenhausen

Chapter 6

The Origins of the Scout Uniform:
Scouting for Boys Part I. January 1908

A scout does not use a showy uniform, because it would attract attention, but scouts in a patrol should dress alike, especially as regards hats or caps and neckerchief.

Flat brimmed hats if possible, or wide awake hat.

Shirt: Flannel

Colours: A bunch of ribbons of patrol colour on left shoulder.

Belt, with coat rolled tight and strapped or tied on behind it.

Haversack: To carry food etc, slung on back across the shoulders.

Shorts: Trousers cut at knee. A kilt if you are a Scotsman.

Stockings, with garters made of green braid, with one end hanging down one inch.

Boots or shoes.

Staff as high as a scout's shoulder. Not shod as it is for feeling the way quietly at night.

Badge on left arm above elbow.

Whistle, with cord round neck for patrol leader.

N.B. The colour of the neckerchief or necktie and the shoulder knot should be the colour of the patrol.

Text and line drawing by Lieut.-General Baden-Powell

The hat

The hat distinguished the Scout from every other boy in the world.[112]

I see in this a value far above a mere pernickitiness in dress. A like uniform hides all differences of social standing in a country and makes for equality; but, more important still, it covers differences of country and race and creed, and makes all feel that they are members with one another of the one great brotherhood.[113]

---

[112] Eileen Wade, 27 Years with Baden-Powell
[113] Baden-Powell as quoted by Eileen Wade, 27 Years with Baden–Powell

Captain Rattray, of the Ashanti Civil Service, wrote to Baden-Powell in December 1923, reminding him that when he (B-P) was with the Ashanti Expedition of 1895-96, the Ashantis called him "*Kantankye*" which means "He of the Big Hat". The founder wore the hat again in the Matabeleland Campaign of 1896. The following year he wrote a short story about it in the Charterhouse School Magazine, *The Greyfriar*. The article was one of a series based on *My Hat*, there having been previous stories entitled for example *My Polo Hat*. This story, predating the birth of the Scout Movement by eleven years describes in loving detail, B-P's affinity for his 'scout hat'

Sketch taken from the Greyfriar's article

It's a scout hat, also known as a cowboy hat or Boss of the plains – of a drab colour with a soft conical crown and a wide flat brim; very light, yet very protectful against the sun, or rain, or thorn bush.

The hat was made by the famous American firm 'Stetson' and had indeed been the hat of choice of many real cowboys[114] since 1865.

It is ironic that the iconic image of B-P wearing his hat should be the one that has burned itself into the subconscious of the British public. Baden-Powell's fame, prior to his Scouting career, stemmed from his famous Boer War defence of Mafeking, but in fact B-P never wore the hat in the besieged town at all.

Newspaper editors could not obtain quality images of Baden-Powell during the siege, so chose to illustrate their articles with the now famous Elliot and Fry photographic image. This was available to them as it was taken in London prior to B-P's departure to South Africa in July 1899.

B-P 1900 cast iron pub table. John Ineson Collection

When Mafeking was eventually relieved it was this image that was used to adorn almost any surface that could take it. Plates, mugs and even cast iron objects such as mangles and pub tables now, and forever more, associate B-P with his big hat.

The letters 'B-P' on the cast-iron pub-table illustrated above, are also the same initials as those given to his 'Boss of the Plains' hat, and indeed the motto of the Scout Movement, *Be Prepared*. B-P was very aware of the amazing co-incidences that seemed to rule his life, but the reader can be forgiven for thinking that some at least may well have been 'self-fulfilling prophecies'.

---

[114] http://www.stetsonhat.com/history.htm

Immediately following the Siege of Mafeking, Baden-Powell was asked to form the South African Constabulary (SAC). This force was really a 'rapid response' military regiment created to pacify former Boer territories, as they were over-run by the 'regular' British Army. It was given its civilian-style name at B-P's insistence, but was involved in active combat until the end of the Boer War, remaining in place until 1908 when its work was complete.

B-P dressed in the uniform of the SAC

B-P was given 'carte blanche' in designing its uniform and badges and this had a bearing on his later plans for the Scout Uniform. The Constabulary's colours were green and yellow which, according to Reynolds[115], were chosen because they were the colours of the Transvaal and the Orange Free State. They became the official colours of Scouting.

The South African Constabulary however was not the first organization to wear the now famous hat. The Canadian North West Mounted Police, (NWMP) who are the forerunners of today's Royal Canadian Mounted Police (RCMP), were formed in 1873 and have worn the same model Stetson since 1894. The 'Mountie' contingent that attended Queen Victoria's Diamond Jubilee in London in 1897 were resplendent in their famous red tunics and 'B-P' hats. Present day 'Mounties' wear the same uniform. B-P held their predecessors in great respect and often mentioned them in *Scouting for Boys*. He denied that he had copied the Scout hat from them, saying quite factually that it was a 'cowboy hat'.

RCMP Constable Nick Dale

Roger Pocock, founder of the Legion of Frontiersmen, had himself been a member of the NWMP in 1895. (See Page 35) When the RMCP contingent came to London, Pocock met up with some of his former colleagues. Part of the celebrations included the Spithead Naval Review. The Canadian Contingent was invited to observe the review from a chartered ship. Pocock [116], in NWMP uniform, took the place of one of the 'Mounties' who had fallen sick. Perhaps

---

[115] EE Reynolds, The Scout Movement, p. 49
[116] 100 Years of the Legion of Frontiersmen, Geoffrey Pocock p. 21

not surprisingly then, when Pocock formed his Legion in1904/5, the uniform included the Boss of the Plains Stetson.

The Legion have worn their Stetsons with pride and distinction for over a century. This did not however, as is often claimed, provide the inspiration for the Boy Scout use of the hat since, as stated earlier, B-P first wore his 'Boss of the Plains' Stetson during the Ashanti Expedition in 1895.

The Legion of Frontiersmen Stetson with a re-strike of their original Stetson badge.
Image courtesy of Countess Mountbatten's Own Legion of Frontiersmen Photo Archives.

B-P specified that his Scouts should wear the same style of hat that he had made famous. This was achieved against some opposition, not least from the Scots. They had received every encouragement from the Founder to wear the kilt, instead of shorts. Some of them felt that their traditional bonnet, the 'Tam 'o Shanter', was the only suitable headgear to wear with it. B-P appealed to their loyalty and his will prevailed. In response he drew the above cartoon with a verse to be sung to the tune of 'Bonnets of Bonnie Dundee'.

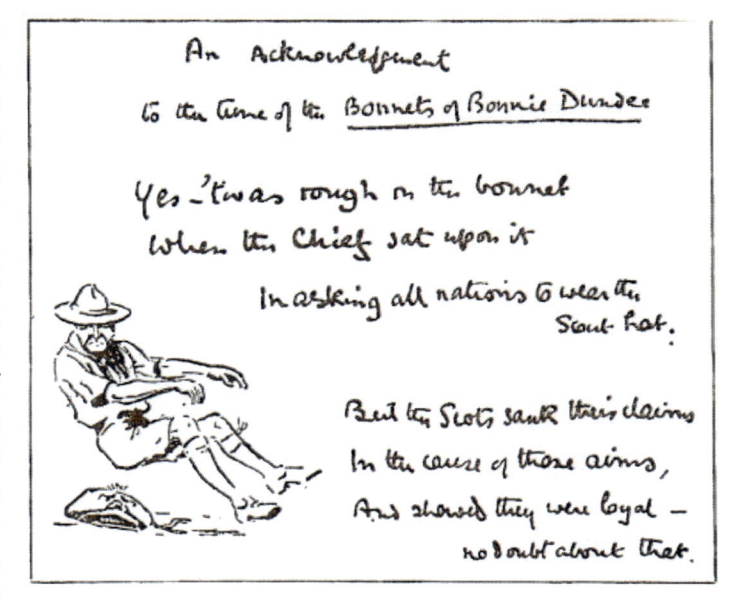

The now familiar piece of headgear was commonly known as the 'Wide Awake' hat, a term which, as far as Scout use is concerned, originated with B-P himself. In the first bound edition of *Scouting for Boys* 1908, *smart and workmanlike* 'Wide Awake' hats are advertised at 2s 6d (12 ½p).

Eileen Wade, B-P's private secretary for 27 years, maintains that the three dents in the crown were to remind Scouts of the three elements contained in the Scout Oath, as it was called in 1908.

1 will do duty my duty to God and the King.
I will do my best to help others, what ever it costs me.
I know the scout law, and will obey it.

It is a fine story, but whether there were three or four dents in the hat seems to have been optional from the evidence of numerous photographs of the period. Generations of Scouts looking at the dents, gave the hat their own affectionate nickname, 'the lemon squeezer', and many were the ways of keeping the dents and brim in pristine shape, tin mugs with hot cinders or boiling water being favourite The photograph opposite is from the 1923 rally at Alexander Palace.

A 2003 MORI poll[117] confirmed that the Scout Motto, 'Be Prepared', was the most often recognised 'logo' from a selection of leading worldwide products. The 'wide awake hat' is also still recognised the world over as a symbol of Scouting, though it has been superseded by the beret in mainstream UK Scouting since the Advance Party Report of 1968.

Baden-Powell Scouts wearing their B-P hats in 2007

It should never be thought however that the famous hat is now only a museum piece. There are a number of Scout Associations throughout the world who still wear it, including the U.K. Baden-Powell Scouts.

The Scarf or Necktie.

Baden-Powell's description of the Scout uniform, from *Part I* of *Scouting for Boys* published January 15th 1908, written over his sketch at the start of this chapter, has a 'postscript',

> *The colour of the neckerchief or necktie ...should be the colour of the patrol.*

This instruction is very interesting because it contains two pieces of information that would surprise most Scouts. It is commonly supposed that Scouts have always worn a Group 'necker'. However in 1908 a group would have had as many different coloured scarves as it had patrols, with the Scouters adding to the colourful array with their green scarves. (See Adult Uniform later in this chapter).

---

[117] http://www.ipsos-mori.com/polls/2003/scouts.shtml

Even less widely known is the fact that, when in 'civvies', boys could tie their neckties (in patrol colours) in a special way to denote that they were Scouts, with a knot both at the neck and lower down the tie. The illustration on previous page, taken from *Part I* of *Scouting for Boys* is entitled, *A Boy Scout's necktie*.

The scarf, like the hat, had been used by generations of cowboys, US Cavalry, wagon train scouts and outdoorsmen to protect the back of the neck against the sun, and the nose and the mouth against the dust of the trail. This item in green with a yellow stripe, was also part of the uniform of B-P's South African Constabulary.

Millions of Scouts worldwide know numerous uses for this instantly recognised piece of Scout apparel. It is a triangular bandage; a blindfold and several scarves can be used with Scout staves to make a stretcher. Knotted together scarves make a rope and, waved from a stave, it can be used to attract attention when help is needed. In games, it serves to show which side a Scout is playing for and, when it is pulled off, the Scout is deemed 'dead' or captured.

'Neckers' are now, as they always have been, an indispensable part of the Scout 'scene'. Every Jamboree has had its own scarf, starting with the Humshaugh Camp in 1908 where all the participants wore a red scarf. A Gang Show was not deemed to be first class until 'the gang' were entitled to wear the prestigious Gang Show neckerchief, which was also red.

From 1908 until at least 1918 knotted neckerchiefs adorned the Scout's neck. The woggle, (boondongle or bolo as it was known in the United States) did not make its appearance in Britain until it was used at Gilwell Park in 1918. Early Scouts were encouraged to knot their scarves round their necks and again lower down to remind them to do their good turn every day. Presumably they untied the knot once that obligation had been completed. Fifty years later Cubs and Scouts made two tiny knots, one at each point at the front of the 'necker', *to stop your luck from running out*.

Shorts

Baden-Powell left the world a legacy that has, in the opinion of the author, been almost extinguished. In 1907 polite society frowned on the very idea that either sex should display bare flesh, other than the head and hands, in public. In the camp kit list for the 1907 Brownsea Camp however, B-P specified that the lads should have shorts.

In 1908 all Scouts wore shorts, but they were not very short! Stockings came up to the knee, and shorts came down to it, but the intervening flash of flesh enabled a degree of movement to the human leg that had previously, in the name of modesty, been denied. Scouts could kneel down to inspect tracking signs or light a fire without ruining their trousers. *Bare Knee Days*[118] were here to stay, and shorts got shorter. When the author went to Grammar School in 1956, third formers (aged 13+) had just been given 'the right' to attend in long trousers. No child at primary school would ever have dreamt of being allowed

---

[118] *Bare Knee Days*, a title of an early Scouting Book by Haydn Dimmock, a one time editor of *The Scout* magazine

to wear long trousers. Shorts, in summer, are still the province of the outdoor enthusiast, but since 1968 they have ceased to be part of the UK Scout Association Uniform, reflecting what is a national trend as far as the wearing of trousers is concerned. Few children in England nowadays, even those of nursery school age, wear shorts even in summer. Yet, our own observations tell us that, due to global warming, average UK temperatures have risen.

Prior to the First World War, Scout shorts were commonly navy blue. There seems very little reason why this colour was chosen. The following explanation is probably quite fanciful, but one that the author would like to be true. Baden-Powell's first contact with a pair of shorts as a boy of Scout age would have been at Charterhouse when he played football. In his later years at the school he was a goalkeeper for the school team, and was, reportedly, *a safe pair of hands, cool under pressure*. The colours of the school team were maroon shirts and navy blue shorts!

The Shirt

There were no precise instructions as to what constituted a 'Scout shirt' in 1908, other than it should be made of flannel, a warm fabric made from light to medium weight, loosely spun wool. B-P wore his South African Constabulary flannel shirt to camp and praised its virtues in that had broad sleeves that were neither too short nor too long. There is no doubt that Baden-Powell associated his flannel shirt with an outdoor existence and, throughout his writings, there are many references to the *flannel shirt life*, a lifestyle that he hoped to open up to 'his' boys who, in the main, lived an urban existence.

The Garter Tab

English male legs in 1908 were, in public, meant to be totally enclosed in tubes of cloth. Shorts were a breakthrough but there were still very few public occasions, other than swimming, when it was acceptable to bare the leg. It was essential then, for the sake of modesty, as well as a smart appearance, that socks did not slip down, and amongst boys of Scout age that was a definite likelihood. The main defence against this possibility was the garter tab. One section of British society had already solved the problem. The Scottish Kilt may or may not have been worn with any under-garment, but stockings, higher than the hem of the kilt, were essential to keep out the Highland cold. They were held securely in place by garters.

Baden-Powell specified that the end of the garter should protrude down under the rolled-over sock by one inch - and should be green. Originally, according to Eileen Wade[119], tabs were made of strands of wool and so formed a wool fringe or 'tab' hanging down from the rolled-over top of the stocking. Tabs were, however, soon to be properly manufactured, made from braid with an inverted 'v' cut into the two descending strips. Later on, Senior and Rover Scouts had their own colours (maroon and red) - though both Wolf Cubs and Scouts wore green. (Logically, cubs should have had yellow tabs - which would have been in tune with B-P's original design, as it too was one of the SAC colours).

---

[119] Eileen Wade, 27 *Years with B-P*

Staff or Stave

According to EE Reynolds[120], the Scout Staff owes its origin to the use made of it by British Engineering Officers who, at the time of the Ashanti Campaign (1895), used staves to test footings and make measurements when laying field telegraph systems. Any seasoned hill walker however, will confirm that walking with a staff is of definite benefit, hence the modern trend for hi-tech sticks and poles.

In 1908 every Scout (and Girl Scout) carried a Scout Staff. The founder stated that they should come to no higher (or lower) than the shoulder, though in his sketch opposite this is clearly not the case. (Scouts in any case grow!) Patrol Leaders added the patrol pennant to their staff signifying their rank and identifying their patrol. Baden-Powell advised that staves should be marked off in foot sections as an aid to measuring and estimations. Though some of their supposed uses might seem a little fanciful, there is no doubt that they were used with great effect in rescues over thin ice, and also in crowd control when Scouts could form a very effective barrier by linking up, a horizontal stave between each boy.

The author has heard several tales at first hand of Scouts growing up, between the First and Second World Wars, in what we would now call 'inner city' areas, where the staff had a very practical value in fending off attacks by those who found it easy to jeer at, rather than join the Movement. One of B-P's favourite sayings was, *A smile and a stick will carry you through every difficulty.*

The Chief, writing of the Scout staff, said:

> *To the outsider's eye the Scouts' staves are so many broomsticks, but to the Scout they are different. His staff, decorated with his own particular totem and signs, is typical. Like his staff, among a mass he is an individual having his own traits, his own character, his own potentialities. He may be one of a herd but he has his own identity.*

As in so many other areas, the Chief Scout led by example and was seldom to be seen without a staff. It became a popular presentation item and Scout Archives at Gilwell Park has a collection of over 40 of his staves/sticks dating back to one presented to him in 1900 by the townsfolk of Mafeking.

---

[120] EE Reynolds, The *Scout Movement* p.49

In any Scout hut, staves would form a ready supply of 'pioneering poles' on which lashings could be practised and 'camp gadgets' built. Like the 'Wide Awake' hat however, few survived the upheavals of the 1968 *Advanced Report* in mainstream British Scouting and regrettably, nowadays, some Scouts will have neither seen or heard of a Scout Staff.

The Haversack

The 2nd edition of *The Scout*, April 25th 1908, carried a catalogue of Scout Uniform and other useful Scout related items. It informed Scouts that they could purchase the items mentioned from The Manager, at the Scout Office in London. B-P wrote,

> *You are not obliged to have all of these things of course. There are just three things as a Scout you should have - namely a haversack, a staff and a shoulder knot.*

Clearly B-P then placed the haversack and the other two items as being fundamental to Scouting, more important even than that Scout hat. Haversacks were often 'blancoed' white and were the repository of all sorts of equipment that a good Scout should carry, not least his lunch. In later years the haversack was dropped as a uniform item though Scout Patrols and troops from the Boys' Brigade and Church Lads' Brigades still retained them.

The Tying of Shoelaces

Though definitely not obligatory, Baden-Powell had developed a way of tying his shoes. He had in fact very strong feelings on the matter of footwear. Like Sir Arthur Conan Doyle's *Sherlock Holmes*, whose methods he much admired, B-P claimed to be able to deduce much from the state of a suspect's footwear[121]. It is not surprising then that he should have an opinion on something as mundane as how to tie a shoelace. Under the heading Tidiness', in *Part III*, chapter IV of *Scouting for Boys*, B-P explains the benefits of his 'Scouts Way', pointing out that in fact it is not really a method of 'tying' a shoelace at all, as no knot is required. Scouts were told that the method made it easy cut to through the laces should the shoe need to be removed in an emergency.

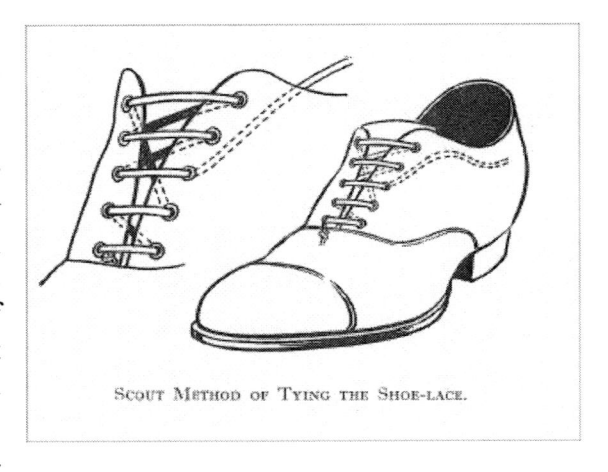

The sketch on the previous page, showing the Scout method of lacing shoes, is not the one Baden-Powell used in Scouting for Boys, but that of Sir Percy

---

[121] Part II *Scouting for Boys*. '*Details of People*'.

Everett.[122] Once shown this method of shoe fastening by B-P in 1908, he used it for the rest of his life. His sketch, with its inset enlargement, is somewhat easier to comprehend than that drawn by the Founder.

Adults: Uniformed or Not?

Whilst *Part I* of *Scouting for Boys* had guidance for Boy Scouts in the matter of uniform, there was no such assistance for Scoutmasters and other uniformed adults. Insisting on uniformity did not fit well with the tactic of trying to encourage adult volunteers, using the carrot that they would be given a freehand in how they ran their troops. On the other hand, the Chief Scout could not allow the public image of his adult leaders to run contrary to the aims of his fledgling Movement.

The biggest criticism levelled at the Hero of Mafeking, was that Scouting was militaristic. This is hardly surprising, given B-P's army rank and the fact that he chose to model his Scout Uniform on his former khaki SAC uniform.

As stated elsewhere in this work, the Founder of the Scout Movement was at pains to emphasise the concept of *Peace Scouting* as a means of training good citizens and dispel the notion[123] that he was preparing 'cannon fodder'.

A very early Scout 'swagger stick'. The fleur, without stars, is pre-June 1909.

In the absence of guidance, Scoutmasters wore whatever they saw fit. The two professions that furnished the greatest number of leaders provided little concern. Clergyman had their own very acceptable garb, and schoolteachers were, as ever, too conventional in their attire to be a problem. The third major group of volunteers were however entirely the problem. Baden-Powell's world had been the army. His friends, in the main, were army officers. Men who had retired from the service after the Boer War, who had served under him or knew his worth were, as he predicted they would, willing to ... *exercise their special gifts and their prestige among boys for doing a great national good at little trouble and expense to themselves.*[124]

Some of these men publicly 'marched out' with their Scouts in their old uniforms complete with medals (medal ribbons, rather than the medals themselves, are still to be found to this day on some Scout Leaders' uniforms). Military uniform included spurs, gauntlets, puttees, swagger sticks, Sam Brown belts, bandoliers and even revolvers worn at the belt. On the other hand, some early Scoutmasters dressed like the boys and, for a time, that found favour with B-P. The main quality he required of a Scouter, he said, was that he should be a *boy-man*. A man who was able to put himself at the level of his boys, be in tune with their needs and provide an exciting brand of Scouting to meet them.

---

[122] Sir Percy Everett, *52 Days* p.69
[123] There have been many such detractors from 1908 to the present day. Rosenthal's, 1984, *The Character Factory*, is perhaps the best-known and longest argued attack.
Baden –Powell *The Boy Scout Scheme,* 1907, a direct plea to ex-army officers to join him in the great game of Scouting.

A logical extension of that philosophy would be that Scouters would dress in the same way, even to wearing the same style of clothes.

As the very early greetings card image of B-P shows, he went some way along this road himself. His sleeve being filled with the same proficiency badges that a Scout might win, and around his neck, the green and yellow ribbon of the Silver Wolf which in 1908 was an award for boys. By August 1908, we find that doubt about this policy had begun to set in. From *The Scout*:

> *It has been suggested to me that Scoutmasters should wear a uniform distinct from the rank and the file. I should be glad to receive the opinions of Scoutmasters on the matter and also their suggestions.*

The debate was to rumble on through the pages of first *The Scout* and then the *Headquarters Gazette* for many years.

Dr Lukis, working from the Toynbee Hall mission, (See Page 84), and another East End 'missioner', Scouter Roland Philipps, were both acknowledged by Baden-Powell as leaders of great potential and importance to the future of the Movement. Tragically they were both to be cut down in Flanders during the First World War. In 1909 Lukis wrote to Baden-Powell to join in the debate and his response was printed on 19th September in *The Scout*.

Philipps, son of Lord St David, habitually wore his Scout Uniform including his shorts. He was one of the first Scouters ever to do, setting a trend that was common place, if not for everyday wear, then certainly on Scout occasions up to the time of the Advance Report in 1968.

Like Roland Philipps, Lukis was almost a maverick in the inspirational way that he organised his East End troop. He was after all running a social experiment. He did not, for instance, wear the specified green neckerchief.

> *My scarf is not the same as the boys being an old school one, I wear my haversack slung at the left side instead of on my back, because I have to be constantly referring to it for odds and ends. I wear the First Class Scout badge on the left side of my hat.*
> *I think it a pity to lay down a regulation uniform for Scout Masters.*

In his reply B-P was happy to endorse Lukis's 'kit' with one or two reservations. Clearly, when fortunate enough to obtain the services of dedicated and brilliant young men, who were bringing Scouting to the masses in the most difficult of circumstances, and moreover at their own expense, the Founder was not going to argue about the colour of a neckerchief or the position of a badge on a hat. Baden-Powell however had to address the problem of uniforms for adults within the Movement, particularly the ex-army brigade. He advised that camp dress ought to be different from that used on parades and listed what he himself wore at the Brownsea and Humshaugh camps and on drills and parades.

Camp
Flat brimmed Scout Hat with white metal badge on the left side; green neckerchief or coloured collar and green tie; khaki flannel shirt with short sleeves; white sweater worn over it or carried on the belt; white shoulder knot on left shoulder, waist-belt brown leather with knife suspended from it; shorts preferably dark blue; stockings preferably khaki, green or brown, garters to show green tabs; shoes.

Parades
Scouts' Hat with badge, coloured collar and green necktie, 'Norfolk' shooting jacket, knickerbocker breeches of the same colour, putties- khaki colour [a bandage like piece of cloth wrapped round the lower leg], *laced boots; walking stick; whistle and lanyard.*

In this photograph of an early but unfortunately unknown Scout band, we have two contrasting styles of Scout 'Officer' dress. Figure 1 shows a young man immaculate in collar, tie, Norfolk jacket and 'Wide Awake' Hat. Figure 2 on the other hand, is obviously ex-Boer War, still wearing his 'Smasher' Hat, Bandoliers and army tunic. Which Scouter best promoted B-P's concept of Peace Scouting?

B-P argued his case that his uniform was neither militaristic nor juvenile.

We do not, I think, want an expensive uniform for a Scoutmaster of Boy Scouts, nor a military one with peaked cap, shoulder cords, belts and badges or rank, and so on; we want, rather, something that can easily be made up, that gives freedom for work, that gives some sort of uniformity and at the same time can serve as a pattern to boys as regards neatness in their own dress.

And, though it took some years to achieve on a 'global level', as in most things, Baden-Powell's will prevailed.

Badges

1.The Brownsea Fleur   2.*The Scouting for Boys* Fleur   3. The Scout Office Fleur

1.The Brownsea Island 1st and 2nd Class badges[125]. If only this was an image of the real thing! There is photographic evidence enough to prove that Brownsea boys wore the badges that B-P made for them out of sheet brass, on their hats and their jackets. No living person however has ever seen an example of what the present Lord Baden-Powell describes as 'the Holy Grail' of Scout Collecting. Note that the Second Class Scroll is 'upside down' compared to the other badges. The later badges, figs 2 and 3, are consistant with the way the 2nd Class badge was worn until it was made redundant in 1968. Fig 1 is a photograph of a replica badge worn by the campers in the re-enactment camp on Brownsea during August 2007, to which the author was an historical consultant. Historical accuracy was achieved by the use of computer-enhanced photographs of the badges worn by the 1907 Brownsea campers.

2.The *Scouting for Boys* Fleur de Lys, hand-drawn by Baden-Powell, appeared in the first part edition of *Scouting for Boys* published January 16th 1908. The second class scroll badge, as well as being reversed, has a central hole at its lowest point through which there appears to be a piece of knotted twine, but in reality in 1908 the 'dangly bit', which was also used on the Medal of Merit, was fashioned from a piece of brass wire.

3. The Scout Office Fleur de Lys appeared on letter-headed paper such as that on which B-P wrote to poet Henry Newbolt on 23rd March 1908. (See Page 50) Though B-P was an excellent artist, the *Scouting for Boys* sketch of the badge is quite amateurish and it may be that Pearsons', who undoubtedly printed the Scout Office letterhead, decided to 'improve' the presentation of the 'logo'. B-P however must have approved the design and certainly would not have used it for his correspondence, had he not been happy with it.

In the first bound edition of *Scouting for Boys* 1908, B-P wrote,

> *The First Class Badge is both the arrowhead and the motto. Second Class Scouts can only wear the motto part of the badge...when on duty or in camp, Patrol Leaders wear the badge in front of the hat, and scouts wear it*

---

[125] B-P copied the Brownsea 1st Class Badge from the badge he designed for his Army Scouts in 1885. See page.28.

on the left arm above the elbow.
Patrol leaders could purchase their badge in 'white metal' for seven pence from the Scout Office, all other Scouts wore brass badges costing only six pence each.

The buttonhole badge is the most common form of the 1908 Scout badge found today. It was very often worn on the uniform as well as on school blazers etc.

Again Patrol leaders had the distinction of wearing the white metal 'silver' badge, but both it and the brass badge cost only two pence each. The Fleur de Lys was also used on 1908 medals and leaders' hat badges.

The distinguishing feature of all 1908 Scouting Fleur de Lys is that they do not have the two five pointed stars in their outer leaves. This new design was registered at the Patent Office in May 1909 and announced in *The Scout* on June 5th of that year. (Actual metal badges based on the registered design were not issued until July 1st 1909.) The stars were added in order that B-P's 'logo' could be protected, restricting its use for his own 'mainstream' brand of Scouting. The plan was to differentiate it from all other forms of Scouting such as those in use in the 'Brother Organisations'.
(See Page 15)

1. Original 1909 Registered Design. Reg .No. 539538

2. The badge as it appeared in *The Scout*.

It was not possible for B-P to try and register the Fleur de Lys itself, as besides being the Scout badge it was also the heraldic emblem of the Kings of France. Similarly he could not protect the name 'Boy Scout' as both words were in current usage.

Proficiency Badges were introduced throughout 1908/9. They were hand embroidered on felt. The Founder added the designs for the Seamanship and Pioneering badges, (opposite) to a letter sent by Everett. Typically B-P did not reply to regular correspondents using fresh paper, but added his notes, sketches and suggestions to their letter and then returned the annotated original to the sender.

109

Humshaugh: B-P's Holiday Camp August 22nd - September 4th 1908

Original 1908 banner image as used in the *The Scout* for Humshaugh articles

The Background

The boys at Baden-Powell's 'experimental camp' on Brownsea in August 1907 were not Scouts in any accepted sense of the word. Ten were members of the Bournemouth and Poole Boys' Brigades and some of the other eleven Public School boys may have belonged to their school's Cadet Corps. As the camp was experimental, pre-dating the Scout Movement, these boys could not have known the Scout Law or have made their Scout Promise, (or the Oath, as it was first known) as B-P had yet to devise them.

Following the publication of *Part I* of *Scouting for Boys* on January 15th 1908, there were a number of organised camps where the Scouts were from recognised troops, the boys having been properly invested in the Scout Movement. One such[126] was held in May by Colonel Vaux D.S.O., a long-standing regimental friend of B-P. Vaux was a member of the famous northern brewing family, and a well-known philanthropist. He arranged for twelve boys, the Peewit Patrol from his own Scout Troop, to camp over Whitsun 1908 on his estate at Grindon near Sunderland with a 'demonstration patrol', the Kangaroos, from a London Hampstead Troop[127]. Baden-Powell 'informally' visited the camp on the May 22nd, 1908. (See Page 76)

Colonel Vaux paid his boys five shillings a week to attend the camp! Articles appeared in the *Sunderland Echo* and the camp was 'written up' by Baden-Powell in *The Scout* of July 4th, 1908.

> *Both patrols looked very smart and well, and seemed to have had a good time in camp.*

B-P's article introducing the Humshaugh Camp, and news of another in the grounds of Woodcote Hall, Wallington, Surrey appeared in the first issue of *The Scout* (April 18th 1908) directly above a 'Nomination Form' for a future 'Baden-Powell camp' to be held that summer at Humshaugh, Northumberland.

The camp at Humshaugh (locally pronounced Hums-alf) was to have the distinction of being the first National Camp for serving Scouts to be led by Baden-Powell. The boys were members of Scout Troops from across Great Britain and they camped at a site close to Hadrian's Wall, north of Hexham, Northumberland between August 22nd and September 4th, 1908.

---

[126] See Page 74, *First Scout Troops*, 1st Sunderland. Col. Vaux's Scouts were mainly newspaper vendors and as they could not attend a meeting about the proposed Whitsun camp until they had sold their copies, Col. Vaux brought up their entire stock.

[127] Also Page 74.

The Build-up. Exciting or Mercenary?

Who of you would want to spend a fortnight under canvas with a troop of other boys, and under the care of General Baden-Powell? Is there a boy in all the land whose heart does not jump with joy at the prospect?

So announced the first issue of *The Scout* on 18th April 1908,

The Most Fascinating Holiday Ever Offered. - Thirty Boys Invited. All Expenses Paid, Including Fares and Food

There had to be a catch, as there were thousands of lads who would have given their eye-teeth to camp with their hero. What *The Scout* was actually announcing was a competition. Scouts simply had to send as many Voting Coupons as they could find/beg to the magazine's editor. Seventeen coupons, in total, appeared in the issues leading up to the event. *The Great Race to the Camp,* as it was called, ran until August 29th when the *Gallant Thirty* winners were announced.

B-P wrote the following in a letter to Keary which, in a modified form, appeared in the first issue of *The Scout* on 18th April 1908. Note there is no mention of 'voting coupons'.

I am very anxious to institute another camp this summer, so that not only may a number of boys come and have a good time and practise real Scouting and life in the open, but also that Scoutmasters and others may come and see how a Scout Camp is carried on...

No Scouts under 11 nor over 16 years[128] of age will be taken; and as I did last year, I should take fellows of any class that like to come whether from Eton College, Elswick Works, or East End Slums. They are all the same to me as long as they are British lads, willing to work at Scouting, obey orders cheerily, and to help each other as much as possible, and provided that they have passed their tests as either first or second class Scouts in a Patrol.[129]

I should expect of them that if they enjoy it (and I rather imagine that they will!) they should afterwards, instead of saying much, do a little towards spreading what they have learnt of the art of Scouting among their friends and neighbours – particularly by raising and teaching new patrols of Scouts.

---

[128] The upper age limit was raised to seventeen.
[129] This requirement was also dropped.

That is all I should ask of them in return for their free Scouting Camp this summer.

By the time the publishers had worked on the idea, it had become a fairly cynical attempt to boost circulation. It has to be admitted however that the extra sales must have also boosted the membership of Scout Groups. Scouts could gain extra votes by sending money for advance orders; six month's subscription cost 2s 6d (12½ pence) and gained 100 extra votes; nine month's subscription costing 3s 3d won 200 extra votes and 12 month's subscription at 4s 4d produced 300 extra votes.

The competition was reported every week under specially drawn headings (see the introduction to this chapter) with lists of the top 50 Scouts. As the date of the camp approached, additional names were listed in divisions A, B and C of young hopefuls who frankly stood no chance. Not surprisingly, there were those who had their doubts about the morality of this competition.

Scouts would encourage friends to buy the papers so they could have their voting coupons. It is very doubtful that Scout F D Watson, who accumulated the most 'votes', had over 29,000 friends! The 50th boy in the league table had over 5350 votes. The scheme must literally have attracted tens of thousands of sales, but must also have disheartened many of the poorer boys.

Arthur Primmer[130], who had attended Brownsea as a member of the Poole Boys' Brigade, sent off his coupons but did not succeed in gaining a place. Happily it did not put him off Scouting. Was B-P ever made aware of Primmer's rejection?

In a letter to Pearson's editor, Peter Keary, dated March 29th 1908, Baden-Powell himself was highly critical of the promotion,

There is something in it, which I fear will put off some readers of the better sort.

1$^{st.}$ The fact is that it touts for subscribers, is to my mind the weakest point: it looks as though we feared not to succeed on our merits....
Secondly it might frighten off boys from trying for the camp competition since it throws it into the hands of the richer ones by giving them 300 votes right off for a year's subscription...

B-P felt somewhat guilty about Pearson's money-making methods and arranged for the first 50 boys, 20 of whom would not go to the camp, to receive a special 'Scout' Camera, and a further 50 a personally signed copy of *Scouting for Boys*.

The image on the following page is from the 1908 Gamages' Catalogue. On October 2nd 1908, B-P visited the famous London store to see two patrols of Scouts who were 'camping' there during a Scouting Exhibition/Promotion. 'Ensign', an established photographic company, had a range of 'Folding Scout' cameras which were on sale in the store at that time. The cheapest camera in the range was 21 shillings (£1.05p in today's terms, though in 1908 this was greater than some working men's weekly wage.) None of the cameras given out at the camp have ever been located, but some photographs taken on them do still exist. (Page 123)

---

[130] Brownsea: B-P's Acorn, p.98

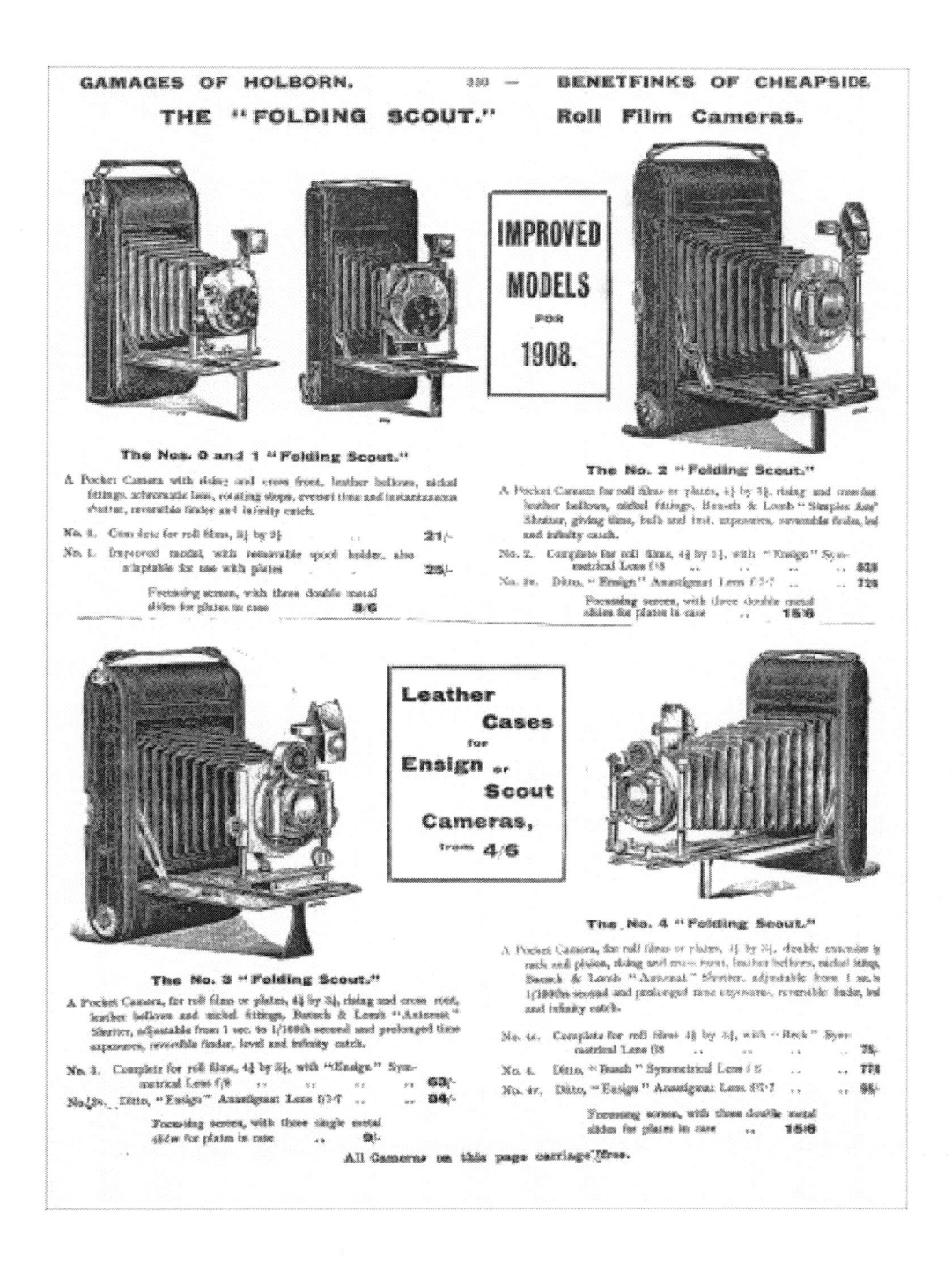

The Location

The exact location of the campsite was kept secret right up to the end of the competition. There was a very good reason for this - it was not finalised until two weeks prior to the camp.

In a letter to Peter Keary, dated May 22nd 1908, B-P states that he was going to look for his campsite that week and on May 30th he wrote again to say he had visited Spurn Point, at the mouth of the River Humber which, *although good is not ideal.* The search for an ideal campsite was still on.

B-P's role as Commanding Officer of the Northumbrian Division[131] of the Territorial Army took him on inspection all over the North-East of England, from York to the Scottish Border. The distances involved in this huge area persuaded B-P to buy a Thorneycroft car (See Page 11) which could be converted to a 'motor-home', with seats that could be made into a bed and slide-out table. The Founder had frequently visited Territorial Camps at Walwick Grange, one of the homes of the Noble family, beautifully situated on the banks of the North Tyne, just south of the Roman Wall near Hexham and was there from the 20th to the 22nd June 1908.

> Saxton Noble was the son of Sir Andrew Noble, a partner in the Armstrong Armaments Company that had a factory on the banks of the Tyne at Eslwick, near Newcastle which, as we shall see, had a part to play in the Humshaugh story.
>
> B-P's friendship with the family came about through his lifetime association with Saxton's brother George who shared many adventures with B-P in India and Afghanistan whilst serving in the 13th Hussars. Saxton Noble, the father of two of the Brownsea lads, underwrote the financial loss of the experimental camp. Humphrey, the elder of his two boys, also attended the Humshaugh camp.

It must have been at this time that B-P decided that the area around the Walwick Grange location offered the necessary conditions for his Summer Camp. He required a campsite close to a railway station, so his campers could arrive from any place in Britain. Yet, it needed to be sufficiently isolated to allow him to get on with training the boys, away from too many prying eyes. (B-P made arrangements with the local police[132] ....*to keep away loafers from the camp.*)

It needed to offer practical camping conditions, being firm underfoot even in wet weather, with a supply of wood and water and, most importantly, able to inspire a real sense of excitement and adventure in his young Scouts. Rural Northumberland, close to the Roman Wall, with its stories of saints, Arthurian knights and border rievers[133] could provide all of this.

Once B-P had made a general decision about the location, it would not have taken him long to find a campsite as he knew the area well, having often fished the river North Tyne. He was also a very good friend of Nathaniel Clayton of nearby Chesters, with whom he stayed just prior to the camp on June 14th 1908, and also of Abel Chapman[134], a noted naturalist (and big game hunter), who lived on the banks of the North Tyne, seven mile north of Walwick Grange.

The exact location B-P chose was just south of the Roman Wall, on a gently sloping hillside adjacent to Carr Edge Plantations, (Grid Ref. NY 890.697) on land belonging to a Mr Henderson. His son still farmed the area in the 1950s

---

[131] The adjective 'Northumbrian' relates either to the modern county of Northumberland or, as in this instance to the former ancient Kingdom stretching north of the River Humber to the Scottish border.
[132] Comment from a B-P letter to Peter Keary, August 9th 1908
[133] Clans of Scottish and Northumbrian cattle thieves.
[134] The Humshaugh Scouts were to visit his home with B-P on Thursday August 27th 1908.

and had memories of the camp, kept fresh no doubt by the signed photo that B-P gave the family as a memento[135].

B-P was then able to write in a letter to Keary on August 9th,

> *I have arranged camping grounds thus: Camp at Walewick Grange [sic] properly spelt Walwick and pronounced Wallick] five miles from Hexham (Station Chollerford) for a week, then Tramps [hikes] to neighbouring spots and bivouac for the nights.*

The view south from the campsite. © CWalker 2008

Fourstones, the nearest station, was the one the Scouts used and is the nearest village to the campsite. However, in a letter of August 17th 1908, giving the *Gallant Thirty* the glad tidings that they had gained a place at the camp, the Scouts are told that they *need ...to travel by the 4.15 train from Newcastle to* **Chollerford***...* where they will be met. Chollerford Station however was not on the main line and no nearer to the camp.

B-P may have had letterheads printed for the camp (as he had at Brownsea), however to date there is no record of any letters sent from the camp, using special paper or otherwise. Humshaugh village is a mile north of the Roman Wall and would seem to have no association whatsoever with the campsite. It was though the nearest telephone exchange and would have served Walwick Grange, so perhaps for that reason B-P may have thought it was also the postal address for the area, and hence the name he gave to the camp.

B-P wrote,

> *I sit writing this letter in the camp on top of a great hill overlooking the Northumbria [sic] moors and dales, with views of the mighty Roman wall, an old grey castle tower where Moss Troopers used to fight. What a country for*

---

[135] On his journey to meet 'Farmer Henderson' that day, B-P was also met Rudyard Kipling whose son John (known as Jack) was part of the B-P's Beaulieu camp the following year. Baden-Powell also visited Comm. Lloyd RNVR on HMS Calliope, moored on the Tyne, to arrange for his Humshaugh Scouts to visit the ship during the camp.

fighting and romance we are in. Scouting today has had its Scouts there before, Scouting for their lives many times in the last two thousand years.
I wish every Boy Scout in Britain could be with us here today.

B-P could not have written these words from the campsite, as there is no view of the Wall. He was on Tourney's Fell at the time, just northwest of the wood above the campsite, which is shown on Henry Thompson's plan.

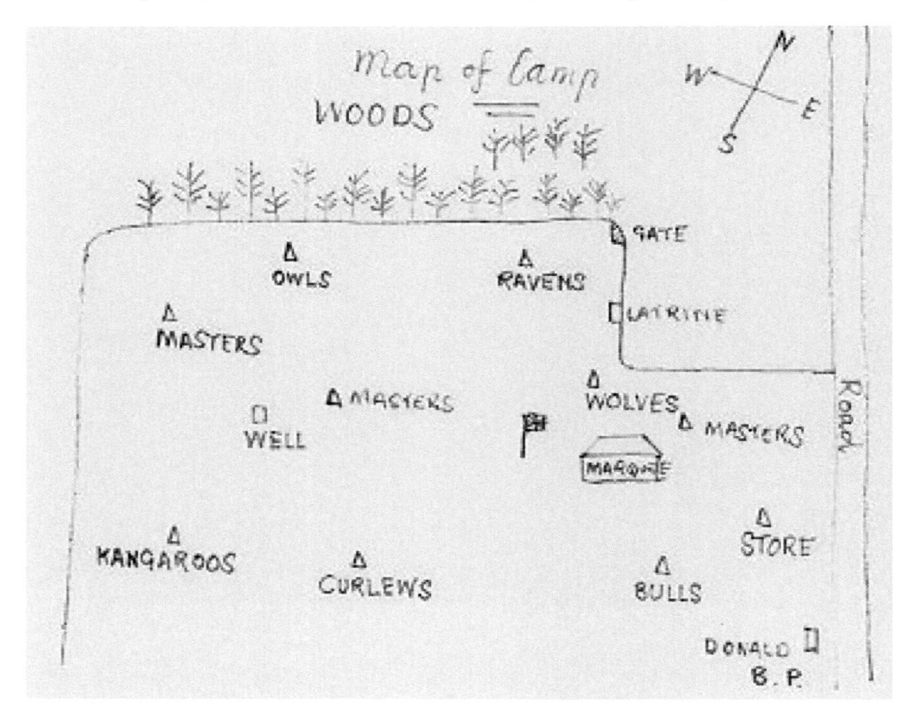

Plan of the campsite from Henry Thompson's diary. The building-like drawing was the large Marquee.

The Camp Quarter-master, Henry Holt, wrote[136]:

The scenery is really lovely, and wherever the eye wanders it falls upon something beautiful, and what with the undulating landscape, the verdant woods and a thousand and one attractions in this picturesque spot, if a boy cannot be happy amid such surroundings he must be a very strange boy indeed.

The 'Conditions'.

On June 6th 1908 Baden-Powell, or someone writing in his name, reported in *The Scout* that an enquirer had asked if it was possible to pay to attend the camp. In other words, was there a way of being able to go to the camp without collecting the voting slips?

To these enquirers I must answer, No, there is no royal road to the holiday camp. If you want to go you must be amongst the 30 on whose behalf are the greatest number of votes. Let me say distinctly, once and for all, there is no other way.

B-P may have intended to take only the competition winners, but this is not what transpired. On August 9th 1908 he wrote to Keary,

---

[136] *The Time of Their Lives*, *The Scout*, 5th September, 1908.

You spoke of sending a few boy friends [sic] to the camp; how many would you like to send? I too would like to send 2 or 3, and we might therefore make up an extra patrol of six between us.

There was then to be a *Royal Road*, which in the end was offered to six boys, five of whom knew Baden-Powell and one only was a friend of Keary's. Parents of the successful competition winners had to sign a parental consent form that had several stipulations, but happily, as at the Brownsea Camp, its sanctions were not required.

6. Any boy who misbehaves himself, or is found otherwise undesirable in camp may be sent home at any time.

The Organisation

SALUTING THE UNION JACK—THE ACTUAL FLAG THAT FLEW OVER MAFEKING.
Boy Scouts at Lieut.-General Baden-Powell's Holiday Camp. No. 5.

Tenting was hired locally, though the giant marquee, or pavilion, as B-P called it[137] was provided by the Territorial Army. He thought it would serve ... *as a mess, store room, etc and staff office*. It proved extremely useful, as it was big enough for the entire camp to be able to carry on patrol activities and games despite the atrocious weather.

The postcard image shows just how large the marquee was. B-P and the other campers are arranged in a 'horseshoe' in front of it, with two of the bell tents being also visible. Under enlargement at least 41 figures can be seen, with four of those for certain being adults. Depicted then are probably all of the 36 boys, but not all of the adults who were known to be present at the camp. There were six leaders who were present and two instructors, who may or may not been there when the photo was taken. (See Page 117) There are also two distant figures to the extreme right outside the 'horseshoe' who are clearly not part of the proceedings. The caption to this original postcard states that the Union Flag is the same as the one flown over Mafeking. It was also used at Brownsea.

---

[137] B-P letter to Keary dated August 9th 1908.

The catering was organised on similar lines to that at Brownsea in that there was an outside catering contractor. Mr James White of Hexham was experienced in catering for large groups camping in the area (probably the TA) and supplied the food, as B-P directed, from local farms. It is not known however where he purchased the *whale for whale burning.* Mr White was able to provide demonstrations of ... *how to make bread without yeast or chemicals*, a task he perhaps accomplished more hygienically than the Brownsea boys whom B-P encouraged to knead dough on the linings of their jackets.

In the same August 9th letter B-P announced his intention of having five patrols of six boys with the 'Special Patrol' of six boys making a total of 36. He and Colbron Pearse (See Page 126) would be joint Commandants, Henry Holt the quartermaster and three Scoutmasters, each in charge of 2 patrols - an excellent staffing ratio.

'The Gallant Thirty'. As reported in *The Scout* 29th August 1908[138]

1	W Ambler	Bradford, W.R. Yorks	16	W Mountford	Wolverhampton, Staffs
2	J S Bartlett	Sheffield, W.R. Yorks	17	T Newton	Wigan, Lancs
3	S S Black	Sheffield, W.R. Yorks	18	J Oakley	Sunderland, Co Durham
4	G Blackmore	Kettering, Northants	19	M A Osborn	Finchley, London
5	J A Carnelley	Halifax, W.R. Yorks	20	A E Page	Sutton, Surrey
6	J A H Coats	Argyllshire	21	R A Piper	Brighton, Sussex
7	R F Crawford	Dublin	22	T W Purves	Glasgow, Lanarks
8	H Davids	Kilmalcolm, Renf.	23	R R Rawson	Epsom, Surrey
9	C S Gibson	Hull, E.R. Yorks	24	R Read	London SW
10	C W Hogg	Middlesborough, Yorks	25	L E Sedgley	Walton-on-Thames Sy
11	A W Horne	Shanklin, I.O.W., Hants	26	H Sharp	Exeter St . Derby
12	L Humphreys	Liverpool, Lancs	27	F Shields	Belfast, Antrim
13	F James	Talbot, Glam	28	C J Thompson	Northallerton, N. Yorks
14	C R Jordan	Middlesborough, N.R. Yorks	29	H Thompson	St. Helens, Lancs
15	J Lewis	Shrewsbury, Salop	30	F D Watson	Beith, Ayrshire

The six boys in the B-P's 'special patrol' are listed on the following page.

> **Interesting Speculation.** Two boys in the postcard image are wearing white tops, yet uniform khaki tops were supplied to all campers (Page 131) Prior to the camp Colbron Pearse's Hampstead Kangaroo patrol and Col. Vaux's Lambton Street special Peewit Patrol (Page 74) were both 'demonstration patrols' and wore similar white jumpers to provide better contrast for photographs. Oakley from Sunderland, was almost certainly from Col. Vaux's troop, and so could well have been at the Grindon Camp It would have greatly assisted B-P to have Scouts of such experience and as stated above, Col.Vaux most likely ensured Oakley's presence. Two boys at the camp, not named in the 'Gallant Thirty' list, (see footnote 132 below) are Scout Adams and PL Pollard who must have been substituted for Scouts who could not attend. Could the other white-topped boy have possibly been Pollard. He wears white on the Curlews photo on p.122. Was he perhaps from Colbron Pearse's Kangaroo Patrol?

The boys came from Ireland, Scotland, Wales and all parts of England except it appears from Northumberland (including the City of Newcastle then its county

---

[138] The table does not include B-P's special patrol of six boys detailed later, or Patrol Leader Pollard and Adams of the Curlews Patrol (see above). Pollard and Adams were reserves replacing two listed boys who could not attend, but exactly who they replaced is not known.

town); Scout Jonathan Oakley lived the nearest to the campsite, some 36 miles away in Sunderland, probably from Col. Vaux's Lambton Troop. (Did the Colonel buy Oakley's Scout Magazines in order that he should have enough votes to win a place, as he had bought newspapers to enable the street vendor Scouts to attend his camp meetings? See page 124) The next nearest participants were Charles Hogg, and CR Jordan from Middlesborough, 56 miles away. B-P's statement that he would take lads from Elswick Works[139] or the East End of London, proved to be one of intent rather than fact, as none of the 'Gallant Thirty' came from either place. The only London participant came from the very expensive address of Buckingham Gate, SW1, very close to B-P's home.

The Patrols

The competition winners were divided into five patrols: Kangaroos, Curlews, Ravens, Bulls and Owls. In addition, the invited boys formed the Wolves Patrol, which consisted of:-

1. Donald Baden-Powell b. October 5th, 1897, died 1973

Donald B-P was the youngest boy in camp though not the least experienced as he had also attended the Brownsea Experimental Camp in 1907 as his uncle's 'adjutant'. Although officially he was not classified as a participant at Brownsea, he took part in all the activities and was awarded his first and second class badges.

His father, Sir George Baden-Powell MP had died when he was only a year old and so his 'Uncle Stephe' (Baden-Powell's family nickname) took a special interest in him. Twenty-one years later Donald[140] recalled memories of the camp.

> We found ... *a miniature tattoo ground which we discovered in another wood below our camping field. Here part of our number sat as an audience on a bank whilst the rest waged mock battles in a small area in front of them. A steep ditch enables the players to come onto the stage without being seen.*

2. Humphrey Noble b. May 9, 1892, died 1968

The Nobles had one of their many homes a few miles away from the Humshaugh site at Walwick Grange. Eton schoolboy Humphrey had also attended the 1907 Brownsea Camp with his brother Marc, (not present at Humshaugh.). The boys' father, Sir Saxton Noble, who had subsidised the Brownsea Camp, went on to become County Commissioner for Northumberland. Because he was not the oldest of the 'special guests' who had been at the Brownsea Camp, (see George Rodney's entry on the next page) he was not the Wolves Patrol Leader but was, most likely, its Corporal.

Rare 1907 image of Humphrey taken from his Eton College Class photo.

---

[139] Elswick Armoury Works was on the Tyne near Newcastle, and does in fact figure in the history of the camp, as it was one of the places visited by all the campers. (See Page 141)
[140] *The Scouter*, August edition 1929.

Humphrey attended the Pax Hill re-union (B-P's home) of the Brownsea Campers in 1928. Like his father he worked in armaments and was awarded the civilian decoration of Member of the British Empire (MBE). When his father died in 1942, he succeeded to the title. He attended the Jubilee Jamboree at Sutton Coldfield in 1957, as well as the Dilston Hall camp visit (See Page 122) to the Humshaugh Site of that year.

Sir Humphrey was residing in Walwick Grange at this time and contributed an article to *The Scouter* about his experiences at both Camps. On the 60th anniversary of the Brownsea Camp he wrote a brief article for the *Eagle*, a boy's comic, where he commented on B-P's magnetic personality.

If he said you had done well, you were in seventh heaven for a week but you would give your eyes rather than let him down.

3. George Rodney b. November 2nd 1891, died 1974.

Rodney attended Brownsea as the Patrol Leader of Wolves.

It is reasonable to assume that he would retain this rank and become the Patrol Leader of the 'special patrol'. Wynne (see below) confirms that his patrol was led by another Etonian. Humphrey Noble - see previous page - was not a PL on Brownsea. He was younger than George being in the following year at Eton. (George's other three brothers had also attended the Brownsea camp but were not present at

Scouting at Eton College.
Despite there being three Etonians at both Brownsea and Humshaugh and Baden-Powell famously addressing the school in 1904 and again in 1914, Scouting never flourished there until 1926, when a School Scout group was formed. Prior to that, but after 1919, Scouting was carried out in House Patrols.

Humshaugh). As the oldest of the brothers, George inherited his father's title and became the 8th Lord Rodney. He married Marjorie, the daughter of Lord Lonsdale, of the Legion of Frontiersmen, (See Page 30) and emigrated to Canada where they became leaders of the Scout and Guide Movement in Alberta.

4. Edward H J Wynne b. 1896, died 1916

In *Headquarters Gazette* July 1912, page 201, there is an article, 'An Old Etonian's Appeal' by 'E.H.J.W.' Its author wrote that he was invited by B-P to attend the Humshaugh Camp ten days before it began. The writer could not have been a Scout at the time, as he said that he met his first Boy Scout at the camp.

> *I was in a tent with five others, one of whom, the patrol leader, was an Etonian like myself.*

Wynne's name was eventually revealed when Mrs P Hatfield, the archivist of Eton College, advised that he was the only boy at the school with the initials EHJW. The *HQ Gazette* article is confirmed, more or less, by B-P's diary as it records on July 30th, (23 days before the camp) that he met 'Eton Boy' Eddie Wynne whilst in Wales. (B-P could of course have followed up this meeting with a written invitation ten days before the camp, just as Wynne recounts.)

The Etonian was invited the following year to B-P's camp at Beaulieu, and proved to be worthy of his place[141], for in the summer of 1910, he held a camp in the *park at home* for 20 boys. The following year the camp, at Coed in Denbighshire, had grown to include over 120 boys.

Lieutenant Edward H J Wynne joined the Grenadier Guards (his father was a Major-General in the regiment) after Christ Church, Oxford and died of wounds on September 16th 1916, joining the horrendous casualty list of campers from Brownsea and Humshaugh. Baden-Powell wrote Wynne's obituary in the December 1916 edition of the *Headquarters Gazette*.

'Teddy' Wynne was heart and soul a Scout. B-P recalled Wynne, on holiday from Eton, spending time washing dirty dishes at the Beaulieu camp *...though his life was a short one, it was a happy one helping others....* Wynne was buried in the La Neuville British Cemetery, Corbie, near Amiens, France.

5. C B P Peake

Peake went on to win great honour in the service of his country. He became Sir C B P Peake KCMG. MC., British Ambassador to Greece. In his letter to Keary, 9th August 1908, B-P writes, *...you spoke of sending a few boy friends to the camp....* Five of the six boys in the special patrol however were B-P's nominees, so it seems likely that Peake was, in the outmoded language of the day, one of Keary's 'boy friends'.

In an article on the Humshaugh Camp in *The Scouter*, December 1954, the Rev. Aiden Pickering wrote that its editor had unsuccessfully tried to put him in touch with one of only two known survivors of the camp, C B P Peake, the other being Humphrey Noble. As Pickering himself recognised there must, at that time, have been many ex-Humshaugh boys still alive. My own researches show that of the three boys of the Curlew Patrol, whose life history is known, two were still alive in 1954. The Humshaugh Pioneers were never fêted or honoured and so, unfortunately, contact with them had been lost.

---

[141] Wynne was not the only Humshaugh boy to follow B-P's instruction and spread the message of Scouting by direct example AW Horne of Shanklin established 2 patrols on his return which, in 1909, merged with a neighbouring group to form the 1st Shanklin (see Appendix)

6. John Cattermole of Humshaugh.

Little is known about this boy, other than from the writings of the Rev. Walter Hatchley[142] who wrote that John was from Humshaugh and a member of the local Boys' Brigade. He had been 'borrowed' by B-P, to act as bugler at the camp and, like the other boys, had been 'kitted-out' with Scout uniform on arrival. Careful examination of the flag-down ceremony image on Page 117, will reveal the detail opposite of John blowing his bugle at the camp. The bugle was sent back to Northumberland, for a special camp commemorating the 100th anniversary of the Founder's birth in 1957.

On a recent visit to the Railway Inn adjacent to the former Fourstones Railway station, undertaken in the interests of historical research, the author of this work found the hostelry to have only two other customers. One, by good fortune, was an ex-Northumbrian Scout, Ronnie Short, who had been present in 1957 at the anniversary camp (100 years since B-P's birth) at nearby **Dilston Hall** (some seven miles from Fourstones), Ronnie recalled the camp had 400 participants, many from outside the region. The campers visited the original Humshaugh Site, catching a train from Dilston to Fourstones, and then walked across fields to the monument (Page 145). Chief Scout Lord Rowallan was present. Ronnie well remembers the Cattermole bugle being blown. Its significance was explained to the boys by Sir Humphrey Noble, one of the original campers- see above. (He died in 1968). Unfortunately, the whereabouts of the Humshaugh bugle is not presently known.

Curlew Patrol

© CWalker 2008

Curlews Patrol. Lawrence Humphreys (most likely) standing extreme right, PL RA Pollard with flag, Charles Hogg (smallest standing). Other members of the patrol include 'Adams'.

---

[142] Hatchley WJ, *The Best Scout England Ever Had*

> **Internet Correspondence.** The photograph of the Curlews Patrol on the previous page was purchased from a postcard dealer by Scout Collector Brian Billington. On the back of the image is written, *Charles Willman Hogg of Middlesbrough High School, born 7.11.94* is identified as *'the small Scout standing'*. Brian consulted the *Scouting Milestones* website and discovered that CW Hogg from Middlesbrough appears on the Humshaugh *'Gallant 30'* list. The photograph was then uploaded to the website and attracted the attention of Chris Ostens of Australia, who is Charles' nephew. They had met in 1960. Chris had a number of photographs left to him by the former Scout, including the one below, which was taken at the Humshaugh camp with Charles' new 'Scout' camera. A further email correspondent, Martin Eggermont of Guisborough, researched Hogg's family tree and suggests, with good reason, that Charles Hogg was closely related to auctioneer Charles Willman, a former Mayor of Middlesbrough (1880). Such is the power of the internet!

In the photograph of Curlews Patrol on the previous page, **Charles Hogg** (smallest standing Scout) is, according to the engraved markings on his Stave, about 4' 6" tall. The four standing Boy Scouts all have lidded tea-cans or billies. Their Scout belts have narrow, rectangular buckles indicating that the purpose-made Scout belt had yet to be invented. All these items were issued as 'kit' at the start of the camp (See Page 132). Two of the boys are wearing metal Scout Badges in their lapels. The Scout seated right is holding a 'broom bessom' (Northumbrian term for a brush made from broom or heather).

B-P taken on a Scout Camera

Curlews' Patrol Leader can probably be visually identified in the photograph, as he would be the one to have the honour of carrying the Patrol Pennant. Fortunately **Lawrence Humphreys**, one of the known Humshaugh Diarists,[143] wrote on the flyleaf to his diary that he was *'No.2'* (or Corporal) of Curlews, and later in his text, we find that **Curlew's Patrol Leader was called Pollard.**

It seems reasonable to assume that Pollard's Corporal, Lawrence Humphreys would be the second oldest boy in the patrol and clearly the boy to the right of the pennant-carrying Patrol Leader fits that description. More information about Humphreys and his diary is to be found on Page 131, as are details from a previously unnamed diary that can now be attributed to P.L. Pollard. Three members of Curlews have then now been positively identified. A fourth member however is also known, as, on Wednesday 2nd September, Humphreys' diary mentions that in a patrol tracking game, ... *Adams was the deer but he was beaten.*

Confusingly neither Pollard's or Adam's names occur in the 'Gallant Thirty' list. RA Pollard was repeatedly mentioned as a contender in Division A (just short of the Top 50) but the only Adams mentioned in the lists, was only once recorded on May 30th as a Division B contender. From the evidence of weekly lists in *The Scout,* boys could make tremendous gains or, having been in the Top 50, disappear from view completely. A likely explanation for the inclusion of

---

[143] The four known Humhaugh's diaries are full documented on Page 131.

both of these boys is that they were replacements for 'winners' who, for whatever reason, could not attend.

It is something of a coincidence that two of the only three boys' diaries known, plus the only named photograph, should all belong to members of the Curlews.

Jonathan Oakley – Patrol Unknown.

It is regrettable that many, if not most of the Humshaugh participants, are not known even in their own Scout Counties. The 'Gallant Thirty' list in *The Scout* provides exact addresses but, one hundred years on, this is insufficient evidence to provide a 'history' of the boy. Apart from B-P's special patrol and the members of the Curlews listed above, there is only one other participant whose life history is known to the author.

As a result of the *Scouting Milestones* website Humshaugh pages, Mr Bruce Hardy, J Oakley's grandson, made contact and was able to supply the following information and images.

Jonathan was the son of a Hyton (near Sunderland) policeman and one of 12 children. Though his father rose to the rank of Sergeant, the family were not wealthy, which makes it very surprising to learn that Scout J Oakley was able to amass 12,254 voting slips!

Living so close to Sunderland, Oakley almost certainly was a member of Col. Vaux's Lambton Street Scouts and so might well have been 'sponsored' by the Colonel, who was known to be very benevolent. (See page 75)

In 1912, Jonathan joined the Royal Army Medical Corp (RAMC), and went to France in 1914. Perhaps fortunately, he was captured in 1915 and sent to a Prisoner of War Camp in Germany, where he escaped making his way back to England. Having escaped from one 'hell-hole', he was part of the ill-fated Gallipoli Campaign of 1916, which he also survived only to be sent to East Africa where he was again captured. When the war ended Oakley joined the Merchant Navy and worked in South Africa and Canada where he met his wife Ann. During the Second World War, Jonathan was again serving his country in one of the highest areas of mortality on the Russian convoys and was sunk three times. After the war he worked for the Admiralty in Scotland before finally following his family to Corby, Northants where he died in 1965 aged seventy-four.

Through his entire adult life, including his wartime experiences detailed above, Jonathan Oakley kept the postcard from the Scout Office and the letter from B-P in his wallet (see next page). This explains their very worn condition, but far from detracting from their usefulness, they speak volumes about the man and the value he placed on his experiences at the camp. Jonathan's parents received the letter, dated 5th September (see following page) from Baden-Powell, shortly after the camp closed. A draft of the example of the same letter in the UK Scout Archives confirms that it was originally headed, The Scouts Camp, Humshaugh, Northumberland, though this was initially typed and then duplicated, rather than properly printed.

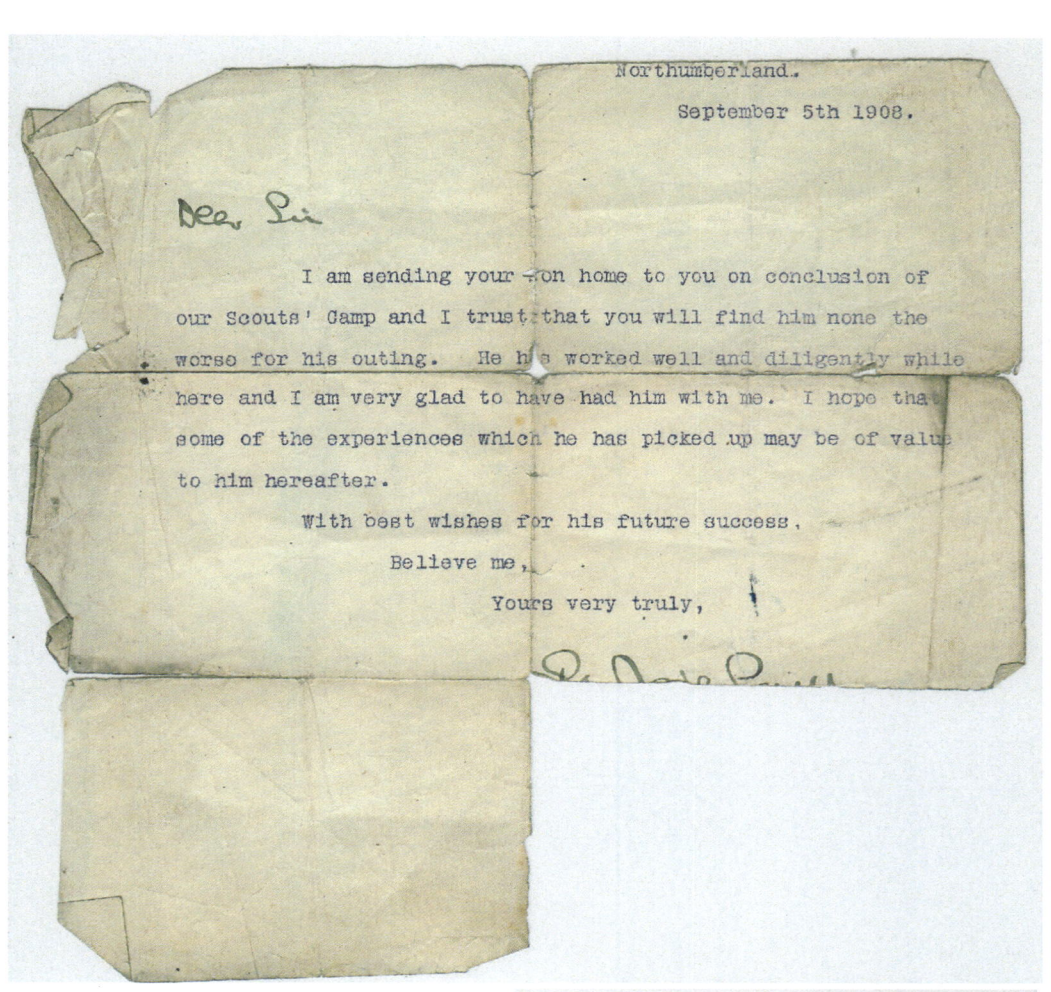

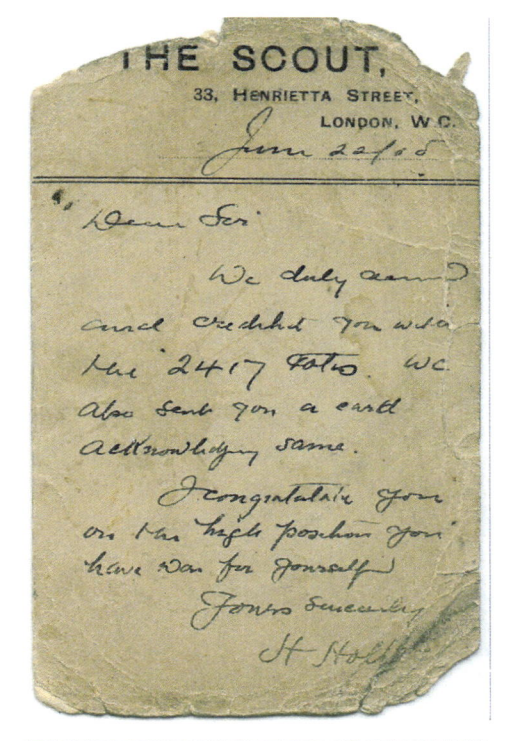

> Northumberland.
> September 5th 1908.
>
> Dear Sir
>
> I am sending your son home to you on conclusion of our Scouts' Camp and I trust that you will find him none the worse for his outing. He has worked well and diligently while here and I am very glad to have had him with me. I hope that some of the experiences which he has picked up may be of value to him hereafter.
>
> With best wishes for his future success.
>
> Believe me,
>
> Yours very truly,
>
> R. Bade-Powell

> THE SCOUT,
> 33, Henrietta Street,
> London, W.C.
> June 22/08
>
> Dear Sir
>
> We duly received and credited you with the "24/17 Fotos. We also sent you a card acknowledging same.
>
> I congratulate you on the high position you have won for yourself
>
> Yours sincerely
> H Holt

Oakley's confirmation that he was in the running to go to the camp, signed H Holt, **Editor of The Scout**.

Oakley pictured seated left in an undated image that is most probably 1908, note his long patrol **ribbons and metal second-class badge**.

> **THE SCOUT**
>
> Editorial Offices:
> 33, Henrietta Street,
> London, W.C.
>
> August 12th, 1908
>
> Dear Sir,
>
> The great Camp race is over, and I am glad to tell you that you are one of the thirty competitors who have sent in the largest number of votes, and you are therefore entitled to spend a fortnight in General Baden-Powell's Holiday Camp, if the inclosed conditions are complied with.
>
> The Camp will commence on August 22nd and will end on September 5th. You will notice this is a day longer than previously announced.
>
> THE SCOUT Camera to which you are also entitled will be presented to you on your arrival in Camp.
>
> I am sending you a Copy of "Scouting for Boys." which is a present from Lieutenant General Baden-Powell.
>
> Yours Sincerely,
> The Editor

The final long awaited confirmation

Adults

I have used this term instead of 'Scouters' because clearly some of the adult leaders/instructors were, at that time, not members of the Scout Movement.

Baden-Powell and Captain Colbron Pearse were Joint Commandants. As already noted, **H. Holt** was Quartermaster. In addition, there were three Scoutmasters, each looking after two patrols.

Captain D Colbron Pearse

Pearse was, with B-P, the Joint Commandant of the camp. He was also responsible for the Bulls Patrol and is mentioned on an almost daily basis in Henry Thompson's diary. In 1908, Baden-Powell encouraged the formation of committees in large centres of population and he appointed Pearse to act as a travelling 'organising secretary', to assist and co-ordinate the emerging Scout Counties. Colbron Pearse was one of the earliest Scoutmasters in North East London, founding the 1st Hampstead Scout Group, (See Page 75) which gave demonstrations of Scouting across the country, prior to the Humshaugh camp. He had camped with his boys at Grindon with Col. Vaux's 'Lampton Street Vendors Club' Scouts, in May 1908, and went on to become the Commissioner for North East London. The Chief Scout presented him with an Honorary Silver Wolf in January 1911. The award, at this time, was

Colbron-Pearse
Poor but unique image from
The Scout Jan. 1911.

normally only for boys who gained the King's Scout badge and 24 proficiency badges but, as a very rare honour, a few early pioneers,[144] such as Pearse, were also given the award. He wrote several books and an early article on *Peace Scouting,* published in *Young England* 1909.

> D. Colbron Pearse disappeared from the British Scouting scene about the time of the First World War. An illustrator of the same *very* unusual name was active in Tasmania, up to the early 1960s, working for the Tasmanian Museum. The museum records show he was born in 1873, and so would have been 35 in 1908 which matches the image on the previous page. He died aged 98 in 1971.

Henry Holt

Quartermaster Holt was not a Scouter at the time of the camp. B-P had a list of three Scoutmasters, any one of whom he would have liked as his QM, but they all had prior engagements. In desperation B-P wrote to Keary on 9th August explaining his lack of success, *...so could Holt take it up?* Holt was another of Pearson's employees and so he did 'take it up', no doubt with some 'encouragement' from his employer. He went on to contribute his observations of the camp to *The Scout,* which he helped to edit.

Holt became the Quartermaster to the Scout Association, and went on to manage the 'Scout Shop'. In December 1913, Percy Everett wrote an article about Holt, as part of the *Some of our Workers* series, in the *HQ Gazette.* Everett claimed that it was he who was *chiefly responsible* for recruiting Holt to the position of Quartermaster at Humshaugh, ... *where his sympathy with the boys and his grasp of detail made him a great success*.

Victor Bridges

Victor Bridges had been invited by Percy Everett to become the first Secretary of the Scout Association in 1908. He combined that role with a career as a prolific and popular novelist.

> Everett wrote that he, ... *is another early worker to whom the Scout Movement is greatly indebted. He acted as Secretary throughout the most anxious periods, and his health has, I am afraid, permanently suffered owing to the enormous pressure he worked under for some months.*

William Birkbeck Wakefield

From Kendal Westmorland, William Wakefield was an enthusiastic organiser of Scouts within the ranks of the YMCA. In the autumn of 1908 he was appointed as Scout Inspector of the North of England, Scotland and Ireland, a role he undertook in a voluntary capacity. In 1910 he visited the USA and helped to start Scouting there. He had a long Scouting career and in 1936 presented Great Tower Campsite on Lake Windermere, to the Association. Lawrence Humphreys' diary records that Wakefield was a member of the Legion of Frontiersmen (See Page 30) as indeed he was, and so in all likelihood he would have worn his spectacular uniform at the camp. He died in Surrey in 1941.

---

[144] Percy Everett gained his 'wolf' six months later, at the Windsor Palace rally on 4.7.1911.

Eric Sherbrooke Walker

Sir Percy Everett wrote of him, *a welcome and familiar friend in every Scouting centre*. Walker was made Inspector for the South of England and Wales at the same time as Wakefield's appointment. Unlike Wakefield however, he did not have sufficient means to volunteer his services.

Walker toured Canada in 1910 with 16 scouts giving demonstrations of Scouting but left Scouting in 1914 to join the Royal Flying Corps. He was subsequently shot down, but escaped from his prison camp using wire cutters disguised as a ham bone sent to him by B-P. Walker enlisted in the RAF in the 2nd World War and narrowly avoided capture in the Western Desert. Between the wars he travelled extensively, at one stage 'rum-running',[145] before building the revolutionary Outspan Hotel at Nyeri, Kenya, that incorporated the famous 'Treetops Hotel'. It was here that Princess Elizabeth learnt, in 1952, on the death of her father King George VI, that she had become Queen Elizabeth II. Walker commented that *...never before had anyone climbed a tree as a princess and come down as a Queen.* Baden-Powell stayed at the hotel and loved to observe the wild animals from 'Treetops'. He had a bungalow built in the grounds of the Outspan Hotel, which became his final home 'Paxtu', where he died in 1941.

Outspan is still open as a hotel today, B-P's cottage has been made into a shrine to Scouting, decorated with badges brought by Scouts from across the world.

John Lionel Calvert 'Banjo' Booth

John Booth[146] was born in 1876 at Killerby Hall, near Catterick, in the North Riding of Yorkshire. His father died when he was only ten years old. John was a very talented artist who, as a child, illustrated and wrote stories for the rest of the extended Booth family

A photo exists of him on-board a ship en-route to South Africa, along with a young Winston Churchill. He spent a total of 15 years with the 1st Volunteer Battalion of the Yorkshire Regiment. He may well then have met Baden-Powell in South Africa, or through B-P's Command of the Northumbrian Territorial Army (Volunteers). When the Founder was garrisoned in Richmond Castle he was responsible for laying out Catterick Garrison Camp, which was very close to the Booth's family home.

---

[145] ES Walker, *Treetops Hotel*, 1962. Rum Runners illegally broke the US prohibition of alcohol between 1920 and 1933 by smuggling liquor into the country mainly from the Caribbean.

[146] Information from Angela Booth of Sydney Australia, the granddaughter of John Booth's brother.

John loved to draw hunting scenes, which had formed a large part of his childhood, as both his parents had been keen members of the Bedale Hunt. His skill led to him to illustrate a number of publications. He had a very keen sense of humour which shines through in both his writing and illustrations.

As a war reporter for *Punch*, John Booth covered the Balkans conflict from 1912 to 1913, after which in 1914, he emigrated with his family to Western Australia. He had only been there for 9 months when The First World War began. He enlisted in the Australian and New Zealand Army Corps (ANZAC) and died on March 28th 1915, like so many of his Corps, as a result of wounds received at Gallipoli. He was buried at sea. Amongst his possessions listed as being returned to his wife was his beloved banjo on which, as we know from the Humshaugh diarists, was John Booth's constant companion.

Percy Winn Everett

A brief summary of Everett's career can be found on p.65. He was yet another employee of Pearson's, but had the distinction of having spent a day at the 1907 Brownsea Camp. He also spent *a few days*[147] at the Humshaugh Camp. He was central to the early development of Scouting and became Deputy Chief Scout.

Everett admires B-P's white SM ribbons worn in 1908

American Instructors

The Newcastle Daily Journal of August 25th 1908, which covered the Humshaugh Camp, records,

> *Two ex-cowboys from America are included in the Scout's Instructors.*

No other hard evidence to support the notion of Americans at the camp has been found. Tantalisingly however, RA Pollard, the Patrol Leader of the Curlews, records in his diary that on Monday 31st August, (see entry for that day, Page 138) there was a new Scoutmaster, but other than the initial letter, his name, F-------- is indecipherable. The name appears to have a total of 10 letters.

The diary of Lawrence Humphreys, Corporal of Curlews Patrol, records on August 29th *Physical Exercises under Mr Wigam,* and on September 1st, *Mr Chance showed us how to jump with a pole.* Mr Chance is mentioned again the same day when,

> *… we tried our hands at basketball, but the baskets were broken so Mr Chance ordered us to go to a small clump of trees and watch the four patrols acting the 'explorers'.*

---

[147] Sir Percy Everett, *The First Ten Years* p. 32 In later life Everett was to infer that he been full-time participant at the Brownsea 1907 Camp.

It may well be clutching at straws but, if there were American Instructors at Humshaugh, the only possible candidates are Wigam, Chance and F---------, as the origins of all the other adults is known. A very thin straw indeed is contained in the reference to basketball, a new game only recently imported from America. If Mr Chance was detailed to teach the Curlews how to play the game, it could well have been because he was familiar with it, as he was an American?

The Daily Programme

06.30 - Turn out, Air bedding. Coffee and Biscuits
07.00 - Physical Exercises or Instruction Parade
07.30 - Stow tents and Wash
08.00 - Prayers & Flag break. (See flag break photo Page 117)
08.30 - Breakfast
09.00 - Scouting Practise
11.00 - Biscuits and Milk
11.30 - Scouting Games
13.30 - Dinner
14.00 - Rest (Compulsory)
15.00 - Scouting Games
17.30 - Tea
18.00 - Recreation and Camp Games
19.30 - Camp Fire
21.00 - Biscuits and Milk. Turn in
21.30 - Lights out

Camp Diaries

To date no single word of diary evidence has ever been discovered that describes the 1907 Brownsea Island Experimental Camp. Four Humshaugh diaries have now been located, Baden-Powell's own, and three of the participants who, with the other boys, were given a diary and a pencil on their arrival at the camp.

These diaries are listed below together with the initials of their authors, which will identify references from their diaries in *The Camp Day by Day* sub-chapter, which follows.

- Baden-Powell's own diary (B-P)
- Henry Thompson's diary, UK Scout Archives (HT)
- RA Pollard's diary (unnamed), Canadian Scout Archives (RP)
- Lawrence Humphreys' diary, in private ownership (LH)

Unfortunately, as is so often the case with historical research, sources sometimes do not all agree. Where there is contradiction, B-P's own diary account is the one used.

> We are fortunate to have the actual weather records, over the period of the camp, from the Meteorological Office at nearby Morpeth. (23 miles distant) These are given at the start of each day, unless the weather was described by a diarist, in which case the diarist's description is used.

Henry Thompson, then aged 15, of the Bulls Patrol was from St Helens, Lancs, probably from the 1st St Helen's YMCA troop (see Appendix). His diary is intact in the UK Scout Archive and is identical to another belonging to a Beaulieu Camper written a year later in 1909. All the boys in both camps were issued with the same diaries by Baden-Powell, enabling them all to take part in the 'Best Diary' competition held at both camps. Henry's diary may not have won the Humshaugh competition but, like all the others, it was inscribed by B-P,

> *This diary records pretty well what you did, but little of what you saw or learnt - that is your experiences and your impressions - which really are the most important things to put in a diary. Your diagrams illustrating the notes are good.* [Author's note: How I wish B-P had followed his own advice.]

Henry was given a signed photo of B-P and a copy of *Scouting for Boys*

Lawrence Humphreys, aged 15, of Walton, Liverpool was Corporal of the Curlews at Humshaugh. His diary was unknown until at a recent Gilwell Reunion, its owner John Day a Worcestershire Scouter, made himself known and kindly furnished me with a photocopy of this amazing document. With the diary was Humphreys' Scoutmaster's Warrant dated February 16th 1909, just six months after the camp, when he could only have been 16 years old, very young indeed for such a role.

Accompanying the diary was a copy of the original, made by Humphrey's on December 1912 when he was at sea, on SS Wayfarer bound from Liverpool to New Orleans, probably on route to a new life in the 'land of opportunity'. The documents only came to light when John Day was offered them by a friend, in the antiques' trade, who had purchased them from another dealer in the process of selling his business.

Lawrence Humphreys' Kit list.

LIST OF THINGS A BOY SHOULD BRING TO CAMP.

- 1 Complete Suit for Travelling to Camp, but not for use while there.
- 1 Great-coat or Mackintosh.
- 1 Pair Shorts.
- 2 Pairs Stockings.
- 1 Brush and Comb.
- 1 Toothbrush, Soap, etc.
- 1 Old Jacket.
- 2 Pairs Shoes or Boots.
- 1 Pair Canvas Shoes.
- 2 Flannel Shirts.
- 1 Sleeping Suit or extra Flannel Shirt Flannel Trousers for night wear.
- 1 Pair Bathing Drawers or Bathing Suit
- 2 Towels.
- 1 Vest.
- 1 Pair Drawers.
- 3 Handkerchiefs.
- 1 Cap.
- 1 Tin of Dubbin for boots

A similarly printed list was also sent to parents of items that would be provided on arrival at the camp,

> *Belt, Haversack, Knife, Lanyard, 'Billy', Scout's Staff, 1 pair of shorts, 1 Pr of Stockings, 1 Pr Garters, 1 Sweater, 1 Neckerchief, 1 Shirt (flannel).*

Patrol Leader R A Pollard. Amazingly, another Humshaugh diary was discovered in the Canadian Scout Archives. Unfortunately, the diary is unnamed, but its author discloses that Mr Wakefield (See Page 127) elected him patrol leader of Curlews. This same sentiment is recorded in Lawrence Humphreys' (Curlews) diary, Monday, 24th August, ...*Mr Wakefield permanently elected our patrol leader.*

Fortunately, Humphreys goes on to record that his Patrol Leader was Pollard. By using the *A Division* lists (runners up after the *Top 50*), provided in *The Scout* it has been possible to establish that P L Pollard had the initials RA.

The Camp, Day by Day

Saturday 22nd August. Dry all day.

© CWalker 2008 The Station Master's House.

Scouts arrived at Fourstones Railway Station and marched a mile along lanes due north to the campsite. Trains still thunder through the Tyne Valley today, but no longer stop at Fourstones. The platforms have all but gone, and the Station Master's house (shown on the left) is now a private dwelling. The Railway Inn, adjacent to the original platforms, is however still in existence.

B-P was not there to meet his boys, as he was inspecting a Territorial Army Unit on that day. His diary sadly records that his little dog 'Taffy' was killed when he fell out of his car and was strangled by his collar and lead which was attached to B-P's 18 h.p. Thorneycroft. (See Page 11) The Humshaugh photo above shows the very car, or would do so if were not obscured by so many Scouts. Sitting at B-P's feet is Colbron Pearse one of the three Scoutmasters. (See photo Page 126) The two patrol flags are those of the Curlews (right) and Bulls.

Charles Hogg of Curlews is to the extreme right, while his white-shirted PL, Pollard is again holding the patrol pennant. (See Curlew Patrol photo on Page 122) As each SM was assigned two patrols, were Curlews and Bulls the two that were under Colbron Pearse's charge?

> *After three quarters of an hour march* [from the Railway Station] *reached camp, waited for luggage and received shirt, shorts, belts and hats. Saw* [our] *SM and he spoke about future* [sic] *and notices.* (LH)

Sunday 23rd August. Occasional Showers.

From Baden-Powell's diary:

> *Motored to Hexham and saw Canon Savage re Service on Sunday for Scouts.*

Afternoon: *Scouts marched to the wall and to Haughton Castle (Mr Cruddas-owner) and had tea in the stable in the rain.*
(Curlews did not visit Haughton Castle on Sunday.)

B-P had set the campers a 'quest'.
(See footnote [148])

The theme for two days and nights is 'The Quest of King Arthur', who has been asleep in some hidden cave in this very area.

As he admitted, there were hundreds of sites connected to Arthurian folklore throughout England. It seems unlikely that the boys visited the cave as it does not feature in any of the diaries. B-P came back to the Arthurian theme however in his final talk to the boys before they left the camp. (See Page 142)

Baden-Powell was much intrigued with Arthurian legends and often used images from these tales in his writings. He was later to use the Knights of the Round Table as the theme for his Rover Scout section

Haughton Castle (shown here in an old print) was built around 1200 A.D. and is an imposing sight on the banks of the North Tyne. The Scouts were entertained by Mr Cruddas who told them the gory tale of a border reiver who, caught stealing cattle, was thrown into the castle dungeons and starved to death. His screams, they were told, could still be heard nightly, echoing through the castle.

p.m. *Visit to Chesters Roman fort and the Roman Wall. Bathing in River Tyne. Campfire with B-P.* (HT)

---

[148] From B-P's 'letter' to *The Scout*, 12th September 1908

> Chester is the best-preserved example of a Roman Cavalry Fort in Britain. Under-floor heat-ing systems are still visible. It was of great strategic importance, as it was once adjacent to a stone bridge over the River North Tyne. English Heritage now manage the site.

B-P had visited Chesters as recently as June 14th 1908 with a Mrs and Miss Swinburne,

> who ... *showed me the Roman camp, barracks, and hot-aired houses....*

> *We had tea as usual, some of the Scoutmasters read us 'Pooh of Pucks Hill'.* (LH)

> **Author's Comment:** Many of the boys were 15 years old, surely this book was far too young for this age group.

Monday 24th August. Overcast and raining a.m.

a.m. *Setting up a loom in the woods and building a hut.* (B-P)
Physical exercises led by Mr Wakefield. (RP) *Ran two lengths of the field and was blown out.* (LH)

Bivouac and straw mattress making. (RP)

A MID-DAY MEAL IN CAMP—THIS HUT WAS BUILT BY THE SCOUTS THEMSELVES.
Boy Scouts at Lieut.-General Baden-Powell's Holiday Camp. No. 3.

The postcard image on the previous page shows the very 'hut' built in the woods on 24th August. B-P had commissioned photographs as a way of instructing other Scouts. In a letter to Everett[149] B-P agonised over the best way to use these images. He settled on postcards with a series of magic lantern slides, drawn in colour by an artist, using the photographs as a basis.

> The second line of the postcard's caption reads: *Boy Scouts at Lieut.-General Baden-Powell's Holiday Camp. No. 3*. Billy Butlin's holiday camp industry began when he opened his first camp near Skegness in 1936, so, in 1908, Baden-Powell's 'Holiday Camp' meant just that and had no other connotation.

p.m. *Made ration bags with needle and thread, short game of football, then a local showed us how to make bread without yeast or chemicals.* (RP)

Evening. *Music round the campfire* (RP) *'Hints on Tracking' by Captain Pearse.* (HT)

Tuesday 25th August. *'Was wet, very wet.'* (Henry Holt – Quartermaster.)

a.m. *After Breakfast we received rest of kit i.e. camera with spool, billy, staff, diary book and pencil.*
Splicing and whipping ropes by the three S.M.s. (B-P)
Built foundation of Campfire. Fire-lighting race between Bulls & Curlews. (HT)
Indoors games in Marquee. Physical Drill. (B-P)

p.m. *Rope splicing and lesson in Photography.* (RP)
Our Scoutmaster showed the time to expose photographs. (LH)
Map Reading and Use of the Compass with Captain Pearse. (HT)

After tea finished bivouac. (RP)

Wednesday 26th August. Sunny morning, rained hard p.m.

a.m. *Collected firewood.* (HT)
Practice in smoke signals and preparation of Hunter's Stew. (RP)

p.m. *Curlews ...went to Haughton Park where we saw the Castle.* (LH)
Scene of cruel deeds, looked round dungeons and made our own tea.
Ambushes on the way home. Saw part of the Roman Wall. (RP)
Captain Pearse instructed in reading compass. Camp Fire. (HT)

Thursday 27th August. *Showery Day* (B-P)

6.30 *Rose. P.E. with Mr Wakefield, changed position of tent.* [
a.m. *Probably because of bad weather.*]
Played 'Scout meets Scout', our Patrol Curlews against Bulls. Draw. (RP)

11.00 *Patrol Activities. First Aid Instruction with Captain Pearse.* (HT)
a.m.

---

[149] B- P letter to Percy Everett, *The First Ten Years*, p. 34. *The photographs are our very best advertisement, they really give the attractive side of the organisation, and photos cannot lie and thus bring it home to boys and parents alike. I don't quite know which is the best way to spread them whether by postcards, or by an extra sheet in the Christmas number of 'The Scout'.*

Marched after dinner via the Wall to Houxty, where Abel Chapman put us up. Ground very wet and rain falling, so we put up in loft and harness room. (B-P) [The stables that the boys stayed in still exist to the rear of the house.]

On the way saw the Roman ditch and mound. Halted at a farm and brewed tea over a camp fire. (HT)

Failed to erect tent, slept in the Horse Hall which contained peat. (RP)

© CWalker 2008

I felt every bone in my body in the morning. (HT)

The present owners were unaware of its B-P connection when I visited the house in 2005 but they were able to tell me of the former owner, Abel Chapman. Classes from the local school used to inspect his collection of 'Big Game' trophies and birds' eggs, before the house (photo above) was sold.

In October, 2002, Tony Jackson of Ontario, Canada wrote to the author:-
My father bought Houxty from Tom Chapman, [the nephew of Abel Chapman] *in 1948.*

I remember arriving there for the first time at the age of eight and being overwhelmed by the heads of big game that were still hanging all over the house. The majority of these trophies were sent to the Hancock Museum in Newcastle, except for one water buffalo, which we retained in the hall. My mother would hang decorations from its horns at Christmas.

Happily, many of these artefacts are still in the Hancock Natural History Museum in Newcastle, where they are very attractively presented in a modern gallery - Abel's Ark, a novel way of displaying the now politically incorrect trophies.

Abel Chapman was born in 1851 and inherited his father's Lambton Brewery and wine-importing business in Sunderland, when he was 18. (Note Col. Vaux's- Scout Troop was in the same area of Sunderland (Page 74) and he too was part of a family brewing business). In the course of Chapman's wine-buying travels, he was able to explore the countries he visited and study his obsession, natural history. After 30 years of hard work in the wine trade, he bought Houxty in 1899 to concentrate on his hobbies. He wrote eleven books on natural history, based on his meticulously-kept and illustrated diaries, and undertook numerous expeditions all over the world. The Hancock Museum cites Abel Chapman as being responsible for the discovery of the wild lynx in Spain, which he saved from extinction, and for the establishment of the first National Park in South Africa, now known as the Kruger National Park. Abel Chapman died in 1929 aged 78 having been a supporter of the Scout Movement throughout its existence.

Friday 28th August. *Cold and rain all day.* (B-P)

a.m. *Physical drill in saddle room with Capt. Pearse.* (RP)
Stretcher drill. p.m. tracking, whistles and hand signals. (HT)

Houxty, Indoors in stables, life saving etc. Chapman showed the boys his collection of heads etc. (B-P) The 'heads' were Chapman's collection of big game trophies.

It was a fine sight well worth going a long way to see. Signalling practice with Capt. Pearse. (RP)

5.30 *Tea. Had campfire, heard phonograph.* (RP)
p.m. *At night P.L.s went out rabbit shooting.* (HT)
Turned in on a bed of peat. (LH)

Saturday 29th August. Cold all day, though cloudy bright.

© CWalker 2008

7a.m. *Got up. P.E. in Mr Chapman's grounds.* (RP)

10.a.m. *Paraded to march to Chipchase Castle. Had lunch at Wark.* (RP)

We left after giving Mr Chapman three hearty cheers. (LH)

Baden-Powell and some of the boys were shown around by Mr T. Taylor. His daughter Miss Taylor as late as 1954, remembered B-P's,

...delightful breezy personality ...and the complete control he had over the boys.

© CWalker 2008

Marched to Wark where we had our dinner in the Town Hall… we had two ambushes on the way. (LH)
Back in camp. 9.30 Turned in. (RP)

Sunday 30th August. A cold day but with some sunshine.

a.m. *Clearing camp.* (HT)
11:30 *Church Parade conducted by B-P.*

After dinner the campers marched to Hexham via Fourstones, to Warden Bridge and along the main road.

Arrived Hexham 3.15 p.m. When we got there we saluted the statue of Benson who was a great scout. (HT) [B-P will have told the boys Benson was a great scout, He would often **call historical heroes 'great scouts'.**]

The Camp Quartermaster, Henry Holt wrote,

> Our visit to Hexham caused considerable stir in the quaint little town. And our route to the Abbey was lined by hundreds of enthusiastic lookers-on who viewed the little regiment of Boy Scouts with awe and wonder.

> Colonel C E Benson, ex-Royal Artillery, was with B-P during the Ashanti Campaign of 1895, and during the Boer War. He was in command of a cavalry column at Elandskloof in 1901 and was responsible for a complete rout amongst the Boers, capturing many men and materials. He died in battle in October 1901. The statue, illustrated on the previous page, was erected by public subscription amongst his Hexham neighbours, with whom he was obviously a popular hero.

© CWalker 2008

There was a short service by the Rev. Sydney Savage, who outlined the history of the Abbey. Afterwards, the Boy Scouts marched to General Sir Loftus Bates house at Spital for tea, and then 'marched' back to camp via the ancient Roman site known as 'The British Camp' near Warden. (See map Page 143).

7.30 pm   *Reached home.*

8.30 p.m. *The General at the camp sang us a song and gave us a recitation about a soldier.* (LH)

Hexham was thronged with onlookers the day that B-P and his Boy Scouts came to town. The Rev. Aiden Pickering met a Hexham businessman in the 1950s, which was proud that B-P had stopped to talk to him on his walk to the Abbey.

Monday 31st August. Fine a.m. but heavy rain p.m. Stormy night.

P.E with new Scout Master Mr F--------. (RP)

Work day. (B-P) Second Class Scout Tests were done today (LH)
Took tent sections into wood and built tent. (HT)

Badge-work. Some second and first class badges completed and presented by B-P.
Those not going in for them (the badges) went to the river for a swim. (HT)
Basketball. Rested expecting night manoeuvres which never occurred. (RP)
        [Obviously cancelled due to the heavy rain.]

Photographer took a number of photos.
     1. *Singing Eengonyama Chorus*
     2. *Sitting round Campfire.*
     3. *Saluting Union Jack.* (LH)

This previously unpublished image shows B-P demonstrating campcraft skills at Humshaugh. Note the two white-topped boys. (See p. 119) Scout staves have been deployed with suitable lashings to construct a 'double tripod' strong enough to suspend a dozen 'billies'.

This was the evening that Donald Baden-Powell was thought to be 'lost'. He had crawled into his tent to get out of the rain, and had crept under his mattress thus escaping the attention of the first searchers. He was eventually found by Baden-Powell, but not before the whole camp had been roused to look for him in the gloom and rain.

Young B-P [Donald] *had not been seen since before tea. A search was made for him and after about 1 ½ hours was found in his own tent.* (LH)

Miss Taylor, of Chipchase Castle, says her family had some fun with B-P about the incident - but the Chief Scout steadfastly maintained that the 'night exercise' had been a useful experience for the Scouts.

The lost boy himself, Donald Baden-Powell in his article in *The Scouter* August 1929, refers to this incident, recalling that it was the *youngest boy who went missing*, but he never revealed that lost boy was himself.

Tuesday 1st September.
Heavy showers all day.
a.m. *Patrol Drill raising section*
Mr Chance showed us how to jump with a pole. (LH)
Made straw ropes.
Played 'Bang the Bear'. (RP)
1st Class tests. (HT)

p.m. *Had debate in Bull's tent, 'Should rabbits be kept in tents' was the first debate of the 'Wall Debating Society'.* (RP)
Evening Lecture by Col. Coulson on 'Kindness to Animals'. (RP)

> And three Scoutmasters with their troops
> In Scout formation went
> With lanterns, poles and tracking irons
> And searched his spacious tent.
>
> Until at last B-P himself
> Declared he would explore
> That mighty cavernous dome where Donald
> Did his nightly snore.
>
> You recollect how all their toil
> Abortive proved in vain
> And how we wandered through the wood
> Amid the pelting rain!
>
> And prodding fiercely in the dark
> He struck some muddy boots
> Invoobo! Zing a zing. Bom Bom!
> Gonyama! We are Scoots!
> *Victor Bridges*, Scoutmaster

Wednesday 2nd September. Changeable. Heavy showers throughout the day.

6.a.m. *Rose. Spent all morning preparing for sports.* (RP)
Sports Day began at 2.p.m.

A considerable number of people assembled, consisting mostly of the friends of the boys, with a few villagers. (BP)

> As only one boy, John Cattermole of Humshaugh lived nearer than Sunderland 36 miles distant, it is a little hard to credit that there would have been many of the boys' friends, but there were certainly guests. Mr George Ward-Price was invited by B-P in a letter dated August 15th, now in the UK Scout Archives.

The various items created considerable interest, and the day proved a perfect success. The audience were delighted with different items, such as tracking, cock-fighting[150], pole-jumping, bang the bear, mattress making, all of which were gone through with commendable skill. The most interesting feature of the day was left until last. This was a highly exciting incident called 'The Attack on the Camp', and the boys that took part in it well deserved the loud applause that rewarded their efforts.
Report in *The Scout* by the Camp Quartermaster (Henry Holt) September19th, 1908.

Glorious tea. (RP)

After tea, the Scouts practised lighting fires using only two matches. The Fire Lighting Competition won by Bulls. In the 'Bang the Bear' competition, H Thompson was the bear! (HT)

Campfire. (RP) *Night Manoeuvres. Adams was the deer but he was beaten.*(LH)

Thursday 3rd September. Overcast but dry.

7 a.m. *P.E.* (PR). *Assisting farmer with fence mending.* (B-P)

Self-Measurement [as in Ch. 4 Camp Life, *S4,e.g. spans and cubits*].
First Aid with Capt. Pearse. (HT)
Did camp fire for 1st Class Badge. (RP)

p.m. *Marched to Fourstones Railway Station and took train to Newcastle upon Tyne where the Armstrong Whitworth Armoury works at Elswick were visited. (B-P) Went on a boat called 'Calliope' and a* [hydraulic] *large crane.* (HT)

Saw motorbuses. Some of us fired guns. Visited old Warship HMS Calliope by the Naval Reserve as a training ship. (RP)
B-P used the history this ship as the basis for one of his yarns.

6.00 *Arrived back in camp. Campfire, B-P yarns about Mafeking.* (RP)

---

[150] Cock-fighting was a game also played on Brownsea, – no animals involved! The Scouts 'rode' their staves like hobby horses crashing into each other until only the winner was left standing.

> The Elswick [pronounced *el-sick*] Works were one of the biggest employers on Tyneside and was founded by William Armstrong, who was knighted in 1859 and ennobled Lord Armstrong of Cragside in 1887. He was largely a self-made man who invented the Hydraulic Crane. Armstrong's factories were responsible for producing warships, armaments and, later on, tanks and planes. Andrew Noble, a gunnery expert resigned his army commission in 1860 to join the company. He became a partner and rose to become Company Chairman on Armstrong's death in 1900. He was created a Baronet in 1902. Sir Andrew Noble was the father of George and Saxton Noble. George served with Baden-Powell in the 13th Hussars from 1886 and shared many adventures with him in Afghanistan and India. His brother Saxton Noble (the 3rd Baronet), lived near to the Humshaugh camp and, as already mentioned, had helped fund the Brownsea Experimental Camp in 1907, attended by his two boys Marc and Humphrey. The latter also taking part in the Humshaugh camp. It is therefore not surprising that the Humshaugh campers were invited to visit the Elswick factory.

Friday 4th September. The Last Day. Dry, though cloudy.

6 a.m. *P.E. Pulled down bivouacs in forest. Bathing parade. (RP)*
    Went down to the river but I only washed my feet, as it was very cold. (LH)
p.m. Flag Raiding (game). [Patrols had to capture each other's flags, whilst of course trying to defend their own.]

In his final address to the lads round the campfire, B-P again conjured up the spirit of King Arthur and the Knights of the Round Table,

> *You must never forget*, he said, *that the distinguishing mark of a Scout should be unselfishness. He should always think of others and try to help them before thinking of himself.*

ROUND THE CAMP FIRE—GENERAL BADEN-POWELL TELLS A SCOUT YARN.
Boy Scouts at Lieut.-General Baden-Powell's Holiday Camp. No. 6.

Sir Percy Everett recalled,

> *In order to mark the occasion, the campfire was bigger than usual and its livid flames brought into bold relief the happy faces of the boys whose glorious holiday was so nearly at an end. I wish all ... could have heard the General's inspiring and encouraging words. He congratulated the boys on their cheeriness and hoped he would meet them all again in similar circumstances. He was cheered into the night.*

The campfires, as at Brownsea, were the best-remembered features of the camp.

> *At the campfire he* [B-P] *was great and kept the pace going with song and story. An amazing amount of latent talent developed as the fortnight went on. The General himself could always be relied upon for a song or recitation of the No. 1 order, whilst the Scoutmaster Booth, with his banjo and his endless repertoire, provided a sure guarantee that proceedings never flagged. The Scouts themselves were great, especially in the chorus line, and the way 'Clementine', 'The Old Folks at Home', and other more modern melodies used to go rolling and echoing over those lonely fells, showed that in lung power at least, every Scout was thoroughly efficient.*
>
> Henry Holt, Report in *The Scout*, September 26th, 1908

The Newcastle *Daily Journal* reported B-Ps final address to the Scouts. He congratulated them on their *soldierly qualities,* and he hoped that they would some day,

> *...be able to render great service to their country.* He reminded them that their *...ideals should be exactly the same as King Arthur's, to serve their country, to be fearless and unselfish, to help the weak, to keep their honour unstained and, if needs be, die in its defence. You must never forget,* he said, *that the distinguishing mark of a Scout should be unselfishness. He should always think of others before thinking of himself.*

© CWalker 2008

An evening view from the campsite.

142

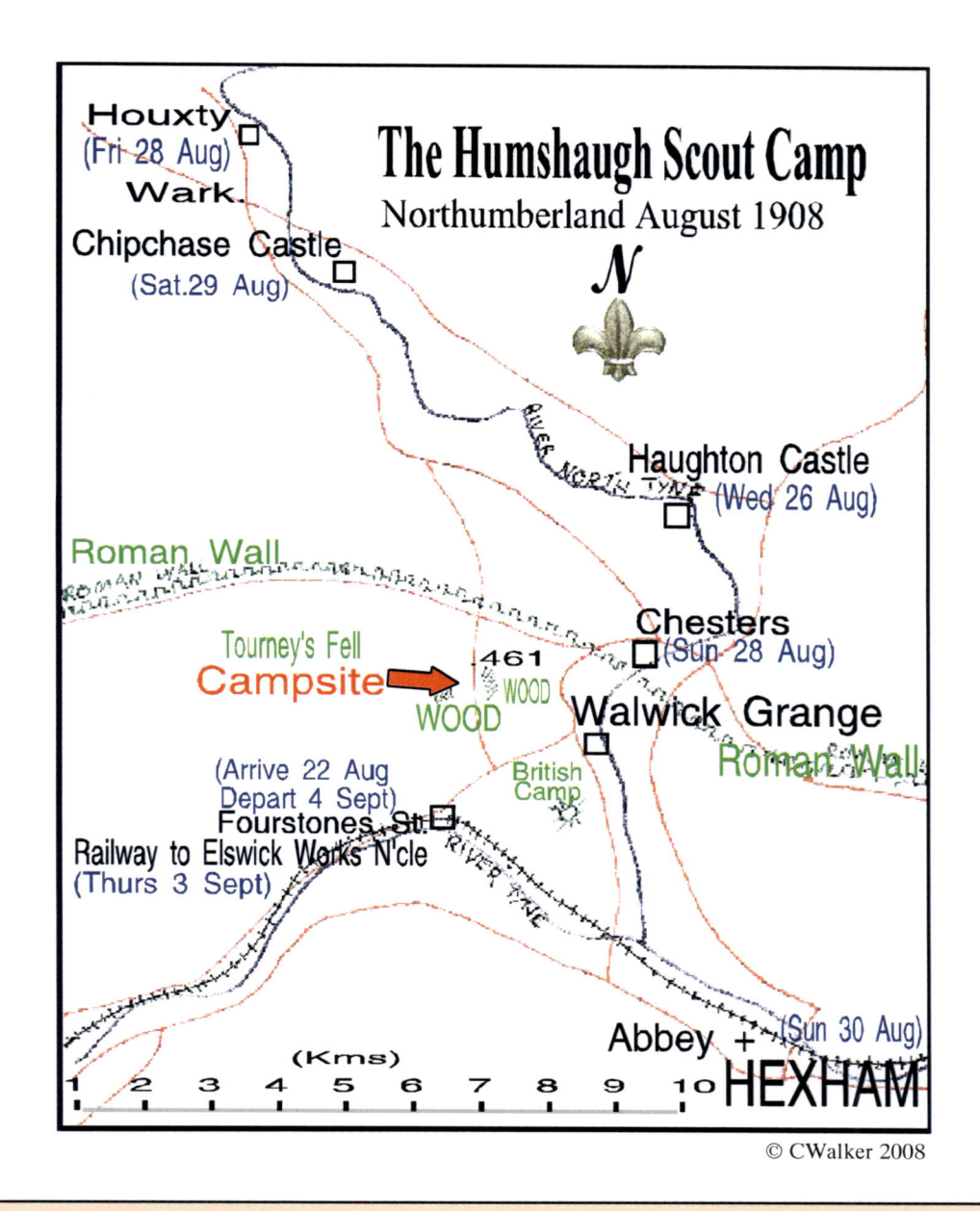

The Humshaugh Scout Camp
Northumberland August 1908

- Houxty (Fri 28 Aug)
- Wark
- Chipchase Castle (Sat. 29 Aug)
- Haughton Castle (Wed 26 Aug)
- Roman Wall
- Tourney's Fell — Campsite → .461 WOOD
- Chesters (Sun 28 Aug)
- Walwick Grange
- Roman Wall
- British Camp
- Fourstones St. (Arrive 22 Aug, Depart 4 Sept)
- Railway to Elswick Works N'cle (Thurs 3 Sept)
- Abbey (Sun 30 Aug)
- HEXHAM

© CWalker 2008

Author's comment. Having lived in Northumberland for three years and led hiking parties in the vicinity of the Humshaugh Camp, I feel that the most obvious choice for a day's hike may have been overlooked. About the same distance from the camp as Houxty is Crag Lough. The lough is a lake lying beneath the Roman Wall which sits airily on top of the Great Whin Sill, a dramatic north-facing cliff, providing one of the most spectacular views in the country.

The parts of the Roman Wall that the boys were taken to see on their 'marches' consists only of mounds and ditches, as confirmed by diarist Henry Thompson who, with the directness of a 15 year old, describes exactly how 'under-whelmed' he was, – ....*visited some Roman Walls* and ...*saw the Roman ditch and mound.*

There was a great deal of 'marching' along lanes to castles and houses which, no doubt, was very instructive but does not, seen in retrospect, appear to be all that thrilling. The weather though was appalling. The local meteorological station at Morpeth, only 23 miles distant, records a total of 2.7 inches of rain over the 10 days of the camp and so, perhaps, some of the visits were only 'wet weather alternatives'?

The Aftermath.

There is no doubt that the camp was a great success, especially from the boys' perspective. John A H Coats wrote:-

> *Although the weather was not of the best, I had the very best holiday of my life. If all camps were like yours, every boy would want to be camping out.*
>
> *As for our good General, how we all loved him! He was also so cheery and kind to us and always willing to show us things we did not understand.*

Old Etonian E H J Wynne was positive,

> *I say without hesitation that I had one of the best times of my life ...*

H Thompson of Bulls agrees:

> *It was the finest time of my life...*

As at Brownsea, the campfires were often recalled as being the most memorable feature of the camp, led of course by B-P himself. This was also the case at Humshaugh. One campfire song written by Scoutmaster J L C Booth (the banjo-player) at the last campfire of the camp had a verse that summed up the weather.

> *You may think that existence is not worth a duckat.*
> *In thirty knot gales that bring rain by the bucket;*
> *But if you start grousing the Scouts'll say, "Chuck it".*
> *Why this is the weather that keeps us in form!*

The Courant, Hexham's long-established local paper, carried but one report on the camp[151] in which it was described as being on *a lonely hill near Chollerford*. This seems a surprising description of the location from a local reporter, though Chollerford is in fact half a mile nearer to the actual site than B-P's own description of Humshaugh. The un-named reporter stated that the boys were to visit the Abbey for the Sunday service the following day. B-P had visited the Abbey to arrange matters with Cannon Savage on the previous Wednesday, the 19th of August. The report however contained real news that even to this day is not generally known.

> *The Scouts were...expected to remain in the district until about the middle of next week when they shift their quarters to Blyth for fresh experience by the sea.*

The report is entirely accurate because in a letter to Keary dated August 9th, B-P outlines the camp's programme, concluding with,

> *... And on to Blyth (sea beach) for the last two days for bathing, boating, etc.*

Blyth, on the Northumberland coast just south of Morpeth, was 40 miles distant from the camp. It would have been surprising if the Founder had omitted water activities completely from his first National Scout Camp. Both the Brownsea camp and at B-P's 1909 National Camp at Beaulieu[152] had water activities as a significant part of their programme.

---

[151] *Hexham Courant*, Saturday, August 22nd, 1908
[152] See Scouting Milestones website at www.scouting.milestones.btinternet.co.uk/beaulieu.htm

The Courant article[153] suggests that *General Baden-Powell of Mafeking fame* was the *teacher* for the 36 boys encamped.

> *The movement which was initiated by the General little over a year ago, has made rapid progress, there being patrols in almost every town in the country ... Scouting ... imparts a valuable training, no matter what his [the boy's] avocation in after life may be.*

Humshaugh Campsite in Later Years

In 1929, a local stonemason, Mr N Peart, with the help of the 3rd Hexham Scout Group, raised a cairn to mark the 21st Birthday of Scouting. There is also an engraved inscription on the rock on which the cairn stands,

B. P. 1908 'LOOK WIDE'

In 1950 a plaque was added to the cairn. It reads:

> *This cairn marks the site of the first Boy Scout Camp held in 1908 by B-P, later Lord Baden-Powell of Gilwell, Chief Scout of the World.*

The cairn from a 1950 postcard. The 're-affirmation of the promise' photo on p.148 was taken from this rock looking in the same direction. The 'Look Wide' view is now totally obscured by trees.

---

[153] Hexham Courant, August 1908.

Since then additional plaques have been added to mark the visits of Chief Scouts Lord Rowallan, Michael Walsh and Garth Morrison. The outcrop however has been engulfed by the plantation, making a nonsense of the inscription, as all that can be seen now is trees. The monument is well maintained by the Northumberland Scouts with a convenient bench, provided close by.

The Baden-Powell Walk.

A 'Heritage Walk' from Fourstones Station to the Humshaugh Campsite has been developed under the auspices of Northumberland Scout Council. Participants can purchase a special badge, certificate and woggle. The scheme is based on the nearby 'Look Wide' Campsite. *Scouting* magazine printed an article by a Finnish Cub Scout, Kari Ranta (see photo on Page 149) who having completed the walk in 2001, signed the special visitors book held at the 'Look Wide Campsite' as participant 14,060.

Certificates issued by Northumberland Scout County to those who complete the walk.

The 'B-P Walk' Badge

90th Anniversary nametape and woggles

The Significance of the Camp.

The Humshaugh camp was planned from first to last as a 'model', not only for those who had already joined the ever-expanding Scout Movement but also for the world at large. It was designed to show what Scouting was all about. It attracted some press coverage in the national newspapers and, as stated previously, postcards and a set of magic lantern slides were commissioned for later use in Scout Huts up and down the country. They were sold through the pages of *The Scout* magazine, but could be borrowed from Scout Headquarters for public use.

The Eengonyama Chorus from Humshaugh photograph

Within days of the closing campfire, *The Scout* announced a new competition. Scouts were again invited to collect coupons to attend, with B-P, a bigger camp for 100 Scouts to be held during the summer of the following year. B-P's qualms about the adverse publicity within the Movement caused by the mercenary nature of the last competition had obviously gone unheeded. Pearson had seen his sales rise and despite his fears, the Founder of the Scout Movement had to admit his Movement was taking the country by storm.

Conclusion

In January 1908, Scouting was little more than a wonderful idea in the mind of one man. By the end of that year there were over 55,000 Scouts in Great Britain, and troops across the Empire. The 'Humshaugh Camp', was inspirational, and a part of the plan for expansion, showing that Scouting was a practical possibility. Camping was firmly established as the central part of the Scouting programme and, 100 years on, remains just as vital and compelling.

Sir Percy Everett last returned to the campsite in 1938 with 1,000 Northumbrian Scouts as well as members of the Scout's 'Train Cruise'[154]. He wrote

> ... the field, the woods, the rocks, just as they were when the Chief gathered his Scouts around him in 1908. No new houses, no new main roads to change the landscape, but just as of old, a perfect camping ground.

Seventy years on, and it is still just the same, and just as hard to find!

The Humshaugh Camp has always been 'in the shadow' of its more famous predecessor, the Brownsea Island Experimental Camp. This was re-enforced by the international celebrations in 2007 that proclaimed that year as the 100th Anniversary of Scouting, so the importance of the experimental camp cannot be denied. Northumberland Scouts, celebrated their centennial in 2008, in the certain knowledge that their County was the home of the first ever National Scout Camp, organised specifically by the Founder to promote Scouting world wide.

English Scouts from Ingleborough and Settle Districts chose to hold their Centennial Sunrise Ceremonies at the 'Look Wide' monument on August 1st. 2007 but Scouts from all over the world have found their way to this historic location and long may they continue to do so.

The author's grandson Harry, reaffirms his promise at the Humshaugh 'Look Wide' monument with his Akela, Tom Peacock, and members of the Yorkshire and Northumberland Scout Fellowships. © CWalker 2008

---

[154] The Scout Train Cruises are documented on Scouting Milestones Scout History website at www.scouting.milestones.btinternet.co.uk/traincruises.htm

The Rest is History?

1908 – 2008 was a century of extraordinary change. Seemingly no element of daily life has been left unmarked by the wheels of progress, and Scouting has kept abreast of the times. This work documents the initial growth of the World Wide Movement that has now expanded to a membership of 40 million Scouts and Guides worldwide. Over the years a staggering 400 million people have worn the uniform and been influenced by B-P's teachings.

On the other hand, very little changes. In Scout Huts throughout the world on troop nights, when a Cub Scout comes to be invested into the Scout Movement, he/she stands in front of their flag and, with the Group, reaffirms the same promise that Scouts made in 1908. They look forward to a world with opportunities that Baden-Powell, visionary as he was, could never have imagined, but he understood well their needs and the contribution that they can make.

Scouts today still enjoy the 'great game' that their Founder initiated, and camping is still the most popular activity. They grow up in today's Scout Movement that enables individuals to achieve their potential and take increasing responsibility for their fellows and the wider environment.

Scouting will continue to prosper and, with global issues coming evermore to the fore, our 'One world – One Promise' tradition seems as sound a basis as any on which to hope, as the Founder anticipated, that our young people will continue to play an active part in meeting its challenges.

© Y Ranta 2008

British, Dutch and Finish Scouts with Cub Scout Kari Ranta at the Humshaugh Cairn.

Appendix

1908 Scout Group Register.

The 1908 troops detailed in the chapter *First Troops* were selected from 375 or so that have been documented in the database that follows. Whilst this is the most extensive listing available, it is by no means complete.

In its first year, the UK Scout Movement was to grow to an estimated[155] 55,000 Scouts. Liverpool had 3000 Scouts alone while other major cities had over 1000. With Scout troops averaging say 25 members, 2000+ groups/patrols would have been in operation. The 2nd Kingston (now Leander Sea Scouts, Surrey) were formed in 1908, but not registered until April 3rd 1909. Their registration document states they were the 3434th group in Great Britain.

The Scout Association has maintained a listing since 1957 of groups that are still operative since they were formed in 1908. The current list is now roughly twice its 1957 length having 99 named groups, despite the fact that quite a few of the groups listed in 1957 have subsequently closed. The new entries have come mainly from groups which have previously amalgamated with a 1908 troop, but kept their own name. There are likely to be many more in this category as it is the exception, rather than the rule, for the complete history of a group, with all its amalgamations, to be properly documented.

The 1908 issues of *The Scout* magazine are a source of much useful information, providing at least the exact date by which groups came to the attention of the its editor. The information, often placed on the last page of the issue, not only names the troop but gives additional facts such as the number of patrols and the name of the Scoutmaster, usually because he/she had written to B-P to tell him news of a particular success. *The Scout* magazine alone has provided evidence of around 250 groups/patrols now on the register.

The Internet, as for most other areas of research, has proved a great boon. Anybody, with the click of a mouse, can access, if not National and District records, then the websites of many of the 1908 troops themselves. In some instances these are extremely well done with clearly presented documentary evidence of their foundation. Others make a claim for 1908 status that is not substantiated, but provide contact details of the group Scout Leader or 'webmaster' to whom questions can be put, and answers found.

On rare occasions, it is possible to find accounts of transcribed interviews with now long-dead Scouts or leaders. These are sometimes to be found in histories published by a 1908 group. Unfortunately such books, produced locally, are hard to find. They were often produced, in very short print runs, for previous anniversaries and so may no longer be in print. They are however a testimony to the dedication of local Scout historians who have taken the time and trouble to record for posterity, history which would otherwise have been lost. It is to be hoped that during 2008, some of these will be reprinted and others initiated. Those known to the author are listed in the Bibliography.

---

[155] There was no official census in 1908, the first being in 1910 when the total number of Scouts was 108,000.

These records of some early groups are kept by local and county archivists, some of which have been lodged in the UK Scout Archives at Gilwell Park. On occasion the records of a defunct troop might well be held in Local Authority run archives.

Trying to verify and locate 1908 troops can present significant problems. St Albans Scout Troop for example could indicate that the group came from the English town of St Albans, but a troop of this name could also belong to any church called St Albans. Unless information can be gleaned from other sources to enable a troop to be properly identified, it has not been added to the register.

The number assigned to a group can also be problematic. Was the 24th Birmingham the 24th Troop in the whole of Birmingham? If it was formed in 1908 the chances are that this was the first troop in its particular district. In the case of the 24th Birmingham, it was previously the 1st Sparkhill and only given the later number when the district or county was rationally organised. It cannot however be assumed that because a troop was numbered the 24th, there were another 23 Scout Troops active in that District. Amalgamations and closures of earlier numbered Troops were commonplace and new groups often were given new numbers rather then utilising an old one.

When troops closed or combined to make them more efficient, their names and numbers were sometimes re-used later e.g. the 1st Birkenhead number has recently been re-assigned to a Scout Fellowship. When the 1st Belfast YMCA was disbanded, its number was deliberately declared 'permanently vacant'.

As the Register lists only 370 or so groups out of a possible total 2000, it has severe limitations. Its compilation however has been a useful exercise and records perhaps for the first time with some provenance the many different forms Scouting took in its founding year. It will at least provide a 'benchmark' for future expansion.

Appendix

> **Key**
> *   Still in operation today.
> **Bold**   The 'First Troops' chapter contains further details.
> SA 2007   This group is on the Scout Association 2007 list of 1908 troops
> <   Prior to
> *Name*   Information is from a book by this author
> GpWS   Information from a current group website.
> A Name   Author of a published work on the group. See Bibliography

	Name	Place	Comment	Started	Source
1st*	Aberdeen City	Scotland	<1921 Scout Marr of the Quest	1908	SA2007
1st	Acton	Birmingham	Plover patrol < 6/6/08. 'held a camp recently'	<26/09/08	The Scout
	Amhurst	Kent	Scout prevented cycle accident	<27/06/08	The Scout
1st *	Arbroath	Angus Scot	<2nd Angus	Jun-08	Wikipedia
*	Arundel	Sussex	Earl of Arundel's Own	May-08	SA 2007
1st	Ashbourne	Derbys	Inaugural Meeting held in town. In comp. 17.10.08	<29/08/08	The Scout
2nd *	Ashbourne	Derbys		<12/11/08	The Scout
1st*	Ashington CLB	North'b'land	Met behind High Market.	<July1908	GSL
1st*	Ashton	Bristol	Became 2nd Bristol, Bert Biden at Marsh Lane	1908	SA 2007
2nd	Aston Manor	Birmingham	Worked with CLB St Paul's Scouts	<21/11/08	The Scout
1st*	Attleborough	Warwickshire	Nuneaton	1908	SA 2007
1st*	Balham & Tooting	London	SM W Langton, later King of Siam's Own 1912	<01/05/08	PB Nevill
1st	Balsall Heath	Birmingham	St Pauls SM Rev Ellison. Boys like strictness,6 am!	<15/8/08	The Scout
	Bangor	Ireland	Start with Wolves, 50 boys,	<12/12/08	The Scout
2nd	Battersea	London	Wandsworth, Attended Carnival< Chums Scouts?	<31/10/08	The Scout
4th	Battersea	London	Wandsworth, Have fine clubroom	<26/12/08	The Scout
1st*	Barnstable	Devon	Reg. 25/5/08 amalg. <1st North Devon 1922.	<25/05/08	P.Jennison
1st	Beccles	Suffolk	SM Allen Formed Empire Day	<24/05/08	The Scout
1st	Belfast YMCA	Ireland	SM A C Black, Camp at Millisle.100 boys by July	<25/04/08	M Bell
	Bexley Heath	London	SM F Wintersgill, 1st Patrol was Otters	<08/09/08	S Harris
1st	Birkdale	Lancs	SM C White. Own large hall with 1st Southport	<26/12/08	The Scout
1st	**Birkenhead** YMCA	**Wirral**	**SM H Clutch, J Evans Formed after meeting**	**1908**	**SA 2007**
2nd*	**Birkenhead**	**Wirral**	**SM S Johnston, Camped at Heswell**	**<19/9/08**	**The Scout**
13th	Birmingham	Birmingham	SM Sam Jenkins	<22/03/08	P Horne
1st	Bishops Latimer	Birmingham	Now 107 Birmingham Central	1908	SA 2007
1st	Birmingham S.	Birmingham	SM Sam Henderson, uses Gym at Dibbeth	<11/07/08	The Scout
18	Birm'ham St Paul's	Birmingham	Lozells	,1908	Horne
	Birmingham YMCA	Birmingham	Held a Field Day	<19/9/08	The Scout
1st	**Blackpool**	**Lancs**	**Lion Patrol, SM F Raynor. PL J Wilkinson**	**Jan.1908**	**M Loomes**
1st	Bloomsbury	London	Camden. Wolves ext. fire on Hampstead Heath	<18/07/08	The Scout
1st	Bordersley	Birmingham	SM EC Willard, ad. on newspaper hoardings	<06/06/08	The Scout
1st	Bounds Green	Islington	SM G Gay, became 151st North London	<27/02/08	PB Nevill
	Bradford	Yorkshire	SM Col.Sgt Evans - meet 2 nights a week	<18/07/08	The Scout
1st	Brechin, Angus	Angus Scot	One of the 4 patrols was for girls	<03/10/08	The Scout
1st	Bridlington Life Boys	Yorks	7 Patrols, SM J Swailes Ineson	<18/07/08	The Scout
1st	Brighton Preston	Sussex	SM H Lascelles, camp at Worthing	<26/08/08	The Scout

1st	Brighton Prep Sch.	Sussex	SM G Davis-Brown	<19/09/08	The Scout
2nd	Brighton	Sussex	SM Beaumont, combined with Ringmer Patrol	<31/10/08	The Scout
1st*	**Broadstone**	**Dorset**	**A Primmer & V Watkin visit Rev. to form Gp**	**1908**	**SA 2007**
	Bromley 'Invicta'	SE London	Flag raiding on Hayes Common	<08/08/08	The Scout
1st	Broughty Ferry BB	Dundee	Field Day and Ascended a lighthouse	<23/05/08	The Scout
1st	Burton on Trent	Staffs	YMCA Group. Have been to camp	<26/09/08	The Scout
1st*	Bury St Edmunds	Suffolk	SM Cyril Smith, 1st Pa Otters > Mayors Own	<05/02/108	Gp WS
	Bushford Patrol	Herts	Attended Bushy British Patrol > 2nd SW Herts	1908	F Brittain
1st	Buxton	Derbys		1908	SA 2007
1st	Camberwell & Peckham	London		<21/11/08	The Scout
1st	Camden	London	Flag raiding with 1st Hampstead	<02/01/09	The Scout
1st	Canterbury	Kent	SM Norman Collard	<18/04/08	The Scout
2nd	Canterbury	Kent	St Peters. Meet in parish hall	<12/12/08	The Scout
1st	Carlisle	Cumbria	SM Rev J Davidson - His journal in Archives	<18/01/08	McNamara
1st	Carlisle Regt CLB	Cumbria		<04/07/08	The Scout
1st*	Carluke Lanark	Lanarkshire	St Johns <6th Lanarkshire	1908	SA 2007
1st	Carmarthen	Wales		<14/04/08	Gp WS
	Caterham	Surrey	Parade for King's Birthday also Haldane's visit.	<18/07/08	The Scout
1st	Catford St Laurence	London	SM Curate Rev Fenton, > BP's Own	1908	Lewisham
1st*	Cheadle Hume	Cheshire		1908	SA 2007
1st	Chelmsford	Essex	SM PC Bragg SM Warrant Oct. 9th 1908	<17/10/08	The Scout
1st	Cheltenham	Glos	SM WP Pyker, 3 patrols	<12/09/08	The Scout
1st	Cheshunt	Herts		1908	SA 2007
1st	Chester	Cheshire	Met in the cellar of a house in Nicholas St.	1908	Chester
2nd	Chesterfield	Derbys	Closed 1993	1908	SA 2007
18th*	Chesterfield	Derbys	Catholic	1908	Dist. WB
1st	Chichester	Sussex	Published a magazine, paper trail 3/10/08	<18/07/08	The Scout
1st	Childs Hill	NW London	SM E Pells after B-P lecture >2nd Hampstead	,Oct. 07	PB Nevill
1st	Chipping Norton	Oxon	SM F Lewis<Pioneers 1907 warranted 11/11/08	<04/07/08	The Scout
1st*	**Chiswick West**	**London**	**SM Tom Foley adopted patrol. PL H Price**	**Sept. -08**	**SA 2007**
1st*	Christchurch Town	Dorset	Reg. doc. 57, 3 Loveless bros and sister ASM	1908	SA 2007
1st	Clapham Crusaders	Derbys	3 Patrols SM Monroe. Exercise on Streatham Com.	<31/10/08	The Scout
1st*	Cleethorpes	Lincs	Kangaroos, tested in Scouting knowledge	<15/08/08	The Scout
1st*	Coatbridge Garturk	Lanarkshire	Scotland	1908	before 2nd
2nd*	Coatbridge Garturk	Lanarkshire	Scotland <90th Lanarkshire	1908	SA 2007
1st	Colchester	Essex	SM Wallace Cole, folded 1988 to be restarted	<1908	SA 2007
	Colwyn Bay YMCA	Denbighsh.	SM Mr Samuel Johnson/ Scout Norman Tucker	<18/04/08	Gp WS
	Constable Works	**Edinburgh**	**Ravens- employees. Walked to Colinton**	**<05/09/08**	**The Scout**
	Cork Hawk Patrol	Ireland	SM formed troop through ad in local paper	<12/9/08	The Scout
	Cork, Glanmire	Ireland	Fox Patrol visit ironworks	<18/07/08	The Scout
1st	Corstorphine	Edinburgh	Camped at Cramond.	<7/11//08	The Scout
1st	Corsham	Wilts	(Lord Methuen's Own)	1908	BBC WS
1st	Coventry	Warwickshire	Camped at Stoneleigh Deer Park	<05/09/08	The Scout
	Coventry G Troop	Warwickshire	21 Boys, SM GH Gould	<19/09/08	The Scout
	Coventry Earsldon	Warwickshire	4 Patrols Camp for a week at Walsgrave.	<05/09/08	The Scout
	Crewe	Cheshire	"Taking up Scouting on a comp. scale"	<18/07/08	The Scout
	Crewton Derby	Derbys	No SM. In demo with other Derby gps	<17/10/08	The Scout
1st	Crosby	Liverpool	SM W Bowker 2 gps 10 day camp Silecroft 40 Sc.	<18/07/08	The Scout
1st*	Crowborough	E Sussex	Met 1908 Whitehill Road. reg. Cert. 1909	1908	Gp WS
1st*	Croyden	S. London	SM HC Simmons. Reg. 16/6/08, camped at Downe	<02/06/08	Gp WS
2nd	Croyden	S. London	SM L Morrant. Members came from Sunday sch.	<22/08/08	The Scout

153

1st	Dalmuir	Clydebank	Making good progress	<02/01/09	The Scout
	Darley Dale	Derbys	Wolves, SM Eric Hunt to camp in Peak District	<18/07/08	The Scout
1st	Denistone	Derbys	In competition with 1st Ashbourne	<17/11/08	The Scout
1st	Denston	Lancs	Were visited by 5th Manchester	<27/12/08	The Scout
2nd	Derby Life Boy Scouts	Derbys	In demo with other Derbyshire groups	<17/10/08	The Scout
4th*	Derby (Derwent)	Derbys	SM DF Foxwell. Met at All Saints House	<11/11/08	Gp WS
1st*	Dereham	Norfolk	SM Howard Cositgan formed Deer patrol	Mar-80	Der.Times
1st	Devizes	Wiltshire	A King saved boy from drowning<amalgamated	<05/09/08	The Scout
1st	Digbeth Institute	Birmingham	SM Sam Harrison, No.1 Birmingham	<22/03/08	P Horne
1st*	Don & Dearne	Yorkshire	Goldthorpe	1908	SA 2007
	Doncaster	Yorkshire	SM Rev A P Gower Rees. ex camp cookery	< 1/8/08	The Scout
	Dover Charlton	Kent	Comp with other Dover patrols	<19/12/08	The Scout
	Dover St Mary's	Kent	Comp with other Dover patrols	<19/12/08	The Scout
1st	**Dublin Cycles**	**Ireland**		**<12/12/08**	**The Scout**
1st*	Duckworth St.	Lancs	Congregational Church. Darwen Lancs.	1908	SA 2007
1st	Dulwich SW	London	(Later 3rd Camberwell -writes PB Nevill)	<14/11/08	The Scout
1st	Durham Easington La.	Durham	SM G Goymer good rooms observation exercise	<08/08/08	The Scout
2nd	Ealing	W. London	SM Arrowsmith. Camped near Perivale	<05/09/08	The Scout
1st	East Ham	London	(St Albans) SM E Wiskern	Apr-08	PB Nevill
1st	E. Lancs Burnley	E Lancs	SMs AT Leatherbarrow, H Baker	<12/12/08	The Scout
6th*	Eccles	Lancs	(1907 Eccles had Seton Indians) <1st Worsley	1908	SA 2007
1st	Edinburgh YMCA	Edinburgh		<17/10/08	The Scout
	Edinburgh St Matth's	Edinburgh	2 Patrols held Field Day	<12/9/08	The Scout
9th*	Edinburgh	Edinburgh		1908	SA 2007
1st	Edmonton, Enfield	London	SM E Crusha, good dispatch running	<02/01/09	The Scout
1st	Egremont, Wallasey	Liverpool	SM Percy White	<22/08/08	The Scout
1st	Elland, Brighouse	Yorkshire	SM A Barber awarded Silver Cross	<28/11/08	The Scout
1st	**Ellstree/Borhamw'd**	**Herts**	**SM Percy Everett 2 patrols incl. his daughter.**	**<13/03/08**	**P Everett**
1st	Elstead	Surrey	Games with Tongham & Headly	<05/09/08	The Scout
1st	Eltham	London	Greenwich, SMs Steele and Munroe	<17/10/08	The Scout
1st*	Eltham Royal	London	(H. Trinity) SM W Anderson. Jan 1908 start?	<June -08	PB Nevill
1st	Enfield	London	SM Rev A Browne	Mar,-08	PB Nevill
1st*	Epping Forest S.	London	Dispatch running. Were 1st Woodford	1908	SA 2007
1st	Erdington	Birmingham		1908	P Horne
19th	Essex (S) BB Sc.	Essex	SM Capt CF Cope - camped recently	<04/7/08	The Scout
	Everton	Liverpool	Scouts helped shipwrecked sailor	<21/11/08	The Scout
1st	Fairfield	Liverpool	45 Scouts	<5/12/08	The Scout
1st	Falmouth	Cornwell	SM J Dinnis to camp in August	<18/7/08	The Scout
1st	Finchley	NW London	Six groups in Finchley	<5/12/08	The Scout
2nd	Finchley	NW London	Six groups in Finchley	<05/12/08	The Scout
3rd	Finchley	NW London	Will hold a concert at Woodside Hall	<28/11/08	The Scout
4th	Finchley	NW London	Six groups in Finchley	<05/12/08	The Scout
5th	Finchley	NW London	Six groups in Finchley	<05/12/08	The Scout
1st*	Flixton	Manchester?	Sc. put out fire in gas pipe casing on rlwy bridge	<19/12/08	The Scout
1st	Folkestone	Kent	SM W Dockrill, in expert signalling	<22/08/08	The Scout
1st*	Forest Hill YMCA	London	SM H Patton (later 9th North London.)	Mar.-08	PB Nevill
1st*	Formby	Liverpool		1908	SA 2007
1st	Fulham	London	Dispatch running Wimbledon Common	<04/07/08	The Scout
3rd*	Fulham	London	SM Rev W Marshall < 25th SW London	Dec.-08	PB Nevill
1st	Garforth Leeds	Yorkshire	GP website documents history	1908	GP WS
1st	Gateshead	Durham	SM GF Wicks - run with 2nd Gateshead	<01/08/08	The Scout

2nd	Gateshead	Durham	SM Shipley, Camp 'some weeks ago' with 1st G.	<01/08/08	The Scout
	Gateshead	Durham	Somerset Troop, SM J Graham	<02/01/09	The Scout
1st	**Glasgow**	**Scotland**	**SM Capt Young, 1st known reg. <120 boys.**	**26/1/908**	**Gp WS**
3rd*	Glasgow Waverley	Scotland	Shawlands, SM J Millar - excellent rooms	>02/01/09	The Scout
4th	Glasgow	Scotland	3 Patrols. On recent wet hike 21 miles in 8 hrs.	<28/11/08	The Scout
	Glasgow Girl Sc.	**Scotland**	**Cuckoos PL A Cargill, >merged 1Glasgow**	**<01/12/08**	**GG Scotl.**
24th*	Glasgow	Scotland	Bearsden	1908	Spalding
1st	Gloucester	Glos	Progress over 3 months, has room lit by gas	<17/10/08	The Scout
1st	Grange o' Sands	Cumbria	SM was vicar	Jul-08	McNamara
1st	Gravesend	Kent	SM A Tutton 25 boys have 2nd Class.	<01/07/08	The Scout
3rd	Grimsby	Lincs		,1908	SA 2007
1st	Guisborough	Yorks	SM Carlton-Stiff, Camped at Grindon, Sund'l'nd	<04/07/08	The Scout
1st	Gypsy Hill Lambeth	London	Field Day on Keston Common	<12/09/08	The Scout
	TS Mercury Gp	Hamble	Rev Bloomfield 5 patrols 'marine scouts'	<May 1908	Gp WS
1st	**Hampstead**	**London**	**SM Colbron Pearse, demo patrol to Cornwall**	**<18/01/08**	**PB Nevill**
1st	Hampstead Gdn C	Camden	SM Sgt P Concannon. Camped Hampstead.	<21/11/08	The Scout
1st	Handsworth,	Birmg.	Camped - surprise 'attacks'	<19/09/08	The Scout
1st	Hanley	Stoke on T	SM FC Millington	<13/06/08	The Scout
1st	Hanwell (St Mary's)	London	Westminster	1908	SA 2007
1st	Harrogate	Yorks	To camp at Redcar YMCA Scout camp	<20/06/08	The Scout
1st	Harrow	Tottenham	2 Patrols in May. SM E Harvey, Camp late Aug.	<15/08/08	The Scout
4th	Harrow	Tottenham	?	<12/12/08	The Scout
1st	Harrow	London	Camped at Folkestone	<17/10/08	The Scout
1st	Hartlepool West	Durham	Greyhounds	<06/06/08	The Scout
1st	Harwich	Essex	SM Barnes-Smith, camp on river bank.	<22/08/08	The Scout
	Hastings	E Sussex	Camp at Brede.	<19/09/08	The Scout
1st	Hatchem, Lewisham	London	Camping in Chislehurst Woods. CLB ICSP?	<12/12/08	The Scout
	Hatfield	Herts	>Viscount Cranbourne's Own. 3 Patrols	1908	F Brittain
	Headly	Surrey	Games with Tongham & Elstead	<05/09/08	The Scout
	Heaton	Newcastle	SM A L Gibson 28/4 was our 1st day, 3 prs of bros	<04/07/08	The Scout
1st	Hednesford	Staffs	SM T Pratchett ex Sunday Sch.	July?-08	SA 2007
1st	Hemel Hempstead	Herts	SM Allen Foxell, after reading 'the parts' S4B	May-08	F Brittain
1st	**Henfield Troop**	**Sussex**	**Started 1907 by 3 girls Hon Sec. AN Wade**	**<05/09/08**	**K Jennings**
1st*	Henley on Thames	London	SM P Sutton, Cpl Lewis saves drowning boy	<22/08/08	The Scout
1st	Herts (SW)	Herts	A Emery and M Scrivener formed Kangaroos	<01/03/08	F Brittain
1st*	Hereford YMCA	Herts	BP spoke Nov 8th 1907 to YMCA	<05/12/08	The Scout
1st	High Barnet	Herts	Met in Hadley woods SM R. Richardson	<21/03/08	F Brittain
	Hillburn	Ireland		<2208/08	The Scout
1st*	Hirst CLB Ashington	Northb'land	SM Jack Dorgan with bro.Tommy from 1st Ashington	1908	SA 2007
1st*	Hockley	Essex	T E Rudhall, President	<08/08/08	The Scout
1st	Holywell, Flintshire	Wales	SM Gordon Jones Pistyll	<31/10/08	The Scout
1st	Horley	Surrey	Pewitts. PL. Whitehouse	<May-08	S Harris
1st	Horwich	Lancs	SM H Peters	<19/12/09	The Scout
2nd	Horwich	Lancs	SM HW Jackson	<19/12/09	The Scout
1st	**Hoxton** Toynbee Hall	**London**	**SM TS Lukis.- Wood-pigeons**	**<27/05/08**	**PB Nevill**
1st	Huddersfield	Yorks	4 patrols and the Kangaroos 'meditate joining'.	<22/08/08	The Scout
	Hull Boys Club Scouts	Yorks	To camp at Hornsea	<18/07/08	The Scout
	Hull	Yorks	SM Rev, A Hitchens	<14/12/08	The Scout
	Hull	Yorks	SM JC Rowson	<17/10/08	The Scout
1st	Hunslet St Silas's	Yorks	Leeds. SM F Beaumont	<19/09/08	The Scout
1st*	Hunts Hartford	Hunts		1908	SA 2007

1st*	Hythe	London	<1st Staines & Egham Hythe Tp. SM Ms Rhodes		1908	SA 2007
1st	Ilford	London	Started by boys 1907, SM Steele 1908		1908	PB Nevill
1st	Ipswich	Suffolk	SM E Hicks, Camp in Martello Tower		<26/09/08	The Scout
1st*	Isleworth	London	Hounslow		1908	SA 2007
1st*	Islington	London	>7th NL SM J Tuckett, made Xmas food for needy		Mar-08	PB Nevill
2nd*	Islington	London	SM E Richardson, (later 5th NL)		Apr,-08	PB Nevill
3rd*	Islington	London			1908	SA 2007
4th*	Islington	London			1908	SA 2007
5th*	Islington	London			1908	SA 2007
1st*	Jarrow St Paul's	Durham			1908	SA 2007
2nd	Jarrow	Durham	A cycle patrol is being 'meditated'		<05/09/08	The Scout
2nd*	Kensington	London	Westminster		,1908	SA 2007
1st	Kentish Town	London	SM R Powell, 3 day camp South Mimms		<31/10/08	The Scout
1st	Kentish Town	London	SM J Patterson Earl of Dartm's Own>1st St Pancras		Jul-08	PB Nevill
1st	Kidderminster	Worcs.	Cuckoo Patrol SM and 3 boys met in Church St		<16/12/08	Dis. WS
1st	Kilburn	London	SM P Watson		<31/10/08	The Scout
1st	Kings Lynn Thornham	Norfolk	SM ex-coastguard. Teaches boys tailoring		<04/07/08	The Scout
1st*	Lambeth South	London	(Blackstaves), West Norwood Brotherhood		1908	SA 2007
	Lancaster Coll.	London	SM Harley-Mason had rifle range. W. Norwood		<12/12/08	The Scout
1st*	Larkhall, Lanarks	Scotland	Became 13th Lanarkshire		1908	SA 2007
1st*	Leeds St Luke's	Yorkshire	St Leeds		1908	SA 2007
2nd*	Leeds Wortley	Yorkshire	SW Leeds Church Gp		1908	SA 2007
1st	Leytonstone	N. London	34 Boys camp at West Bay Bridport		,05/09/08	The Scout
1st	Liscard N Crusaders	Liverpool	3 Patrols<1st New Brighton FC Bullen<3rd Wallasey		<19/9/08	Gp WP
?	Liverpool	Liverpool	SM J Murphy, Scout A Bennet killed in lift acc.		<11/07/08	The Scout
8th *	Liverpool YMCA	Liverpool	1st Toxteth		1908	SA 2007
1st	London (City of)	London	SM A Poyser 1st boys from choir Ld Mayor's Own		May-08	PB Nevill
1st	London (East)	London	SM J Landsberg, later 2nd Stepney		1908	PB Nevill
2nd	London (North)	London	SM AN Francis, Islington		Nov.-08	PB Nevill
12th	London (North)	London			1908	SA 2007
23rd	London (North)	London			1908	SA 2007
1st	London BB Scouts	London	SM Gordon, had first camp		<12/11/08	The Scout
4th	London BB Scouts	London	Tottenham		<12/12/08	The Scout
49th	London BB Scouts	London	4 patrols, Camped Alfreton (Derbys?)		<04/07/08	The Scout
	London BB Scouts	London	St. Paul's. Onslow Square. SM Inns		<18/07/08	The Scout
	Notting Hill	London	Nr Hyde Pk. SM Barrs used parades		<06/06/08	The Scout
1st	Long Eaton	Derbys	In demo with other Derbys groups		<17/10/08	The Scout
1st*	Longford Manchester	Lancs	Amalgamated with 1st Stretford		1908	SA 2007
1st	Loughborough	Liecs	SM Rev AJ Swiney		<17/10/08	The Scout
	Loughborough	Leics	SM Sgt Instructor Higgins		<12/12/08	The Scout
1st	**Lowestoft Sch**	**Suffolk**	**SM Pyke, Scouts help drifter crew**		**<27/06/08**	**The Scout**
	Lowestoft Coll.	**Suffolk**	**Played Cricket against Oulton Ladies**		**<22/08/08**	**The Scout**
1st	Lymington	Hamps	Ex cadets, Camp at coast, Insp. by Eric Walker.		<11/07/08	The Scout
	Lytham St Annes	Lancs	(Mistakenly called Burnley in The Scout)		<02/01/09	The Scout
1st	Macclesfield	Cheshire	Met Christchurch Sch. 1908		1908	Gp WS
11th	Maidstone Kent	Kent	SM Jack Green > Loose Swiss Gp 1910		<June-08	M Proctor
1st*	Malvern Link	Worcs	Jack Rodway joined in 1908 became leader		1908	SA 2007
1st	St John's Lads	Manchester	Lads Club Scout Gp. Outing to Trafford Park,		<12/12/08	The Scout
5th	Manchester	Lancs	Is forging ahead, had cycle patrol		<17/10/08	The Scout
1st	Market Harborough	Liecs			1908	SA 2007
1st*	Marylebone	London			<April-08	SA 2007

	Troop	County	Notes	Date	Source
8th	Motherwell BB	Scotland	Capt DJ Love sent photo of Scouts	,1908	The Scout
1st	Nairn	Inverness	Church St Sch. SM Mr Riach, teacher, 3 patrols,	Sept.-08	R.Preece
1st*	New Cross	London	< The Greys, SM JE Curd, Lewisham	May-08	PB Nevill
	Newcastle N.I.	Ireland	SM Chippindall, Donard Park has plaque.	>09/03/08	M Bell
1st*	**Newport**	**I. of Wight**	**The Old Guard, SM J Burgess, Jan 08 reg.**	**,08/02/08**	**Reynolds**
	Newport	I. of Wight?	70% 1st class Also has a cycle sect.	<4/7/08	The Scout
1st	Newry	Co Down	Ireland. Under 'captaincy' of John Kavanagh	<22/08/08	The Scout
1st	Normanton	Derbys	In demo with other Derbys groups	<17/10/08	The Scout
1st	North Berwick	North'b'land	Founded August	Aug.-08	Town WB
1st	Norwich	Norfolk	Cuckoos stopped stampeding horses	<26/12/08	The Scout
1st*	Norwich	Norfolk	Capt. Bower's Own. >Earliest Sea Scouts?	1908	SA 2007
1st	Norton Stockton	Durham	Provided honour guard for Prince of Wales	<21/11/08	The Scout
1st*	Nottingham YMCA	Notts	200 scouts in Nottin'ham by 22/8/1908	1908	SA 2007
3rd	Nottingham	Notts	SM J Harrison. Camp, surprise attacks	<05/09/08	The Scout
	Not' ham New Basford	Notts	Palm St Baptists SM Rev A Hitchens (to start)	<14/11/08	The Scout
1st	Offerton	Sunderland	Met 1st Guisborough at Grindon Camp	<21/11/08	The Scout
1st	Oldham	Lancs	With 2nd Oldham have 100 Scouts.	<18/07/08	The Scout
2nd	Oldham	Lancs	Went with 1st O to YMCA camp at Windermere	<18/07/08	The Scout
20th	Paddington	London	Also known as 28th Paddington	,1908	SA 2007
2nd	Paisley, Nr Glasgow	Scotland	SM Charles McLardie, meet 3x per wk.	<22/08/08	The Scout
21st	Paisley BB Scouts	Scotland	(Inchinnan), SM Capt W McClelland.3 Patrols	<15/08/08	The Scout
1st*	Parkstone, Poole	Dorset	J Aitken, F Williams <Lady Baden-Powell's Own	<May1908	WS Seller
	Peckham, Southwark	London	Cuckoos, SM Councillor Harley	<03/10/08	The Scout
1st	Pimlico, Westminster	London	SM F Mann, ex Cheer Boys> 15th Westminster	<18/07/08	The Scout
2nd	Pimlico, Westminster	London	SM Miss H Cunningham. > 2nd Westminster	,1908	PB Nevill
1st	Pitlochry	Scotland	SM JG Dixon, only has 'habitual' kilt wearers	<08/08/08	The Scout
1st	Pool Otley	Yorkshire	2 Patrols	<05/09/08	The Scout
2nd	Plumstead Greenwich	London	Ch of Ascension. Concert to help band fund.	<28/11/08	The Scout
1st*	Plymouth	Devon		,1908	SA 2007
	Port Talbot Sch.	**Glams**	**5 patrols (Had Scout F James at Humshaugh)**	**<18/07/08**	**The Scout**
3rd*	Portobello St James	London	Kensington	,1908	SA 2007
1st	Portsmouth	Hampshire	10 ten camp on Hayling Island, attacked BB camp	<19/09/08	The Scout
1st	Preston, Brighton	Sussex	SM Rev H Lascelles Camp at Worthing	<26/09/08	The Scout
1st*	***Putney (East)**	**London**	**Started by WP Adams. SM Delcomyn SA2007**	**Jan.-08**	**PB Nevill**
1st	Rawmarsh	Nr Sheffield	SM slept in hammock, fell on two boys	<21/10/08	The Scout
1st*	Reading YMCA	Berks	SM SG Sainsbury, dispatch carrying	<23/05/08	The Scout
1st	Retford	Notts	Have a QM to help boys save	<06/06/08	The Scout
1st	Richmond St Pauls Sch	London	SM Capt W G White - met in park	Dec.-08	W White
1st*	Rochdale St James	Lancs	SM Waller	,1908	SA 2007
1st*	Romsey	Hampshire		,1908	SA 2007
	Rotherham YMCA	Yorkshire	To go to Yorks YMCA Camp Redcar in Aug	<20/06/08	The Scout
1st	Roundhay Leeds	Yorkshire	3 patrols	<18/07/08	The Scout
	Salford	Manchester	Met St Johns Deansgate on night hike	<12/12/08	The Scout
1st	Salisbury	Wilts	SM PJ Southam + 4 other SMs reg. Cert.	<02/07/08	Certificate
	Sandown	I. of Wight	SM's Parks, A Grapes, Date from J Porter's E Card	<19/12/08	B Groves
	Sandy	Beds	Peewits. SM St A Saunders	<19/12/08	The Scout
1st	Sawbridgeworth	Herts	formed by Marcus Woodward author	,1908	F Brittain
1st	Seacombe	Wallasey	Nr Liverpool. Night camping at coast	<26/09/08	The Scout
1st	Sefton Park	Liverpool	Published a magazine	<14/8//08	The Scout
1st	Shadwell St Georges	London	SM Chudleigh, Weslyan Troop	<25/07/08	The Scout
1st*	Shanklin IoW	I. of Wight	SM AJ Horne returning from Humshaugh	,Sept-08	B Groves

	Slough Stoke Hs Sch	Bucks	Practise dispatch running and disguise	<23/05/08	The Scout
1st	Sloytor Newton Abbot	Devon	S E Smerdon, Involved wide games	<05/12/08	The Scout
1st	Southfields	London	Competed on Wimbledon Com. with 2nd Wands	<17/10/08	The Scout
1st	Southport	Lancs	SM C White, Own Hall with 1st Birkdale	<26/12/08	The Scout
8th*	Southport	Lancs		SA 2007	The Scout
	Southsea	Portsmouth	Wolves	<26/09/08	The Scout
1st	Southwark	London	SM RA Puttick	Aug.,-08	PB Neville
1st	South Woodford	London	30 boys with cycle patrol<1st Epping Forest S.	<05/09/08	The Scout
1st*	Sparkhill	Birmingham	24th Birmingham	,1908	SA 2007
1st	Spondon	Derbys	SM GR Chetwynd	<31/10/08	The Scout
2nd	Spondon	Derbys	Met Spondon House Sch, did demos.	<31/10/08	The Scout
1st*	St Albans	Herts	Fox Patrol PL Wilfred Crofts< 1st St Albans	,1908	F Brittain
	St George's	E London	Mile End Rd. New Patrol every week	< 04/07/08	The Scout
1st*	**St Helens YMCA**	**Lancs**	**(Pilkington's?) Dispatch running coal mine visit**	**<23/05/08**	**The Scout**
	St Johns Lads	Manchester	Deansgate, 4 Patrols Outing to Trafford Park.	<12/12/2008	The Scout
1st	St Paul's CLB	Glos	Progressed will over 3 months	<17/10/08	The Scout
1st	Stafford	Staffs	SM Maj. Weigall, had had camp	<05/09/08	The Scout
1st*	Stirlingshire	Scotland	D McAree J Jamieson Scouts<Maj. Crumm 1910	<21/12/08	S. Park
1st	Stockport	Manchester	Washed out of camp but had no tents!	<19/09/08	The Scout
8th*	Stockport	Manchester	With break 31/3/48 to 30/6/49	,1908	SA 2007
1st*	Stoke Newington	London	SM N Rohmer became 11th N. London	,1908	PB Nevill
1st*	Stoke on Trent	Staffs	St Andrews SM, W Hockett warrant 14/12/08	<14/12/08	Gp WS
1st*	Strathblane	Stirlingshire	SM Miss E. Gairdner. Curlews>18th>36th	Aug. 1908	Parish WS
1st	Stretford	Manchester	SM Gordon (1st Longford, 18th Manchester)	<21/11/08	The Scout
1st	Streatham Common	London	SM FW Stacey	<01/07/2008	PB Nevill
1st*	Streatham	London	SM Capt Grome Merilees. 3 day camp	<18/06/08	The Scout
2nd	Streatham	London	Camped with 1st Upper Tooting then merged	<31/10/08	The Scout
1st	Stretford Longford	Manchester	SM Gordon, had first camp	<21/11/08	The Scout
3rd*	**Sunderland**	**Durham**	**Vaux's Own ex Lampton St Boys' Club**	**,1908**	**SA 2007**
1st	Swinton	Manchester	SM WRA Usher	<12/12/08	The Scout
2nd	Swinton	Manchester		<31/10/08	The Scout
1st	Syston	Liecs	SM H Franklin, formed. First Scout band	,Feb-08	Gp WS
1st	Thirsk	Yorkshire	,M Rev. AJE Swiney	<21/11/08	The Scout
1st	Thornaby	Yorkshire	3 Patrols	<19/09/08	The Scout
1st*	Tonbridge	Kent	Green Hares	1908	SA 2007
	Tongham	Surrey	Games with Headly & Elstead	<05/09/09	The Scout
1st	Tooting	London	Very good rooms	<12/12/08	The Scout
2nd	Tooting	London	Amalgamated with Upper Tooting	<31/10/08	The Scout
1st	Torquay	Devon	Wolf patrol PL Bill Mortimer, >SM Steinmetz	1908	GG Halliday
2nd	Torquay	Devon	SM Aallams, met Trinity Church Hall.	Aug.-08	GG Halliday
3rd	Torquay	Devon	SM Mr Frost, Cobra and Kingfisher Patrols	Oct.-08	GG Halliday
	Totnes Gram. Sch.	**Devon**		**<04/07/08**	**The Scout**
1st	**Toynbee**	**E. London**	**SM TS Lukis, St Barts Hosp<Sir Stanley Vane**	**<27/05/08**	**B-P Nevill**
1st	Toxteth YMCA	Liverpool		1908	SA 1957
1st	Trammere	Liverpool	Field day with Oxton BB	>03/10/08	The Scout
1st	Truro BB	Cornwell	Inspected by Col. Vyvyan ex Mafeking	>13/06/08	The Scout
1st	Twickenham	London	Now have cyclist patrol	<19/12/08	The Scout
1st	Upper Tooting	London	SM W Laughton amalgamated 2nd Streatham	<31/10/08	The Scout
1st	Wakefield	Yorkshire	To YMCA Yorks Scout camp Redcar	<13/06/08	The Scout
3rd	Wallasey Emmanuel	Wirral	SM R Samuel Reg. 6/10/08, was1st N Liscard	<06/10/08	Gp WS
1st*	Wallington SW	London	SM Tobot, camp at Woodcote Hall + 3LoF	<04/0708	The Scout

1st	Walthamstow NE	London	Camp two nights a week	<26/09/08	The Scout
1st	Walthamstow	NE London	Forest Troop. Epping Forest. Camp 2 nights a wk.	<26/09/08	The Scout
	Walthamstow BB	London		<25/04/08	The Scout
2nd	Wandsworth	London	Comp on Wimbledon Com. with 1st Southfields	<17/10/08	The Scout
3rd	Wandsworth	London	SM TA Officer, for Public sch. Boys	<28/11/08	The Scout
4th	Wandsworth	London		<31/10/08	The Scout
1st	Wanstead Slip	London	SM Rev Hughes	1908	Nevill PB
1st	Watford	Herts	Started with lone patrols, enrolment cards	Oct.-08	F Brittain
1st *	Watford	Herts	Kangaroos >1st SW Herts, (Countess of Clar.'s Own)	<01/03/08	SA 2007
	Watford Grammar Sch	Herts	Bulls of Bushy House W. GS Sch.	<01/03/08	F Brittain
1st*	Welwyn	Herts	SM Arthur Davies, 'some rowdy boys'	<12/12/08	The Scout
1st	West Hampstead	London	SM PH Lehman. Adv. for boys by bill sticking	<28/12/08	The Scout
	West Hartlepool	Durham	Greyhounds 6/6/08.SM R Leonard<Mounted Tp	<15/08/08	The Scout
1st*	Westcliffe on Sea	Essex		1908	SA 2007
1st	Westminster Sch.	London	Panthers (Kensington)	<12/12/08	The Scout
1st*	Weybridge	Surrey	(Brooklands Own)	1908	SA2007
1st	Wharfdale, Pool,	Yorkshire	SM Lt N Barker	<12/12/08	The Scout
	Whitehaven YMCA	Cumbria	3 Patrols. SM O Paige, Camped at Ennerdale	<05/09/08	The Scout
	Whitehead	Co. Antrim	Ireland. Owls, good at tracking	<07/11/08	The Scout
1st	**Wigan Gram. Sch.**	**Lancs**	**SM Headteacher R Chambres <day after B-P visit**	**28/1/08**	**Sch Log**
1st	Windhill	Bradford	SM Rev Ewbank > 13th Bradford North	<22/03/08	L Nunn
1st	Winston Green	London	Handsworth. Want more members	<7/11/08	The Scout
1st	Withington	Clos	Patrol. SM EFE Fisher	<04/07/08	The Scout
4th*	Woking	Surrey	(Christchurch)	1908	SA 2007
1st	Wolverhampton	Staffs	Reg. No. 4671, ran till 1938.	1908	W. Archives
5th*	Wolverhampton	Staffs	Reg. No. 4673, ran till 1964.	1908	SA 2007
1st*	Wolverton	Bucks		<23/02/08	Gp Website
1st	Wombourne	Staffs	Col. Shaw Hellier SM until 1914 then his sister.	1908	3rd GpWS
1st	Woodford	Kettering	Northants. Has bugle band	<26/09/08	The Scout
	Worcester B	Worcs	SM Kerred, no tents sleep around campfire	<05/09/08	The Scout
	Worcester East	Worcs	Organised a camp	<04/07/08	The Scout
4th*	Worth	Yorkshire?		1908	SA 2007
1st	Wosborough Dale	Barnsley Yorks	SM R Addy, Hound and Cuckoo Patrols	<31/10/08	The Scout

Bibliography

Baden-Powell Bt-Col RSS, Aids to Scouting, Gale& Polden, 1899
Baden-Powell Lt Gen RSS, The Boy Scout Scheme, Pearson, 1908
Baden-Powell Lt.-Gen RS, Scouting for Boys, Pearson, 1908
Baden-Powell Lt. Gen. C.B., Scouting for Boys PartsI-VI, H.Cox 1908
Baden-Powell's Diary, UKScout Association - on Microfiche
Baden-Powell, Lt-Gen Sir R, My Adventures as Spy, Pearson, 1915
Bellamy Rev RL, Hints from Baden-Powell, Gale & Poldon, 1900
Brittain Frank, 100 Years of Hertfordshire Scouting, Herts Scout Archives 2008
B-P Scout, Cycle Scouts Training, Brown 1910
Boys of The Empire Magazine, Melrose, Alexander and Shepheard, 1900-01
Chick Avril, Wynn Everett's Story, Girl Guide Association 19??
Culliford SG, New Zealand Scouting, The First 50 Years, SG, BSA of NZ 1958,
Dimmock Hayden, Bare Knees Days, Pearson, 1939
Everett Percy, The First Ten Years, The East Anglian Daily Times, 1948
Everett Percy, 52 Days, The East Anglian Daily Times, 1946
Harris S, Legalised Mischief, Vol. 2, Lewarne Publishing, 2003
Hatchley WJ, The Best Scout England Ever Had, Newcastle E. District Sc. Counc.1985
Heasman R, Who Was Cyril Arthur Pearson? Pearson's Holiday Fund, 2006
Jeal TJ, Baden-Powell, Hutchinson, 1989
MacDonald, Sons of the Empire, Toronto, 1993
Milne AR & Herward, CB Those Boy Scouts, A Story of Scouting in Victoria,
Mizzi JA, Scouting in Malta, Progress Press, Valletta, 1989
Nevill B-P, Scouting in London, London Scout Council, 1966
Park S, A Brief History of the 1st Stirlingshire Scout Group, 1979, revised 2008
Pickering Aiden, B-P in the North, The Humshaugh Camp, in The Scouter, Dec 1954
Pocock G, One Hundred Years of The Legion of Frontiersmen, Phillimore, 2004
Pocock R The Frontiersman's Pocket Book, Murray, 1909
Preece R , Scouting around Inverness, 1907-2007"
Proctor Tammy, On My Honour, American Philosophical Society, 2002
Reynolds EE, The Scout Movement, Oxford University Press, 1950
Richards Paul, Ed, The Founding of the Boy Scouts, Ed. P Richards, Standish Mus. 1973
Roebuck M & Wenham J, The New History of Broadstone, 2006
Rosenthal M, The Character Factory, Pantheon, 1984
Simpson HS, Old Burnside, Uni. of Kentucky, 1996
Scouts Canada, 75 Years of Scouting in Canada, 1982
Scout Association, HQ Gazette, 1909
The Scout, Pearsons, 1908
Spalding AJ, A History of the 24th Glasgow (Bearsden) Scout Group, Board book, 1988
Wade E K, 21 Years of Scouting, Peasons 1929
Wade E K, 27 Years with Baden-Powell, Blandford 1957
Walker CR, Brownsea: B-P's Acorn, Write Books, 2007
Walker CR, Mafeking Siege Register Write Books, 2007
Walker ES, Treetops Hotel, Robert Hale, 1962

Websites. Scouting Milestones   www.scouting.milestones.btinternet.co.uk
All other websites are credited with a checked ULR on the page of use.

Index.

<u>The Humshaugh Campers, adults and Scouts are listed in Chapter 7</u>

A database of 1908 troops in to be found in the appendix, those commented on in Ch.4 (First Groups) are highlighted
Foreign troops started in 1908 are described by Country in Chapter?, Page 87.

Aids to Scouting	17,18,19,24,38,41,65,70,73
Armstrong, Lord	9,140
Baden-Powell, Agnes	83
Baden-Powell, Donald	5,119,139
Baden-Powell, Henrietta	15,34,42,44,46,49,50,83
Baden-Powell, Lady	7
Baden-Powell, Lord (present)	108
Baden-Powell, Maj. Baden	44
Baden-Powell, Sir George	19
Bass, Mrs Myra	95
Beard, Dan	25-26
Beaumont, Elizabeth de	80,81
Beaumont, Marguerite de	80-81,83
Booth, John 'Banjo'	128,129,142,144
Boy Scouts Scheme	5,7,8,15,17,19,20,21,23-24,30,34,41,43,45,48-49,59,62,66,73,74,90-1,93-4
Boys' Brigade	5,15-19,21,24,41,42,58,61,63,83,104,110,112,122
Boys of the Empire	41,66
Brownsea Camp	5-6,7,9,10,17,19,26,38,42,43,44,48,63,64-65,66,70,74,75,91,101,107,108,109 110,112,115,117,118,119,120,121,129,130.142,144,145,148
Burchardt-Ashton, Arthur	21,30,38-9
Cargill, Allison	82
Chaloner, Richard	74
Chance Mr, US Instructor?	129-130,139
Chapman, Able	114,136,137
Charterhouse	14,15,84,97,102
Church Lads' Brigade	15,18-20, 21,48,58,74,83,104
Clayton Nathaniel	114
Colbron Pearse, Capt. D	75,118,126,127,132,100
Conan Doyle, Sir Arthur	30,104
Connaught, Duke/Duchess	9,18,51
Continance	29-30
Coulson, Colonel	6,138,147
Cruddas Mr	113
Cutcliffe Hyne CJ	29,30
Eengonyama Chorus	138
Everett, Sir Percy	6,28,46,49,65-67,105,109,127,128,129,135,142,148
Fry, CB	8,30
Gee, Walter	18-19
Girdlestone, Frederick	14,
Girl Scouts	67,78-83
Green , Captain George	17,19,63
Guisborough CLB	19,74
Haig Brown, Dr W	14,
Haldane RB	9,51
Hassall, John	52
Henderson, 'Farmer'	114,115

161

Holt, Henry	116,118,125,126,127,128,136,139,141,143
Hume Pollock, Mr	84
Keary, Peter	43,44,51,58,60,76,89,91,112,113,114,116,121
Kipling, Rudyard	35-36,52,115
Kyle, Archibald	68,95
Legion of Frontiersmen	21,29-40,48,58,70,87-88,98,120,127
Lonsdale, Lord	29,30-31,120
Louis, Prince of Battenberg	37,87-88
Lukis, Dr TS	84-85,106
Mafeking	5, 13,14,16,19,30,34,35,40,43,53,65,66,76,86,90,93,97,98,104,105,117,140
Markham, Violet	83
McLaren, Maj. Kenneth	44,45
Meath, Earl of	29,30
Mercers' Company	13,39
Motto	53,60,97,100,108
Noble, Saxton	10,74,114,119
NW Mounted Police	29,32,33,35,98-99
Pearson, Sir Arthur	5,6,9,15,23,30,34,42,43,44,45,48,50,52,55,59,60,62,65,66,72,74,89,92,108,112,147
Philipps, Roland	106
Pocock, Roger	29-40,44,58,98,99
Primmer, Arthur	63-65,112
Ranta, Kari & Joppi	146,149
Robson, Captain Henry	17,19,42
Roosevelt, Franklin D	25,51
Rowallan, Lord	146
Royal United Services Inst.	13
Scouting for Boys	6,8,9,13,15,17,19,23,24,25,27,28,30,31,35,38,41-57, 59,62,64-66,70,71,77,80,81,86,87 89,91,92,94-96,98-101,104,105,108,110,112,131
Seaton, Ernest Thompson	10,22-28, 30,38
Seton-Karr, Sir Henry	29,31
Smith, William	16-18,24,41
South African Constabulary	30,32,98,101,102,103,105
Steele, Colonel Sam	30
The Scout magazine	9,15,27,32-34,37,51,57-59,62,64,68,70,75-82,84-87,89-95,104,106,109-111,116,123,124,127, 132,140,142,147,150
Thomlinson Mildred	82
Toynbee Hall	84,106
Van Raalte, F & C	9,30
Vane, Sir Francis	30,32
Vaux, Col. Ernest	10,74-77,84,110,119,124,126
Wade, Eileen	99,102
Wade, Maj. A	78
Wakefield WH	21,38,49,127,128,132,134,135
Walker, Eric S	128
Watkin, Victor	64,65
White, James (Caterer)	118
Wigam, Mr US Instructor?	129-130
Wilkinson, John "Wilkie'	71
Williams, George	20
YMCA	8,15,20-21,25,31,38,39,48,49,58,72-73,83,85,127,151
Young, Capt. Robert	67-68